Sandra Lee

Fast-Fix Family Favorites

This book belongs to:

....

Meredith® Books Des Moines, Iowa

Copyright © 2008 Sandra Lee Semi-Homemade® All rights reserved. Printed in the USA.
Library of Congress Control Number: 2008922211 ISBN: 978-0-696-24182-6

Special thanks to Culinary Director Jeff Parker

sem·i·home·made

adj. **1:** a stress-free solution-based formula that provides savvy shortcuts and affordable, timesaving tips for overextended do-it-yourself homemakers **2:** a quick and easy equation wherein 70% ready-made convenience products are added to 30% fresh ingredients with creative personal style, allowing homemakers to take 100% of the credit for something that looks, feels, or tastes homemade **3:** a foolproof resource for having it all—and having the time to enjoy it **4:** a method created by Sandra Lee for home, garden, crafts, beauty, food, fashion, and entertaining wherein everything looks, tastes, and feels as if it was made from scratch.

Solution-based **E**nterprise that **M**otivates, **I**nspires, and **H**elps **O**rganize and **M**anage time, while **E**nriching **M**odern life by **A**dding **D**ependable shortcuts **E**very day.

dedication

To every Semi-Homemaker®
Who juggles a full load every day
This book will help you make meals quick
And still have time to play.

Make comfort food or family faves
Save time with my best tricks
Starters, entrees, serve-alongs
They're all a real fast fix.

A sit-down home-cooked meal
Makes memories you'll long treasure
With Semi-Homemade®, it's easy
And always such a pleasure.
XO—SL

Table of Contents

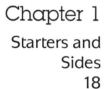

Chapter 1

Starters and
Sides
18

Chapter 3

Comfort Food
54

Chapter 2

Soups and
Salads
34

Chapter 4

Quick Weeknight
Meals
80

Sm | Sandra Lee Semi-Homemade. grilling 2 | Meredith

Sm | Sandra Lee Semi-Homemade. slow cooker recipes 2 | Meredith

Sm | Sandra Lee Semi-Homemade. 20-minute meals 2 | Meredith

Sm | Sandra Lee Semi-Homemade. cooking 3 | Meredith

Sm | Sandra Lee Semi-Homemade. gatherings | Meredith

Sm | Sandra Lee Semi-Homemade. cooking made light | Meredith

Sm | Sandra Lee Semi-Homemade. 20-minute meals | Meredith

Sm | Sandra Lee Semi-Homemade. slow cooker recipes | Meredith

Sm | Sandra Lee Semi-Homemade. grilling | Meredith

Sm | Sandra Lee Semi-Homemade. cooking 2 | Meredith

Sm | Sandra Lee Semi-Homemade. desserts | Meredith

Sm | Sandra Lee Semi-Homemade. cooking | Meredith

Sm | Sandra Lee Semi-Homemade. Cool Kids' Cooking | Meredith

Letter from Sandra

Food, family, and friends—these are my favorite things. Mix them well, season with love, and you have the recipe for a happy life.

It was my Grandma Lorraine who taught me to love food. Like many women, she was a single working mom, juggling a full-time job with cooking, cleaning, and caring for two little girls. Time was precious and money was tight, but we had hot, home-cooked meals every night. Though far from fancy, they were nutritious and filling and made with love. Mealtime was our time together, a time to stop and smell the spices after a busy day.

Grandma Lorraine adored being in the kitchen. To her—and now to me—it is the heart of a home, the place where family and friends gather to share food and conversation. Memories are made in the kitchen; bonds are strengthened as we pour, stir, sprinkle, and enjoy the fruits of our labor with the people who make it all worthwhile. A kitchen is a happy place, filled with life and laughter, but most of all it's filled with love.

Today, meals have become an either-or proposition—either feed the family fast with takeout or spend hours shopping and cooking meals you can feel good about serving. Semi-Homemade® combines the best of both, with savvy shortcuts and smart timesaving tips that help you make wholesome, scratch-tasting meals in minutes. It's all part of my 70/30 philosophy: Mix 70% quality prepackaged foods with 30% fresh ingredients and a dash of your own creativity to fix a meal that's 100% fast and fabulous! It's a solution that works for all kinds of homemakers—busy parents, professionals, students, and especially those who juggle it all.

My *Fast-Fix Family Favorites* is the best of the best, containing everything I love about cooking in one convenient go-to book. You'll find more than 300 of my favorite recipes for starters, sides, soups, salads, entrées, and desserts that you can mix and match to make a complete meal. Reinvent comfort food with American family favorites or treat your palate to culinary adventures from around the world. Add variety to weeknight meals or celebrate holiday gatherings with fancier fare. Streamline meal prep with one-dish delights or stay fit with light and healthful selections that make eating well easy. Keep dinner stress-free by letting my slow cooker meals simmer all day while you're away—or fire up the grill and show off your skills with my grilling greats.

Whatever the occasion, the building blocks for a wonderful meal are right on your own shelves. I'll let you in on my best secrets for stocking staples that give you a head start on dinner, plus share quick tricks for everything from supereasy serve-alongs to speedy cleanup. There's even my own Grilling 101 to ensure your patio parties sizzle with style. It's twice the recipes, twice the shortcuts, twice the value, in one supersized book.

Gather your family, invite your friends, and turn my favorite things into yours. In a fast-paced world, these are the solutions that go the distance, delivering dinner on the double in half the time, then letting *you* take all the credit. That's the best of Semi-Homemade®.

Cheers to a happy, healthy life!

Sandy

Extra-Easy Entertaining

Food equals fun! When you're getting ready to throw a party—big or small—plan your appetizers, desserts, and drinks accordingly. Assume that each guest will have about 3 appetizers and 2 drinks.

Gather Together!

Parties are a great way to gather friends and family for good times and good food. You must be sure to provide enough food—too much is better than not enough. A general rule of thumb is to assume that each party guest will have 2 to 3 drinks and appetizers per person. Once you calculate that number, throw in a couple of extra of each to make sure you have plenty. I like to keep extra appetizer-type foods on hand just in case I run out—for example, I keep bread and crackers in the pantry to serve with dipping oil or other spreads. A selection of cheeses, such as nutty Parmigiano Reggiano, creamy Brie, and pungent Maytag blue all go great with bread and crackers. I also keep fresh fruit, such as seedless grapes and sliced pears and apples in the house to go with the cheese and crackers. I provide an adult punch or two, but always stock up on extra red and white wine.

Help from the Slow Cooker

If you don't have enough room in the oven for all your party dishes, employ the use of your slow cooker. Appetizers—such as meatballs, dips, and beverages—can be cooked to perfection in the slow cooker and then kept toasty warm throughout the party. Just set the heat to low and stir the contents several times during the celebration. If you're already baking something in the oven, consider using the slow cooker for preparing the dessert or side dish.

Quick-Prep Appetizers

When you need fast and creative starters, look no further than the pantry and refrigerator. For example, Johnsonville® summer sausage can be cut into slices and served on skewers with cherry tomatoes, artichoke hearts, ripe olives, cheese, pepperoncini peppers, and anything else you like. Brush with Italian salad dressing for a satisfying antipasti kabob.

Slow cooker meatballs

Slow cooker dessert pears

Red wine

Breads and crackers

Cheese and fresh fruit

Supereasy Serve-Alongs

Turn any dish into a full-course meal by adding some quick and easy side dishes and desserts. Spruce up cakes and cookies from the bakery with sprinkles, coconut, fruit, ice cream, and more!

Vegetables

Add vegetables to the meal for a healthful kick with bagged salad mix, canned vegetables, frozen vegetable mixes, or steam-in-the-bag vegetables (look in the produce section of your supermarket). For extra flavor on your canned, frozen, and steamed vegetables, stir in butter and some of your favorite fresh chopped herbs, such as basil, parsley, thyme, dill, and/or tarragon. Add dazzle to your salads by topping the greens with a balsamic vinaigrette, strawberries, and almonds.

Deli Salads

Search the deli case at your supermarket for delicious side dish salad options, such as coleslaw, and pasta, bean, and potato salads. Customize these premade favorites by adding additional chopped fresh vegetables—such as onion or tomato—herbs, or nuts and seeds.

Deli Salads

Vegetables

Side Dishes

Breads

Side Dishes

Make it different every night by trying choices such as stuffing mixes, quick-cooking rice, refrigerated pastas, frozen french fries, or refrigerated mashed potatoes. Add extra flair by stirring in an assortment of fresh chopped herbs, cut-up vegetables, and butter.

Bread

Soft on the inside, crusty on the outside—that's the best kind of bread! Cut thick slices from loaves or break dinner rolls in half, spread with plenty of butter, and use to mop up any sauce or juice left on your plate. As a great appetizer or starter dish, flavor olive oil with herbs (such as basil, oregano, and/or thyme) and some chopped garlic. Serve the oil mixture with a basket of rustic bread chunks or slices and use the oil for dipping.

Quick Cleanup

Kick kitchen cleanup into high gear by thinking ahead!
A quick trick: Spray measuring cups with nonstick cooking
spray before filling with sticky ingredients such as honey.

Disposable foil pans

Make Life Easier

Tidying up the kitchen is simple with a little planning. When making bar cookies or other messy foods, line the baking pan with aluminum foil for easy removal and even easier cleanup. Or use disposable foil pans and just throw the mess away when you're done cooking! Grate cheese and citrus zest, peel vegetables, and sprinkle sugar on cookies over waxed paper. This keeps the mess in one place and makes it easier to clean the counter when you're done. Use a zip-top plastic bag to marinate meats and combine messy mixtures. Toss the plastic bag and cleanup is done!

Waxed paper

Foil-lined pan for bar cookies

Foil-lined baking pans

Zip-top plastic bag

13

Choosing a Slow Cooker

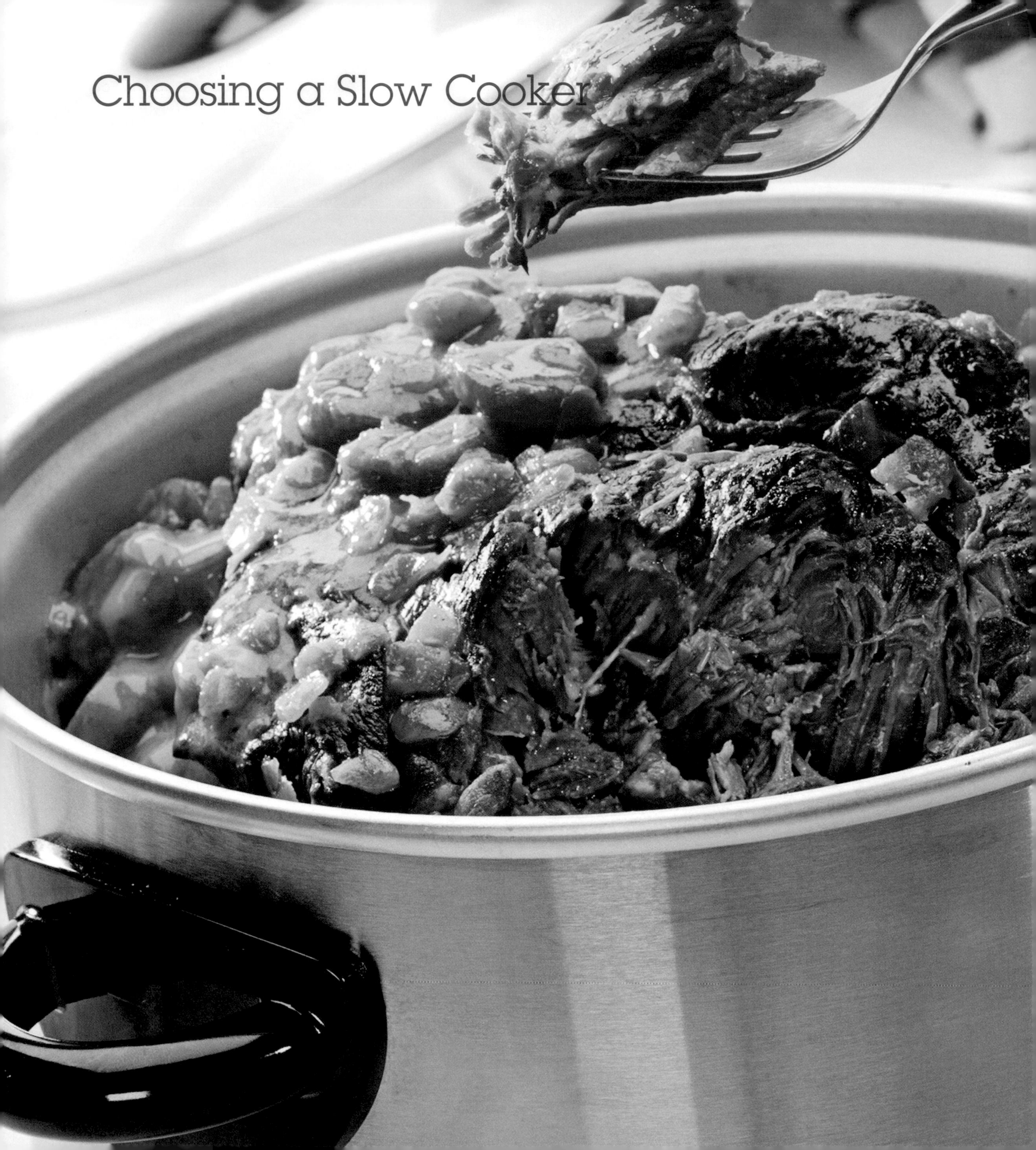

Cooker Sizes and Styles

Totable slow cooker: Say good-bye to the days of trying to transport the very "untransportable" slow cooker! With the new totable device (photo, bottom left) food can be cooked to perfection, then carried to potlucks and parties with ease. Just slip the safety catches for the lid in place and snap the magnetized handles together for piping hot, portable food.

Small cookers: Not everybody needs to prepare mass quantities of slow-cooked food. For single people, couples, and party appetizers, the 1½-quart cooker is the best option. For couples (who want leftovers) and small families, choose a 3½- to 4½-quart cooker. This size is perfect for soups, stews, and chilies.

Large cookers: Most of the recipes in this book call for larger cookers—between 4 and 5 quarts. This size of slow cooker will work well for any size family because large families have plenty to eat and small families and couples will have enough leftovers to freeze or eat the next night. For super-large families, the biggest slow cookers—6- to 8-quart—are probably the best bet.

Slow Cooker Savvy

Keep these hints in mind when it comes to slow cooker success:

Slow cookers work best when filled at least one-half full and not more than two-thirds full. Pay attention to the size of slow cooker called for in each recipe. Layer ingredients as directed in the recipes or follow manufacturer's directions.

Never put frozen meat in a slow cooker; thaw it first. Browning meat such as roasts and chops is a preference, not a necessity. If you're short on time, skip the skillet and go straight to the slow cooker.

Be careful not to peek too often! Each time you open the lid, another 15 minutes must be added to your cooking time.

Large and small cookers

Totable cooker

Grilling 101

Before you start flipping and flaming fabulous food, remember, timing and temperature are key. Use these charts to control your grill's heat and decide between direct or indirect heat.

Grilling 101

Gas grills generally come with thermometers but you can also find grill thermometers that sit right on the grate for charcoal grills. If you're feeling brave, you can test the temp with your hand by holding it several inches over the grate and count how many seconds you can keep it there comfortably (see "hand method" below).

Grill thermometer

Heat Level	Temperature	Hand Method
Hot	450° F to 500° F	2 seconds or less
Medium-Hot	400° F to 450° F	3 to 4 seconds
Medium	350° F to 400° F	4 to 5 seconds

Direct Heat Grilling

Direct heat grilling is just that … placing meat directly over the heat source. Typically this is used for smaller pieces of food, such as steaks, chicken breasts, pork chops, and vegetables. For direct grilling on a charcoal grill, cover the charcoal grate with a layer of briquettes, then pile the briquettes into a pyramid. Add lighter fluid and light the charcoal. Let the coals burn for 25 minutes or until covered with a gray ash. Use long-handled tongs to spread coals across the grate. **Oil the cold cooking grate just before beginning to cook and then place it on the grill. Never spray the grate with cooking spray when it is over hot coals.**

Indirect Heat Grilling

Indirect grilling "bakes" food over a longer period of time, because the heat source is off to the side instead of directly under the food. This is ideal for larger cuts of meat like roasts. For indirect grilling on a gas grill, light the grill, leave one burner off, and place the food on the grate above the unlit burner. Close the grill. Use the grill knobs to control the heat. For indirect grilling on a charcoal grill, follow "Direct Heat Grilling" directions for arranging and lighting charcoal, using about 50 briquettes. When the coals are covered with gray ash, divide them in half and place them on opposite sides of the grill. Put a disposable foil drip pan between the piles. Open vents to increase temperature; close to decrease temperature.

Direct

Indirect

Indirect

17

Starters and Sides

There's something about beginnings. Maybe it's the clean plate that lures me or maybe it's the promise that, lovely as this dish is, it's just a sample of more to come. Whatever the appeal, you have to start somewhere … and this chapter is a wonderful place. If you're looking for small bites with big flavor, try Shrimp Crostini. When company's coming, Caesar Artichoke Dip lets you impress with ease. And for something perfect on the side, try the elegant Pommes Soufflé for dinner parties or Texas Mashed Potato Salad for a perfect BBQ pair up. These dishes—whether starter or side—are wonderfully flexible, so mix and match to your heart's content.

The Recipes

Crabmeat Cucumber Rounds

Prep 15 minutes **Chill** 30 minutes **Makes** 16 rounds

¼	cup mayonnaise, *Best Foods*® or *Hellmann's*®
1	teaspoon prepared horseradish, *Morehouse*®
½	teaspoon Dijon mustard, *French's*®
½	teaspoon Worcestershire sauce, *Lea & Perrins*®
1	can (4.25-ounce) crabmeat, well drained, *Geisha*®
½	large unpeeled English hothouse cucumber, cut crosswise into 16 thin slices (about ¼-inch slices)
8	pimiento-stuffed green olives, sliced, *Star*®

1. In a small bowl, mix together mayonnaise, horseradish, mustard, and Worcestershire sauce. Stir in well-drained crabmeat, cucumber, and olives. Cover and chill in the refrigerator for 30 minutes.

Shrimp Crostini

Start to Finish 20 minutes **Makes** 8 servings

24	baguette slices, ¼-inch thick
½	cup butter
1½	teaspoons crushed garlic, *Christopher Ranch*®
1	pound frozen cooked and peeled large shrimp (26/30 count), thawed
2	tablespoons chopped fresh parsley
1	package (5.2-ounce) soft cheese with garlic and herbs, *Boursin*®
12	cherry tomatoes, cut in half
	Fresh chives (optional)

1. Preheat oven to 400 degrees F. Place baguette slices on a baking sheet. Bake for 7 to 10 minutes or until just toasted and golden around the edges.

2. Meanwhile, in a large skillet, melt butter over medium heat. Add garlic; cook and stir for 1 minute. Add shrimp, cooking and stirring for about 5 minutes or until heated through. Add parsley; toss to combine. Remove from heat.

3. Spread toasted baguette slices with soft cheese and top with a shrimp and a cherry tomato half. Garnish with chives (optional).

Caesar Artichoke Dip

Prep 10 minutes   **Bake** 40 minutes   **Makes** 4 cups

	Olive oil cooking spray, *Pam*®
⅔	cup fat-free Caesar salad dressing, *Girard's*®
⅓	cup light mayonnaise, *Hellmann's* or *Best Foods*®
⅓	cup fat-free sour cream, *Knudsen*®
⅓	cup grated Parmesan cheese, *DiGiorno*®
2	cans (15 ounces each) artichoke quarters in water, drained and chopped, *Maria*®
1	can (14.5-ounce) organic diced tomatoes with basil and garlic, drained, *Muir Glen*®
5	ounces low-fat Swiss cheese, shredded, *Alpine Lace*®
½	teaspoon hot pepper sauce, *Tabasco*®
	Baked tortilla chips and/or vegetable dippers

1. Preheat oven to 350 degrees F. Coat a 1-quart baking dish with cooking spray; set aside. In a medium bowl, whisk together salad dressing, mayonnaise, sour cream, and Parmesan cheese until smooth. Stir in artichokes, tomatoes, Swiss cheese, and hot pepper sauce. Transfer to prepared baking dish. Bake for 40 to 45 minutes or until mixture is set and top is golden. Serve dip with baked tortilla chips and/or vegetable dippers.

Antipasti

Start to Finish 10 minutes   **Makes** 4 servings

1	bag (5-ounce) mixed torn salad greens, *Fresh Express*®
1	pound assorted deli meats (such as salami, mortadella ham, cappocola)
1	container (8-ounce) fresh mozzarella cheese, *Fiorella Fresh*®
4	ounces provolone cheese, sliced
1	jar (16-ounce) mixed olives, *Giuliano Olive Antipasto*®
2	tomatoes, quartered
1	cup pepperoncini
1	can (15-ounce) garbanzo beans, rinsed and drained, *Progresso*®
1	cup (½ bottle) balsamic vinaigrette, *Newman's Own*®
	Packaged breadsticks

1. Place greens on a large platter. Arrange deli meats, cheeses, olives, tomatoes, pepperoncini, and garbanzo beans on top. Drizzle with vinaigrette. Serve with breadsticks.

Pâté "Pop Tarts"

Prep 15 minutes   **Cook** 20 minutes   **Makes** 4 servings

	Canola oil cooking spray, *Pam®*
1	package (6.5-ounce) pizza crust mix, *Betty Crocker®*
¼	teaspoon ground black pepper
¼	cup cognac
¼	cup water
¼	pound foie gras mousse pâté, *D'Artagnan®*
1	egg, lightly beaten
1	tablespoon cream

1. Preheat oven to 375 degrees F. Lightly spray a baking sheet with cooking spray; set aside. In a medium bowl, combine pizza crust mix and pepper.

2. In a microwave-safe bowl, combine cognac and water. Microwave on high heat setting (100 percent power) for 30 seconds to 1 minute. Add to pizza crust mix. Fold together thoroughly, then stir 20 times until dough forms a ball. Let rest 5 minutes.

3. On a lightly floured work surface, roll out dough to ⅛-inch thick. Cut out eight 3×5-inch rectangles. Spread approximately 1 tablespoon of the foie gras mousse pâté onto each of four rectangles, leaving a ¼-inch border. Brush borders with beaten egg and top with remaining rectangles. Using the tines of a fork, crimp edges of "pop tarts." Poke vent holes in top crusts with fork. Transfer "pop tarts" to prepared baking sheet.

4. Beat the remaining egg with cream. Using a pastry brush, lightly brush tops of "pop tarts" with egg mixture. Bake for 20 to 25 minutes or until golden brown.

Phyllo Cheese Straws in Pesto

Prep 20 minutes **Bake** 12 minutes **Makes** about 36 straws

1	package (8-ounce) cream cheese, softened, *Philadelphia®*
¼	cup grated Parmesan cheese, *Kraft®*
1	egg, lightly beaten
¼	teaspoon salt
1	box (16-ounce) phyllo dough, thawed, *Athens®* (40 sheets)
1	stick (½ cup) butter, melted
	Store-bought basil pesto, *Buitoni®*

1. In a small bowl, combine cream cheese, Parmesan cheese, egg, and salt. Mix well. Spoon cream cheese mixture into a pastry bag fitted with a ¼-inch diameter round tip. Set aside. Preheat oven to 375 degrees F. Lay out thawed phyllo dough. Working quickly to keep dough from drying out, brush top sheet with melted butter and pipe cheese filling along long edge of phyllo ½ inch from each end. Fold over ends to enclose filling and roll up phyllo to make a straw. Place straw on a baking sheet. Repeat with remaining sheets of phyllo. Bake straws for 12 to 15 minutes or until golden. Serve straws with basil pesto for dipping.

Artichokes Gratinée

Prep 10 minutes **Cook** 18 minutes **Makes** 4 servings

	Plain breadcrumbs, Progresso®
1	jar (12-ounce) marinated artichoke bottoms, drained and patted dry, *Luna Rossa®*
1½	teaspoons grated Parmesan cheese, *DiGiorno®*
¼	pound soft sheep's milk cheese or Brie, rind removed
1	cup European-blend salad greens, *Ready Pac®*
2	tablespoons balsamic vinaigrette, *Newman's Own®*

1. Preheat oven to 350 degrees F. Line a baking sheet with parchment paper. Sprinkle 1 teaspoon of breadcrumbs onto parchment where each artichoke will sit. Set artichokes, cup sides up, on breadcrumbs. Sprinkle each with additional breadcrumbs and ¼ teaspoon of Parmesan cheese.

2. Bake for 15 minutes. Remove baking sheet from oven; preheat broiler. Divide sheep's milk cheese among each artichoke bottom. Broil filled artichokes, 6 inches from heat source, for 3 to 4 minutes or until cheese melts and starts to bubble and brown. In a bowl, toss salad greens with balsamic vinaigrette. Serve artichoke bottoms on greens.

Fondue Party!

Start to Finish 20 minutes **Makes** 6 servings of each fondue

Kids love fondue too! Try making these two variations for some slumber party fun. The Cheese Fondue is a kid-friendly version of the Fiesta Fondue (below) and the Chocolate Fondue is a sweet way to end the evening.

FOR CHEESE FONDUE:
1   package (8-ounce) cream cheese, *Philadelphia*®
1   can (10-ounce) condensed cheddar cheese soup,
         Campbell's®
½   cup half-and-half or light cream
½   cup shredded cheddar cheese, *Kraft*®
        Assorted dippers (such as cut-up vegetables
           and pretzel sticks)

FOR CHOCOLATE FONDUE:
12   ounces semisweet chocolate pieces, *Nestlé*®
1   cup half-and-half or light cream
1   teaspoon ground cinnamon, *McCormick*®
        Assorted dippers (such as marshmallows
           and cut-up fruit)

1. For Cheese Fondue, cut cream cheese into 1 inch pieces. Place in a microwave-safe bowl. Microwave, covered, on medium-high heat setting (80 percent power) for 1½ minutes. Stir in cheddar cheese soup, the ½ cup half-and-half, and the cheddar cheese. Microwave, covered, on medium-high heat setting for 5 minutes more, stirring every minute. Serve with dippers.

2. For Chocolate Fondue, in a microwave-safe bowl, combine chocolate pieces, the 1 cup half-and-half, and the cinnamon. Microwave, covered, on medium-high heat setting (80 percent power) for 1½ minutes. Stir chocolate mixture for 1 minute; cover. Microwave on medium-high heat setting for 1 minute more. Stir until chocolate is melted completely. Serve with dippers.

Fiesta Fondue

Prep 5 minutes **Cook** 10 minutes **Makes** 6 servings

Fondue is back! Some restaurants have entire menus consisting of different kinds of fondue. Hard to imagine this dish could be so popular, but it is—which is why I've included a couple of options. Simple to make, this dish always earns glowing reviews.

1   can (10.75-ounce) cheddar cheese soup, *Campbell's*®
1   package (8-ounce) shredded sharp cheddar cheese, *Kraft*®
1   cup chunky chipotle salsa, *Pace*®
1   cup whole milk
        Assorted dippers (such as cubed French bread and
           tortilla chips)

1. In a heavy medium saucepan, combine cheese soup, cheddar cheese, salsa, and milk. Cook and stir over medium heat until shredded cheese melts and the mixture is smooth. Transfer cheese mixture to a fondue pot or ceramic bowl. Serve with dippers.

Borracho Beans

Prep 15 minutes   **Cook** 25 minutes   **Makes** 4 servings

South of the border, they call these beans "drunk" beans because a bottle of beer is used as the broth. When brewed with pinto beans, bacon, and tomatoes and green chiles, it all becomes a peppery puree—cooled with a chaser of cilantro and fresh lime. Serve with tortilla chips for dipping.

2	cans (16 ounces each) pinto beans, *Bush's*®
1	can (10-ounce) diced tomatoes and green chiles, *Ro-Tel*®
1	can (4-ounce) diced green chiles, *La Victoria*®
½	cup frozen diced onions, *C&W*®
1	teaspoon crushed garlic, *Christopher Ranch*®
1	bottle (12-ounce) Mexican beer, *Negro Modelo*®
⅓	cup real bacon pieces, *Hormel*®
¼	cup finely chopped fresh cilantro
1	lime, sliced into wedges

1. In a medium saucepan, over medium-high heat, stir to combine all ingredients (except cilantro and lime wedges). Bring to a boil; reduce heat to medium-low heat. Simmer, uncovered, for 20 minutes. Transfer bean mixture to a serving bowl. Stir in cilantro. Serve with lime wedges.

Waldorf Slaw

Prep 10 minutes   **Chill** 1 hour   **Makes** 4 servings

1	bag (16-ounce) 3-color slaw mix, *Fresh Express*®
2	large Granny Smith apples, cored and diced small
1	cup chopped walnuts, *Blue Diamond*®
½	cup mayonnaise, *Best Foods*® or *Hellmann's*®
⅓	cup poppy seed dressing, *Knott's*®

1. In a large bowl, combine slaw mix, diced apples, and chopped walnuts; set aside.

2. For dressing, in a small bowl, combine mayonnaise and poppy seed dressing. Pour dressing over slaw mixture and toss to cover.

3. Cover with plastic wrap; chill 1 hour before serving.

Jalapeño Potato Salad

Prep 5 minutes **Chill** 1 hour **Makes** 6 servings

- 2 pounds deli potato salad
- 2 tablespoons diced jalapeños, *La Victoria*®
- 1 scallion (green onion), chopped
- 1 tablespoon finely chopped fresh cilantro
- 1 teaspoon Mexican seasoning, *McCormick*®
- 6 dashes chipotle pepper sauce, *Tabasco*®
  Whole jalapeño peppers (optional)

1. In a large bowl, stir to combine all ingredients (except whole jalapeño peppers). Cover with plastic wrap and chill in the refrigerator for 1 hour to allow flavors to blend.

2. Garnish with whole jalapeño peppers (optional). Serve chilled.

Texas Mashed Potato Salad

Prep 10 minutes **Cook** 10 minutes **Chill** 2 hours
Makes 6 servings

- 1 bag (28-ounce) frozen potatoes O'Brien, *Ore-Ida*®
- 1 tablespoon water
- 2 hard-cooked eggs, chopped
- ½ cup mayonnaise, *Best Foods*® or *Hellmann's*®
- ¼ cup yellow mustard, *French's*®
- 2 tablespoons sweet pickle relish, *Vlasic*®
  Salt and ground black pepper
  Paprika (optional)
  Fresh parsley leaves (optional)

1. Place potatoes in a large microwave-safe bowl with the water. Cover; microwave on high heat setting (100 percent power) for 8 minutes. Stir; cover and cook for 2 to 4 minutes more or until potatoes are tender; drain water. Transfer potatoes to a large serving bowl; chill about 2 hours or until completely cool.

2. Remove potatoes from the refrigerator. Add eggs, mayonnaise, mustard, and relish. Mash mixture with a potato masher until combined and potatoes are in small pieces. Season to taste with salt and pepper. Sprinkle with paprika (optional). Garnish with parsley (optional).

Pommes Soufflé

Prep 15 minutes   **Cook** 60 minutes   **Makes** 4 servings

Soufflés have a reputation for being temperamental, but this stress-free soufflé eliminates the traditional stovetop stirring to make it practically foolproof. Just don't open the oven door until you're ready to remove it!

	Butter
2	tablespoons grated Parmesan cheese, *DiGiorno*®
1	packet (3.6-ounce) instant roasted garlic mashed potatoes, prepared according to package directions and cooled, *Betty Crocker*®
4	eggs, separated and reserved in different bowls
¾	cup cream
1	tablespoon snipped fresh chives
½	teaspoon salt
¼	teaspoon ground black pepper

1. Preheat oven to 350 degrees F. Butter the bottom and sides of a 1½-quart soufflé dish. Add Parmesan to dish and roll dish to coat inside with Parmesan.

2. In a medium bowl, combine cooled potatoes, the egg yolks, the cream, chives, salt, and pepper. In a separate medium bowl, use an electric mixer to beat egg whites until stiff peaks form, taking care to not overbeat them. Stir ⅓ of the egg whites into potato mixture. Add the remaining egg whites, gently folding to combine.

3. Transfer mixture to prepared soufflé dish. Bake for 60 to 65 minutes or until puffy, golden brown, and a knife inserted near center comes out clean. Serve immediately.

Six-Cheese Tortellini

Start to Finish 20 minutes **Makes** 4 servings

2	tablespoons butter
1	cup whole milk
¼	cup cheese dip, *Kraft® Cheez Whiz®*
1	package (8-ounce) shredded Italian cheese blend (mozzarella, smoked provolone, Parmesan, Romano, fontina, and Asiago cheeses), *Sargento®*
⅛	teaspoon cayenne pepper, *McCormick®*
2	packages (9 ounces each) refrigerated fresh cheese tortellini, *Rosetto®*

1. For cheese sauce, in a large heavy saucepan, melt butter over medium heat. Add milk and bring to a simmer. Whisk in the cheese dip. Gradually whisk in shredded cheese blend. Cook and stir about 5 minutes or until cheeses melt and mixture begins to bubble. Whisk in cayenne.

2. Meanwhile, in a pot of boiling salted water, cook tortellini about 4 minutes or until just tender. Drain. Add tortellini to cheese sauce; gently toss to coat. Divide tortellini and sauce equally among 4 pasta bowls and serve warm.

NOTE: This dish can be made up to one day ahead. Prepare as directed above; cover and chill tortellini and cheese sauce in separate containers. When ready to serve, transfer tortellini and cheese sauce to a 2-quart baking dish. Preheat oven to 350 degrees F. Cover and bake about 25 minutes or until heated through.

Gnocchi Dippers

Start to Finish 15 minutes   **Makes** 4 servings

1	package (9-ounce) gnocchi (dry pasta section), *Alessi®*, or cheese tortellini pasta, *Rosetto®*
2	teaspoons olive oil, *Bertolli®*
¼	onion, minced
2	teaspoons bottled minced garlic, *McCormick®*
1	package (8-ounce) cheese product, *Kraft® Velveeta®*
½	cup low-fat milk
¼	teaspoon hot sauce, *Tabasco®*
	Fresh thyme sprigs (optional)

1. Prepare gnocchi according to package instructions.

2. In a medium saucepan, heat oil over medium heat. Cook onion and garlic in hot oil about 2 minutes or until onion is tender. Add the cheese product, milk, and hot sauce. Cook and stir about 4 minutes more or until sauce is smooth and cheese has completely melted.

3. Add cooked gnocchi to sauce; gently fold to coat. Transfer gnocchi and sauce to 4 bowls. Garnish each with thyme sprigs (optional). Serve immediately.

Curried Bow Tie Salad

Prep 10 minutes   **Cook** 5 minutes   **Chill** 15 minutes
Makes 4 servings

³/₄	cup sour cream
2	teaspoons curry powder, *McCormick®*
2	cans (8 ounces each) pineapple chunks, drained, *Dole®*
1	ripe medium avocado, peeled, pitted, and sliced
1	medium red apple, cored and sliced
8	ounces bow tie pasta/farfalle (half of a 16-ounce package), *De Cecco®*
	Salt

1. In a large bowl, combine sour cream and curry powder. Gently fold in pineapple, avocado, and apple.

2. Meanwhile, in a pot of boiling salted water, cook pasta about 5 minutes or until just tender. Drain. Rinse pasta; drain well. Fold pasta into sour cream mixture. Chill about 15 minutes or until cold. Season to taste with salt and serve.

French Bean Casserole

Prep 15 minutes **Bake** 20 minutes **Makes** 6 servings

1	tablespoon olive oil, *Bertolli®*
1	small onion, minced
6	ounces crimini mushrooms, sliced
1	can (10.75-ounce) condensed cream of mushroom soup, *Campbell's®*
1	cup heavy cream
1	pound baby green beans, trimmed and cleaned
½	cup toasted almonds

1. Preheat oven to 350 degrees F. In a medium skillet, heat oil over medium heat. Add onion and cook until soft. Stir in mushrooms. Increase heat to medium-high and cook until mushrooms are golden and most of the moisture has evaporated.

2. Add soup and cream. Cook and stir until simmering. Stir in the green beans. Pour mixture into a buttered 9×13-inch baking dish and top with toasted almonds. Bake for 20 to 25 minutes or until beans are tender.

Maple Sweet Potatoes

Start to Finish 10 minutes **Makes** 4 servings

1	can (29-ounce) cut sweet potatoes, drained, *Princella®*
2	tablespoons butter
2	tablespoons pure maple syrup, *Spring Tree®*
½	teaspoon pumpkin pie spice, *McCormick®*
	Salt and ground black pepper
	Chopped toasted pecans (optional)
	Additional pure maple syrup, *Spring Tree®* (optional)

1. Place drained sweet potatoes in a microwave-safe bowl. Cover and microwave on high heat setting (100 percent power) for 5 minutes. Drain well.

2. Stir in butter, maple syrup, and pumpkin pie spice. Use a fork to mash sweet potatoes. Season to taste with salt and pepper. Sprinkle with chopped toasted pecans (optional). Drizzle with additional maple syrup (optional).

Sweet Potato Fries

Prep 10 minutes **Bake** 30 minutes **Makes** 4 servings

2   pounds sweet potatoes, peeled
1   tablespoon canola oil, *Wesson*®
1   teaspoon pumpkin pie spice, *McCormick*®
1   tablespoon low-sodium chili seasoning, *McCormick*®
    Dipping sauces (such as mayonnaise, sour cream,
       and/or ketchup) (optional)

1. Preheat oven to 400 degrees F. Line a baking sheet with aluminum foil; set aside.

2. Cut potatoes in half lengthwise, then cut into ½-inch-thick fries. In a large bowl, combine sweet potatoes, oil, pumpkin pie spice, and chili seasoning. Toss until potatoes are thoroughly coated. Spread fries in a single layer on prepared baking sheet.

3. Bake fries in for 30 to 35 minutes, turning once to evenly cook. Serve with dipping sauces (optional).

Buttermilk-Garlic Smashed Potatoes

Start to Finish 20 minutes **Makes** 6 servings

1   bag (16-ounce) fresh diced red-skin potatoes,
       Reser's®
1   cup buttermilk
4   cloves roasted whole garlic, finely chopped,
       Christopher Ranch®
4   teaspoons butter seasoning, *Molly McButter*®
½   cup sour cream, *Knudsen*®
    Chopped fresh chives (optional)

1. In a large microwave-safe bowl, combine potatoes, buttermilk, garlic, and butter seasoning. Cover and microwave on high heat setting (100 percent power) for 12 to 15 minutes, stirring halfway through cooking time. Add sour cream. With a potato masher, mash potatoes until creamy but with lumps and peels visible. Garnish with chives (optional).

Soups and Salads

Served as a snack, light lunch, side dish, or main meal, soups and salads are always welcome. The savviest of chefs know that soups and salads as stand-alones or as starters to a main course are foolproof ways to ensure a successful meal. Who doesn't love to have a fresh, crisp salad? Or a steaming bowl of flavorful soup? Both are staples of any diet.

By adding the smallest accoutrements, you can change the flavor, texture, and presentation of your soups or salads. Garnishes as simple as toasted almonds, sweet candied walnuts, a dollop of cumin-flavored sour cream, or a decorative piece of puff pastry are easy to add and a great way to show off your culinary creativity.

The Recipes

Thai Chicken Soup

Prep 15 minutes   **Cook** 3½ to 4½ hours (High)   **Makes** 6 servings

1¼	pounds boneless, skinless chicken breast halves, diced
2	cans (14 ounces each) reduced-sodium chicken broth, *Swanson*®
2	cans (14 ounces each) light coconut milk
1	can (15-ounce) straw mushrooms, drained, *Polar*®
3	tablespoons refrigerated chopped lemongrass
1	tablespoon bottled chopped ginger
2	teaspoons Thai seasoning, *Spice Islands*®
2	tablespoons bottled lime juice, *ReaLime*®
2	tablespoons chopped fresh cilantro

1. In a 4-quart slow cooker, stir together chicken, chicken broth, coconut milk, mushrooms, lemongrass, ginger, and Thai seasoning until thoroughly combined. Cover and cook on high heat setting for 3½ to 4½ hours.

2. Stir in lime juice and cilantro. Serve hot.

Chicken Edamame Chowder

Prep 3 minutes   **Cook** 3 to 4 hours (High)   **Makes** 6 servings

1¼	pounds chicken tenders, cut into bite-size pieces
2	cans (14.75 ounces each) cream-style corn, *Green Giant*®
3	cups frozen shelled edamame
2	cups diced potatoes, *Reser's*®
½	cup frozen chopped onions, *Ore-Ida*®
¼	cup crumbled bacon, *Hormel*®
2	cups reduced-sodium chicken broth, *Swanson*®
½	cup half-and-half
	Salt and ground black pepper

1. In a 4-quart slow cooker, combine all ingredients except half-and-half and salt and pepper. Mix thoroughly.

2. Cover and cook on high heat setting for 3 to 4 hours.

3. Stir in half-and-half; season to taste with salt and pepper. Serve hot.

Creamy Green Chile Soup

Prep 15 minutes **Cook** 20 minutes **Makes** 6 servings

1	cup frozen chopped onion, *Ore-Ida*®
1	teaspoon crushed garlic
2	cups frozen corn kernels, divided, *Birds Eye*®
6	whole green chiles, coarsely chopped, divided, *Ortega*®
2	cans (14 ounces each) reduced-sodium chicken broth, divided, *Swanson*®
1	teaspoon Mexican seasoning, *McCormick*®
2	tablespoons butter
1	package (8-ounce) sliced fresh mushrooms
¼	cup gold tequila, *Jose Cuervo*®
¾	cup Mexican crema, *Cacique*®
	Salt and ground black pepper
	Fresh chopped cilantro (optional)
	Crumbled Cotija cheese (optional)

1. In a medium saucepan, combine onion, garlic, 1 cup corn kernels, half of chopped chiles, 1 cup chicken broth, and Mexican seasoning. Bring to a boil over medium-high heat. Reduce heat and simmer for 10 minutes.

2. Meanwhile, in a medium skillet, melt butter over medium-high heat. Add remaining corn and green chiles. Add mushrooms; cook and stir for 10 minutes or until water from mushrooms is released and evaporated.

3. Transfer onion mixture to a blender and add additional 1 cup chicken broth. Puree until smooth, working in batches if necessary. Pour into skillet and add remaining broth, tequila, and cooked vegetables. Bring to a boil. Reduce to low heat, stir in crema, and season to taste with salt and pepper. Serve soup hot garnished with cilantro and Cotija cheese (optional).

TIP: To keep hot liquid from splashing while being blended, cover blender with dish towel and pulse.

Sante Fe Five-Bean Soup

Prep 8 minutes   **Cook** 10 minutes   **Makes** 8 servings

1	can (15-ounce) black beans, drained, *S&W*®
1	can (15-ounce) kidney beans, drained, *S&W*®
1	can (15-ounce) garbanzo beans, drained, *S&W*®
1	can (15-ounce) red beans, drained, *S&W*®
1	can (15-ounce) navy (or white) beans, drained, *S&W*®
1	can (14.5-ounce) chopped tomatoes, *Del Monte*®
1	can (14-ounce) chicken broth, *Swanson*®
¾	cup chunky salsa, *Pace*®
2	teaspoons ground cumin, *McCormick*®
1	teaspoon dried red pepper flakes, *McCormick*®
	Fresh cilantro (optional)

1. Puree black beans in a blender. In a large pot, stir together all the remaining beans, the tomatoes, broth, salsa, cumin, and red pepper flakes. Stir in pureed black beans. Cover and simmer for 10 minutes or until hot, stirring occasionally.

2. Ladle soup into bowls. Garnish with fresh cilantro (optional). Serve hot.

Gazpacho Monterey

Prep 15 minutes   **Chill** 1 hour   **Makes** 6 servings

1	can (28-ounce) whole peeled organic tomatoes in juice, *Muir Glen*®
1	bag (16-ounce) frozen pepper stir-fry, *Birds Eye*®
1	cup organic chicken broth, *Swanson*®
1	cup orange juice, *Minute Maid*®
4	cloves whole peeled garlic, *Christopher Ranch*®
1	jalapeño chile pepper, seeded and chopped
1	slice whole grain bread, torn into pieces, *Oroweat*® *Health Nut*
	Salt and ground black pepper
3	tablespoons fresh cilantro leaves

1. In a blender, combine tomatoes, pepper stir-fry, chicken broth, orange juice, garlic, chile pepper, and bread (work in batches, if necessary). Cover and blend until smooth. Transfer to a large bowl. Season with salt and black pepper. Cover and chill for 1 hour. To serve, top soup with cilantro.

Enchilada Soup

Start to Finish 20 minutes   **Makes** 6 servings

	Olive oil cooking spray, *Pam*®
1 ¼	pounds ground uncooked turkey breast
1	cup chopped red onion
4	cups organic chicken broth, *Swanson*®
1	cup reduced-fat cheese dip, *Tostitos*®
¾	cup tomato puree, *Muir Glen*®
1	can (4-ounce) diced green chiles, drained, *La Victoria*®
1	tablespoon enchilada sauce mix, *Lawry's*®
1	teaspoon bottled crushed garlic, *Christopher Ranch*®
¼	cup finely chopped fresh cilantro
	Jalapeño chile peppers, sliced (optional)
¾	cup baked blue corn chips, *Guiltless*® *Gourmet*

1. Coat the bottom of a large pot with cooking spray; heat over medium-high heat. Add turkey and onion. Cook and stir until turkey is no longer pink, stirring to break up clumps. Add broth, cheese dip, tomato puree, chiles, enchilada sauce mix, and garlic. Bring to a boil; reduce heat. Simmer for 10 minutes. Stir in cilantro. Garnish with jalapeño peppers (optional). Serve with corn chips.

Mushroom Soup

Prep 5 minutes   **Cook** 10 minutes   **Makes** 2 servings

2	tablespoons olive oil, *Bertolli*®
1	large, fresh portobello mushroom, gills scraped off and mushroom finely chopped
1	can (10.75-ounce) condensed golden mushroom soup, *Campbell's*®
1	cup water
¾	cup heavy cream
1	teaspoon bottled minced garlic, *McCormick*®

1. In a large saucepan, heat olive oil over medium-high heat. Add mushroom and cook about 2 minutes or until tender.

2. Mix in soup, water, cream, and garlic. Bring soup to a simmer, stirring occasionally. Ladle soup into 2 bowls and serve.

NOTE: If desired, garnish each serving with a white mushroom slice and fresh thyme.

French Onion Soup

Prep 5 minutes   **Cook** 4 hours (High) or 8 hours (Low)   **Makes** 8 servings

5	cups sliced onions
2	cans (14 ounces each) reduced-sodium beef broth, *Swanson*®
2	cans (10 ounces each) beef consommé, *Campbell's*®
1	packet (0.9-ounce) onion soup mix, *Lipton*®
8	slices French bread
1	cup shredded Gruyère cheese

1. In a 3½- or 4-quart slow cooker, combine onions, broth, consommé, and soup mix. Cover and cook on high heat setting for 4 hours or low heat setting for 8 hours.

2. Preheat the broiler. Ladle soup into 8 broilerproof soup bowls arranged on a foil-lined baking sheet. Top each bowl with a slice of French bread. Sprinkle 2 tablespoons of cheese over each bread slice. Place the pan with the soup bowls under a broiler just until cheese is melted.

Herb Tortellini Soup

Prep 10 minutes   **Cook** 3 hours (High) or 7 hours (Low), plus 1 hour (High)
Makes 8 servings

3	cans (14.5-ounce) reduced-sodium chicken broth, *Swanson*®
1	can (28-ounce) crushed tomatoes, *Hunt's*®
1	can (11-ounce) sweet corn (no added salt), *Green Giant*®
1	package (10-ounce) frozen cut-leaf spinach
1	small red onion, diced
1	zucchini, diced
½	cup chopped fresh herbs (such as parsley, thyme, oregano, and basil)
1	tablespoon bottled minced garlic, *McCormick*®
1	tablespoon Italian salad dressing mix, *Good Seasons*®
½	teaspoon red pepper flakes, *McCormick*®
1	package (8-ounce) cheese tortellini, *Barilla*®
	Salt and ground black pepper
	Additional fresh chopped herbs (optional)

1. In a 3½- to 4-quart slow cooker, combine broth, tomatoes, corn, spinach, onion, zucchini, herbs, garlic, salad dressing mix, and red pepper flakes. Cover and cook on high heat setting for 3 hours or low heat setting for 7 hours.

2. Add tortellini; season to taste with salt and black pepper. Cover and continue cooking for 1 hour. (If cooking on low heat setting, turn to high heat setting to cook tortellini.) Garnish with additional fresh herbs (optional). Serve hot.

Crabby Bisque

Prep 5 minutes   **Cook** 6 minutes   **Makes** 2 servings

This is a soup among soups. Not much compares to this flavorful Crabby Bisque. This "must make" is super to serve in coffee mugs and makes a unique appetizer sipper.

1   can (10½-ounce) restaurant-style condensed
         crab bisque, *Bookbinder's*®
¾   cup plus 2 tablespoons heavy cream
1   tablespoon chopped fresh parsley
1   can (4.25-ounce) crabmeat, *Geisha*®
1   tablespoon lemon juice, *ReaLemon*®
         Salt and cayenne pepper

1. In a medium saucepan, combine bisque, ¾ cup of the heavy cream, and parsley. Bring to a boil. Stir in crabmeat with juices. Bring to a simmer. Add lemon juice. Season to taste with salt and cayenne pepper.

2. Spoon soup into 2 bowls. Divide the remaining 2 tablespoons cream between the bowls; swirl with butter knife to create design. Serve hot.

Curried Apple Squash Soup

Start to Finish 10 minutes   **Makes** 4 servings

2   boxes (18.3 ounces each) butternut squash soup,
         Campbell's Select®
1   cup cinnamon apple sauce, *Mott's*®
2   tablespoons ketchup, *Heinz*®
2   teaspoons curry powder, *McCormick*®
1   teaspoon pumpkin pie spice, *McCormick*®
         Plain yogurt or sour cream (optional)
         Pumpkin pie spice, *McCormick*® (optional)

1. In a medium saucepan, combine butternut squash soup, apple sauce, ketchup, curry powder, and the 1 teaspoon pumpkin pie spice. Bring to boil over medium-high heat.

2. Reduce heat and simmer for 5 minutes. Ladle soup into 4 bowls. Drizzle yogurt into soup and sprinkle with additional pumpkin pie spice (optional). Serve hot.

Quinoa Salad

Start to Finish 30 minutes **Makes** 6 servings

2	cups organic chicken or vegetable broth, *Swanson*®
1	cup quinoa
1	cup seeded and chopped cucumber
½	cup chopped roasted red bell peppers, *Delallo*®
½	cup crumbled feta cheese, *Athenos*®
¼	cup finely chopped flat-leaf parsley
2	scallions (green onions), sliced
3	tablespoons slivered almonds, toasted, *Planters*®
1	tablespoon fines herbes, *Spice Islands*®
9	cups Bibb lettuce leaves, torn
¼	cup light roasted garlic and balsamic salad dressing, *Bernstein's*®

1. In a medium saucepan, combine chicken broth and quinoa. Bring to a boil; reduce heat. Cover and simmer for 10 to 15 minutes or until liquid is absorbed. Spread quinoa on a foil-lined baking sheet; cool.

2. In a large bowl, combine cooled quinoa, cucumber, roasted peppers, feta cheese, parsley, scallions, almonds, and fines herbes. Toss to mix. Toss lettuce with quinoa mixture; divide among 6 chilled salad plates. Drizzle with salad dressing.

Grilled Caesar Ranch Salad

Prep 5 minutes **Grill** 1 minute **Makes** 6 servings

1	cup ranch dressing, *Hidden Valley*®
¼	cup shredded Parmesan cheese, *Kraft*®
2	tablespoons fresh lemon juice
2	teaspoons Dijon mustard, *Grey Poupon*®
½	teaspoon bottled crushed garlic, *Christopher Ranch*®
	Salt and ground black pepper
1	package (3-ounce) romaine hearts, *Earthbound Farm*®
2	tablespoons extra virgin olive oil, *Bertolli*®
	Caesar salad croutons, *Pepperidge Farm*®
	Additional Parmesan cheese

1. In a bowl, combine ranch dressing, the ¼ cup Parmesan cheese, the lemon juice, mustard, and garlic. Season with salt and pepper.

2. Set up grill for direct cooking over medium heat (see page 17). Oil grate when ready to start cooking. Cut romaine hearts lengthwise, keeping core intact. Drizzle cut sides with olive oil and season with salt and pepper. Place romaine hearts, cut sides down, on hot, oiled grill. Grill 1 to 2 minutes or until grill marks form and romaine lettuce just begins to wilt. Transfer romaine hearts to plates; drizzle with dressing. Garnish with croutons and additional Parmesan cheese.

Grilled Tuna Niçoise

Prep 25 minutes **Marinate** 1 hour **Stand** 20 minutes
Grill 8 minutes **Makes** 4 servings

4	tuna steaks, 1 inch thick
⅓	cup olive bruschetta topping,* *Delallo®*
1	tablespoon capers, drained, *Star®*
1	teaspoon bottled crushed garlic, *Christopher Ranch®*
1½	cups Italian dressing, *Newman's Own®*
4	cups mixed salad greens, *Fresh Express®*
2	hard-cooked eggs, sliced
1	cup frozen French-cut green beans, thawed and drained
1	tomato, cut into wedges
1	can (15-ounce) sliced potatoes
	Fresh basil sprigs (optional)

1. Using a sharp knife, cut a pocket into the side of each tuna steak, cutting about halfway through the tuna steak; set aside. In a medium bowl, combine olive bruschetta topping, capers, and garlic. Set aside 1 tablespoon of olive mixture. Stuff remaining olive mixture into pockets in tuna steaks and secure openings with toothpicks.

2. Place stuffed tuna steaks in a large zip-top bag; cover with Italian dressing. Squeeze air out of bag and seal. Marinate in refrigerator 1 to 3 hours.

3. Set up grill for direct cooking over medium heat (see page 17). Oil grate when ready to start cooking. Remove tuna steaks from marinade; discard marinade. Let tuna steaks stand at room temperature about 20 minutes.

4. Place tuna on hot, oiled grill. Cook 8 to 12 minutes or until fish flakes easily when tested with a fork, turning once. (Be careful not to overcook; tuna will dry out quickly.) Remove tuna from grill; set aside.

5. Divide mixed salad greens among 4 plates. Remove toothpicks from tuna steaks. Place a grilled tuna steak on top of each salad. Top each tuna steak with some of the reserved olive mixture. Around the edges of the plates, arrange egg slices, green beans, tomato wedges, and sliced potatoes. Garnish with fresh basil sprigs (optional).

*NOTE: If olive bruschetta topping is not available, substitute purchased olive tapenade or chopped black olives.

Bay Shrimp and Avocado Salad

Prep 5 minutes   **Makes** 2 servings

8   ounces cooked, peeled, and deveined bay or other shrimp
1   cup shredded carrots, rinsed and drained, *Ready Pac®*
½   cup frozen petite peas, thawed, *Green Giant®*
½   cup frozen cut corn kernels, thawed, *Green Giant®*
4   tablespoons Champagne vinaigrette, *Girard's®*
    Salt and ground black pepper
1   firm, ripe avocado, halved and pitted

1. In a medium bowl, toss shrimp, carrots, peas, corn, and 3 tablespoons of the vinaigrette to coat.

2. Season shrimp salad to taste with salt and pepper.

3. Place one avocado half onto each of 2 plates. Spoon shrimp salad on top of avocado halves. Drizzle remaining 1 tablespoon vinaigrette over avocado halves and serve.

Cajun Salmon Salad

Prep 15 minutes   **Grill** 8 minutes   **Makes** 4 servings

1   1-pound fresh or frozen salmon fillet
1   tablespoon extra virgin olive oil, *Bertolli®*
2   tablespoons Cajun seasoning, *McCormick®*
½   cup fat-free Thousand Island salad dressing, *Kraft®*
1   teaspoon hot pepper sauce, *Tabasco®*
¼   teaspoon Cajun seasoning, *McCormick®*
4   cups packaged lettuce mix, *Ready Pac®*
1   cup cooked brown rice, *Uncle Ben's® Ready Rice*
1   cup no-salt-added organic kidney beans, rinsed and drained, *Eden®*
½   cup chopped roasted red bell peppers, *Delallo®*

1. Thaw fish, if frozen. Set up grill for direct cooking over medium-high heat (see page 17). Oil grate when ready to start grilling. If present, remove bones from salmon. Brush both sides of fish with olive oil and sprinkle with the 2 tablespoons Cajun seasoning; set aside.

2. Place fish on hot oiled grill. Cook for 4 to 6 minutes per side or until fish flakes easily when tested with a fork. Do not overcook.

3. For dressing, in a small bowl, combine salad dressing, hot pepper sauce, and the ¼ teaspoon Cajun seasoning. Divide lettuce among 4 chilled plates. Top each plate with ¼ cup rice, ¼ cup beans, 2 tablespoons bell peppers, and one-quarter of the fish. Serve with dressing.

Spinach and Tomatoes With Feta

Start to Finish 10 minutes   **Makes** 4 servings

2	tablespoons extra virgin olive oil, *Bertolli®*
1	teaspoon bottled crushed garlic, *Christopher Ranch®*
2	bags (12 ounces each) baby spinach, *Fresh Express®*
1	can (15-ounce) petite diced tomatoes, drained, *S&W®*
2	teaspoons lemon juice, *ReaLemon®*
1	package (4-ounce) crumbled feta cheese, *Athenos®*

1. In a large skillet, heat oil over medium-high heat. Add garlic and swirl around pan. Add spinach and cook until almost wilted, using tongs to turn occasionally.

2. Add drained tomatoes and wilt spinach completely. Transfer to a serving bowl; stir in lemon juice. Top with crumbled feta cheese. Serve immediately.

Herb and Rib-Eye Salad

Prep 15 minutes   **Cook** 7 minutes   **Makes** 2 servings

1	beef rib-eye steak, 1 inch thick
	Salt and ground black pepper
1	tablespoon canola oil, *Wesson®*
1	head butter lettuce, leaves removed and torn
¼	cup fresh thyme leaves
¼	cup chopped fresh chives
¼	cup fresh tarragon leaves
¼	cup torn fresh basil leaves
2	roma tomatoes, seeded and diced
	Balsamic vinaigrette, *Newman's Own®*

1. Season the steak generously on both sides with salt and pepper. In a large heavy skillet, heat oil over medium heat. Add the steak and cook for about 4 minutes or until seared and well-crusted on 1 side. Turn and cook 3 minutes more for medium-rare or 4 minutes more for medium.

2. Transfer steak to cutting board and let rest, covered loosely with foil. Meanwhile, combine lettuce and herbs; divide between 2 plates. Thinly slice steak across the grain, trimming away fat. Arrange steak slices on top of greens. Sprinkle with diced tomatoes and drizzle with vinaigrette.

BBQ Chicken Salad

Start to Finish 10 minutes **Makes** 4 servings

10	cups (about 12 ounces) Italian lettuce mix, *Fresh Express®*
½	cup ranch salad dressing, *Hidden Valley®*
2	packages (6 ounces each) grilled chicken strips, *Oscar Mayer®*
⅓	cup BBQ sauce, *Bull's Eye®*
½	cup shredded cheddar cheese, *Kraft®*
1	can (11-ounce) mexicorn, *Green Giant®*
1	can (4-ounce) diced green chiles, *Ortega®*
¼	cup real crumbled bacon, *Hormel®*
1	cup french fried onions, *French's®*

1. In a large bowl, toss salad mix with ranch dressing and set aside. In a medium bowl, toss chicken strips with BBQ sauce and set aside.

2. Divide dressed salad among 4 chilled dinner plates. Top each with chicken strips. Arrange remaining ingredients on salads. Serve immediately.

Fried Chicken Salad

Start to Finish 20 minutes **Makes** 4 servings

1	box (12-ounce) popcorn chicken, *Tyson®*
½	cup ranch dressing, *Hidden Valley®*
2	teaspoons BBQ seasoning, *McCormick® Grill Mates®*
8	cups romaine and/or iceberg lettuce, chopped
1	cucumber, thinly sliced (optional)

1. Preheat oven to 425 degrees F. Line baking sheet with foil. Place popcorn chicken on baking sheet. Bake in preheated oven for 8 to 10 minutes or until crispy and heated through.

2. For dressing, in a small bowl, mix together ranch dressing and seasoning; set aside. Divide lettuce onto 4 cold plates. Top with chicken pieces and, if desired, cucumber slices. Drizzle dressing over salad.

Chicken-Tarragon Salad

Start to Finish 15 minutes **Makes** 4 servings

½	cup fat-free mayonnaise, *Hellmann's®* or *Best Foods®*
¼	cup fat-free plain yogurt, *Horizon Organic®*
2	teaspoons chopped fresh tarragon
1	teaspoon poppy seeds, *McCormick®*
2	pouches (7 ounces each) chunk chicken breast meat, rinsed and drained, *Tyson®*
1	cup seedless red grapes, cut in half
2	ribs celery, chopped
¼	cup chopped walnuts, *Planters®*
6	cups packaged spring mix lettuce, *Ready Pac®*
¼	cup chopped red onion

1. For dressing, in a small bowl, whisk together mayonnaise, yogurt, 1 teaspoon of the tarragon, and poppy seeds; set aside.

2. In a medium bowl, combine chicken, grapes, and celery. Set aside 1 tablespoon of the walnuts. Add remaining walnuts to chicken. Pour ½ cup of the dressing over mixture and stir to combine.

3. In a large bowl, toss lettuce with the remaining ¼ cup dressing. Divide mixture among 4 chilled plates. Divide chicken mixture among plates. Sprinkle each plate with some of the remaining 1 teaspoon tarragon, the reserved walnuts, and the onion.

Tropical Chicken Salad

Prep 15 minutes **Grill** 8 minutes **Makes** 4 servings

4	boneless, skinless chicken breast halves
2	teaspoons extra virgin olive oil, *Bertolli®*
	Refrigerated pineapple chunks, *Del Monte®*
⅓	cup fat-free plain yogurt, *Horizon Organic®*
1	tablespoon orange juice concentrate, *Minute Maid®*
4	cups packaged chopped romaine lettuce, *Ready Pac®*
1	cup refrigerated mango chunks, drained, *Del Monte®*
8	whole strawberries
1	avocado, sliced

1. Set up grill for direct cooking over high heat (see page 17). Oil grate when ready to start cooking. Brush both sides of chicken breast halves with olive oil. Place chicken on hot oiled grill. Cook for 4 to 6 minutes per side or until chicken is no longer pink (170 degrees F).

2. For dressing, drain pineapple, reserving ⅓ cup juice. Measure 1 cup pineapple chunks; set aside. (Refrigerate remaining juice and pineapple for another use.) In a small bowl, whisk together the ⅓ cup reserved pineapple juice, yogurt, and orange juice concentrate. Set aside.

3. On a large serving platter, arrange romaine lettuce, chicken, pineapple chunks, mango chunks, strawberries, and avocado slices. Serve with dressing.

Smoked Turkey and Pear Salad with Pomegranate Vinaigrette

Start to Finish 20 minutes   **Makes** 4 servings

FOR POMEGRANATE VINAIGRETTE:
3   tablespoons extra virgin olive oil, *Bertolli*®
2   tablespoons pomegranate juice, *Pom*®
2   tablespoons red wine vinegar
1   tablespoon garlic and herb salad dressing mix, *Good Seasons*®

FOR PROSCIUTTO CROUTONS:
3   ounces prosciutto, thinly sliced
1   tablespoon extra virgin olive oil, *Bertolli*®

FOR SMOKED TURKEY AND PEAR SALAD:
1   bag (5-ounce) prewashed baby arugula, *Ready Pac*®
12   ounces smoked cooked turkey breast, thinly sliced and rolled
1   can (15-ounce) sliced pears, drained, *Del Monte*®
2   ounces goat cheese, cut into ⅛-inch slices, *Silver Goat*®
⅓   cup glazed walnuts and almonds, *Emerald*®

1. For Pomegranate Vinaigrette, in a small bowl, whisk together olive oil, pomegranate juice, vinegar, and salad dressing mix; set aside.

2. For Prosciutto Croutons, separate prosciutto slices and roll up slices, starting from short ends. Cut into ½-inch pieces. In a medium skillet, heat olive oil over medium-high heat. Add rolled prosciutto pieces to hot oil; cook for 3 to 4 minutes or until brown on all sides. Using a slotted spoon, remove prosciutto from skillet; drain on paper towels.

3. For Smoked Turkey and Pear Salad, divide the arugula among 4 plates. Top each portion with rolled turkey slices, pear slices, goat cheese, glazed nuts, and Prosciutto Croutons. Drizzle with the Pomegranate Vinaigrette.

Greek Turkey Salad

Start to Finish 20 minutes **Makes** 6 servings

	Olive oil cooking spray, *Pam®*
1	package (1.25-pound) turkey breast strips, *Jennie-O®*
2	tablespoons lemon juice, *ReaLemon®*
1	tablespoon Greek seasoning, *Spice Islands®*
	Salt and ground black pepper
12	cups (about 20 ounces) packaged chopped romaine lettuce
1	cucumber, seeded and chopped
2	medium tomatoes, cut up
½	medium red onion, thinly sliced
½	cup pitted kalamata olives, drained, *Mezzetta®*
⅓	cup crumbled feta cheese, *Athenos®*
¾	cup light roasted garlic balsamic salad dressing, *Bernstein's®*
¼	cup fresh oregano leaves

1. Coat a large nonstick skillet with cooking spray. Heat skillet over medium-high heat. Add turkey, lemon juice, and Greek seasoning. Cook and stir for 5 to 7 minutes or until turkey is cooked through. Season with salt and pepper. Set aside to cool.

2. In a large salad bowl, combine romaine, cucumber, tomatoes, red onion, olives, and feta cheese. Toss with salad dressing. Top with turkey strips. Garnish with oregano leaves.

Steak Salad

Start to Finish 10 minutes **Makes** 4 servings

¾	cup evaporated milk, *Carnation®*
¼	cup mayonnaise, *Hellmann's®* or *Best Foods®*
1½	tablespoons finely chopped fresh chives
1	tablespoon lemon juice, *ReaLemon®*
1	tablespoon prepared horseradish, *Morehouse®*
1	tablespoon finely chopped fresh flat-leaf parsley
	Salt and ground black pepper
12	ounces leftover cooked beef steak, sliced on the bias
1	bag (7-ounce) mixed greens, *Ready Pac®*
½	cucumber, sliced
1	tomato, sliced
1	cup croutons

1. In a bowl, whisk together milk, mayonnaise, chives, lemon juice, horseradish, and parsley. Season with salt and pepper. Microwave leftover steak on medium-high setting (80 percent power) for 2 to 3 minutes or until hot, stirring once. Divide mixed greens among 4 chilled dinner plates. Divide sliced cucumber and tomatoes evenly among the salads. Divide steak among salads. Pour dressing over each and top with ¼ cup of croutons.

Comfort Food

Comfort food is cold weather food. I went to college in Wisconsin, where the air turns nippy in September and stays chilly until May. Even when the temperature dipped and the leaves fell from the trees, inside the cafeteria, we knew that food equaled warmth.

No matter how old we become—or how far we roam—simple foods wrap us in a sense of security. This chapter is filled with the foods from our past, nostalgic favorites updated with a nouveau twist. Every mouthful is a cure-all, soothing us, cheering us, giving us comfort as only food can.

The Recipes

Country Biscuits And Gravy

Prep 5 minutes   **Cook** 12 minutes   **Makes** 4 servings

8	ounces (bulk) pork sausage, crumbled, *Jimmy Dean®*
1	can (10.5-ounce) white sauce, *Aunt Penny's®*
¾	cup whole milk
	Salt and ground black pepper
1	package (10.2-ounce) buttermilk biscuits, *Pillsbury® Grands!®*

1. In a small skillet, cook sausage over medium heat for about 4 minutes or until cooked through. Add white sauce and milk. Bring to a simmer. Cover and simmer 2 minutes to blend flavors. Season to taste with salt and pepper.

2. Meanwhile, bake biscuits according to package instructions. Split baked biscuits in half; place two halves on each plate. Spoon sausage mixture over biscuits. Serve hot.

Cream of Wheat Brûlée

Prep 5 minutes   **Cook** 3 minutes   **Makes** 4 servings

4	packets (28 grams each) instant *Cream of Wheat®*
2⅔	cups milk
1	teaspoon almond extract, *McCormick®*
4	tablespoons packed light brown sugar
	Fresh blueberries
	Half-and-half

1. Move oven rack to top shelf of oven (4 inches from heat source). Preheat broiler. Line a baking sheet with foil.

2. In each of 4 ceramic soufflé dishes, combine one Cream of Wheat packet, ⅔ cup milk, and ¼ teaspoon almond extract. Microwave individually on high heat setting (100 percent power) for 1½ to 2 minutes. Remove and stir. Sprinkle each dish with 1 tablespoon brown sugar.

3. Place dishes on prepared baking sheet. Broil for 2 to 3 minutes or until caramelized and bubbling. Remove from oven. Serve immediately with blueberries and half-and-half.

Pumpkin Cinnamon Pancakes

Prep 5 minutes   **Cook** 6 minutes   **Makes** 2 servings

If you're a pumpkin lover like me, I've got your number—six, that is! This stack of six pancakes is every pumpkin fan's dream. This idea came to me on a fall trip to New York. It was "pumpkin everything" at the Regency Hotel, and the pumpkin pancakes were the best I'd ever tasted—so here's my Semi-Homemade® version for you to enjoy!

PECAN SYRUP:

1	cup maple-flavored pancake syrup, *Log Cabin Original Syrup®*
5	tablespoons chopped pecans, toasted, *Diamond®*

PUMPKIN CINNAMON PANCAKES:

1	cup buttermilk pancake mix, *Aunt Jemima®*
⅔	cup cold water
⅓	cup canned pumpkin, *Libby's®*
½	teaspoon ground cinnamon, *McCormick®*
⅛	teaspoon ground ginger, *McCormick®*
	Nonstick vegetable cooking spray, *Pam®*
	Butter

1. For Pecan Syrup, in a small microwave-safe bowl, combine maple syrup and pecans. Microwave on high heat setting (100 percent power) for about 25 seconds or until hot. Set Pecan Syrup aside and keep warm.

2. For Pumpkin Cinnamon Pancakes, in a medium bowl, whisk pancake mix, water, pumpkin, cinnamon, and ginger just until blended (do not overmix; batter should be lumpy).

3. Spray a heavy griddle with nonstick spray; heat griddle over medium heat. Spoon 2 tablespoons of the batter onto griddle to form each pancake. Cook about 2 minutes or until bubbles appear. Turn pancakes over and cook 2 minutes longer. Transfer pancakes to plates. Top with butter and warm Pecan Syrup.

Ricotta Pancakes

Prep 10 minutes **Cook** 8 minutes **Makes** 4 servings

1	cup part-skim ricotta cheese, *Precious®*
4	eggs, separated
½	cup baking mix, *Bisquick®*
½	stick (¼ cup) butter, melted
3	tablespoons lemon juice, *ReaLemon®*
2	tablespoons sugar
1	teaspoon lemon extract, *McCormick®*
½	teaspoon ground nutmeg, *McCormick®*
	Raspberry or boysenberry syrup, *Knott's Berry Farm®*
	Fresh berries (optional)

1. In a large bowl, use an electric mixer on low speed to combine ricotta, egg yolks, baking mix, butter, lemon juice, sugar, lemon extract, and nutmeg. Using clean beaters,* in a small bowl, beat egg whites until stiff but not dry. Carefully fold one-third of the egg whites into batter to loosen batter. Gently fold in remaining egg whites. Lightly grease a heavy griddle; heat griddle over medium heat. Pour ⅓ cup of the batter at a time onto griddle. Cook until edges are dry. Turn pancakes over and cook until golden brown. Serve hot with fruit syrup and garnish with fresh berries (optional).

*TIP: Egg whites will not whip properly if any oil is on equipment.

Apple-Raisin Sandwiches

Prep 5 minutes **Cook** 8 minutes **Makes** 2 servings

2	eggs
¼	cup whole milk
¼	teaspoon ground cinnamon, *McCormick®*
4	slices raisin bread, *Wonder®*
½	cup prepared apple pie filling, *Comstock®* or *Wilderness®*
1	tablespoon butter
	Powdered sugar, *C&H®* (optional)

1. In a large baking dish, whisk together eggs, milk, and cinnamon. Make 2 sandwiches with the bread and apple pie filling. Place sandwiches into egg mixture. Let soak about 3 minutes or until egg mixture is absorbed into the bread, turning sandwiches over occasionally.

2. On a griddle, melt butter over medium-low heat. Add sandwiches and cook about 4 minutes per side or until brown and heated through. Cut each sandwich in half. Sprinkle with powdered sugar (optional).

Crepes Benedict

Prep 10 minutes   **Cook** 8 minutes   **Makes** 2 servings

4	slices turkey bacon, *Butterball*®
2	10-inch prepared crepes, *Frieda's*®
4	eggs
2	tablespoons butter
	Salt and ground black pepper
⅓	cup canned hollandaise sauce, *Aunt Penny's*®

1. Prepare bacon according to package instructions. Place crepes in plastic wrap. Microwave on high setting (100 percent power) for 20 seconds. Whisk eggs in a bowl.

2. In a medium skillet, melt butter over medium heat. Add eggs; stir constantly for about 2 minutes or until light and fluffy. Season eggs to taste with salt and pepper.

3. Place hollandaise sauce into a microwave-safe cup; microwave on high setting (100 percent power) about 45 seconds, stirring every 15 seconds. Season sauce to taste with salt and pepper. Set aside.

4. Place 1 crepe on each breakfast plate. Spoon half the scrambled eggs into the center of each crepe and top with 2 bacon slices. Roll up enchilada-style. Top crepes with hollandaise sauce and serve.

Pesto Chicken Panini

Start to Finish 10 minutes   **Makes** 4 servings

¼	cup plus 2 tablespoons purchased pesto, *Delallo®*
¼	cup mayonnaise, *Hellmann's®* or *Best Foods®*
1	loaf (16-ounce) ciabatta bread, sliced in half horizontally
2	packages (6 ounces each) grilled chicken strips, *Oscar Mayer®*
1	cup baby arugula or spinach, rinsed and patted dry
2	tomatoes, sliced
15	fresh basil leaves
4	slices presliced mozzarella, *Tillamook®*

1. In a bowl, stir together ¼ cup of the pesto and the mayonnaise. Spread mixture on both halves of ciabatta bread. In a medium bowl, toss chicken strips with remaining 2 tablespoons pesto.

2. On bottom half of bread, place arugula, then pesto chicken mixture. Top with tomatoes, basil leaves, cheese, and top half of bread. Cut into 4 portions and serve.

Tuscan Tomato Soup with Basil

Start to Finish 10 minutes   **Makes** 4 servings

1	can (28-ounce) whole peeled tomatoes with basil, *Progresso®*
1	tablespoon extra virgin olive oil, *Bertolli®*
1	cup frozen chopped onion, *Ore-Ida®*
1	teaspoon bottled crushed garlic, *Christopher Ranch®*
1½	teaspoons Italian seasoning, *McCormick®*
1	cup white wine (such as Chardonnay)
2	tablespoons chopped fresh basil leaves

1. Place tomatoes in a blender; puree. In a medium saucepan, heat olive oil over medium-high heat. Add onion and garlic; cook and stir for 1 to 2 minutes. Add pureed tomatoes, Italian seasoning, and wine. Bring to a boil. Reduce heat and simmer for 5 minutes. Serve garnished with chopped basil.

Cafeteria-Style Macaroni and Cheese

Prep 15 minutes **Bake** 55 minutes **Makes** 12 servings

Sure, the blue box is easy, but a little extra effort pays off big in taste. Evaporated milk makes it rich, hot pepper sauce and paprika add spice, but it's the crunchy crumb topping that nudges it near nirvana.

	Nonstick cooking spray, *Pam*®
1	pound elbow macaroni, uncooked, *Anthony's*®
5	tablespoons melted butter, divided
1	pound American cheese, grated, *Kraft*®
2	cans (12 ounces each) evaporated milk, *Carnation*®
2	cups water
4	eggs, lightly beaten
2½	teaspoons ground mustard, *Coleman's*®
2	teaspoons Worcestershire sauce, *Lea & Perrins*®
1	teaspoon salt
¼	teaspoon hot pepper sauce, *Tabasco*®
1	cup bread crumbs, *Progresso*®
1	teaspoon paprika, *McCormick*®

1. Preheat oven to 350 degrees F. Lightly coat a 9×13-inch baking dish with cooking spray.

2. In a large bowl, toss uncooked macaroni with 3 tablespoons of the melted butter to coat. Add cheese and combine thoroughly. Transfer to prepared baking dish.

3. In a medium bowl, whisk together evaporated milk, water, eggs, ground mustard, Worcestershire sauce, salt, and hot sauce. Pour evaporated milk mixture over macaroni mixture. Bake in preheated oven for 55 to 60 minutes. Remove from oven.

4. Move top rack of oven to highest position under broiler. Preheat broiler. Meanwhile, combine bread crumbs, paprika, and remaining 2 tablespoons butter. Sprinkle over baked macaroni and cheese.

5. Place macaroni and cheese under broiler. Broil for 1 to 2 minutes or until golden brown.

Comfort Food | 61

Grilled Cheese Dippers with Tomato Soup

Prep 10 minutes **Cook** 10 minutes **Makes** 4 servings

GRILLED CHEESE DIPPERS:
1	can (10.75-ounce) condensed Southwest-style pepper Jack soup, *Campbell's*®
8	ounces shredded Mexican cheese blend, *Kraft*®
1	French bread baguette, sliced ½ inch thick
½	stick (¼ cup) butter, softened

TOMATO SOUP:
1	can (10.75-ounce) condensed tomato soup, *Campbell's*®
1	can (10.75-ounce) condensed cheddar cheese soup, *Campbell's*®
3	cups spicy vegetable juice, *V8*®
2	teaspoons hot pepper sauce, *Tabasco*®
1	teaspoon dried basil, *McCormick*®

1. For Grilled Cheese Dippers, in a bowl, combine pepper Jack soup and the shredded cheese. Spread mixture on half of the baguette slices; top with the remaining baguette slices. Butter the outside of the sandwiches.

2. In a large skillet, cook sandwiches over medium-high heat for about 2 minutes per side or until golden brown. (Cover skillet to ensure the cheese melts.)

3. For Tomato Soup, in a medium saucepan, combine tomato soup, cheddar cheese soup, vegetable juice, hot pepper sauce, and dried basil. Heat over medium heat until heated through, stirring occasionally. Serve soup in mugs with Grilled Cheese Dippers.

Western Meat Loaf Sandwich

Start to Finish 10 minutes   **Makes** 4 servings

1	package (17-ounce) prepared meat loaf, *Hormel*®
2	tablespoons tartar sauce, *Best Foods*®
1	tablespoon Dijon mustard, *Grey Poupon*®
1	tablespoon chili sauce, *Heinz*®
4	onion rolls
4	leaves romaine lettuce
1	tomato, sliced
4	slices pepper Jack cheese, *Tillamook*®
⅓	cup french fried onions, *French's*®

1. Cook meat loaf in microwave according to package directions. Remove from package; cut into thick slices and set aside. Meanwhile, in a small bowl, stir together tartar sauce, mustard, and chili sauce.

2. Split onion rolls. Spread sauce on bottom half of rolls. Place lettuce and tomato slices on each. Top with a meat loaf slice, cheese slice, fried onions, and top half of roll. Serve immediately.

Black Bean Salad

Start to Finish 10 minutes   **Makes** 4 servings

1	can (15-ounce) 50-percent-less-sodium black beans, drained and rinsed, *S&W*®
¾	cup premade pico de gallo, *Ready Pac*®
½	cup diced tri-color peppers, *Ready Pac*®
2	tablespoons cilantro and pepita Caesar dressing, *El Torito*®

1. In a large bowl, toss together all ingredients.

2. Serve immediately.

Blue Cheese -Bacon Burgers

Prep 20 minutes   **Broil** 8 minutes   **Makes** 4 servings

BLUE CHEESE BUTTER:
½   **stick (¼ cup) butter**
2   **tablespoons blue cheese crumbles, *Treasure Cave*®**

BLUE CHEESE-BACON BURGERS:
1½   **pounds lean ground beef**
½   **cup blue cheese crumbles, *Treasure Cave*®**
¼   **cup real bacon pieces, *Hormel*®**
1   **tablespoon Montreal steak seasoning, *McCormick*®**
     ***Grill Mates*®**
     Onion rolls
     Lettuce, tomato, onion

1. For the Blue Cheese Butter, in a small bowl, use a fork to smash together butter and blue cheese crumbles; set aside.

2. Preheat broiler. Line a baking sheet with foil; place a wire rack over foil. For the Blue Cheese-Bacon Burgers, in a large bowl, stir together ground beef, blue cheese crumbles, bacon pieces, and steak seasoning. Wet your hands to prevent sticking and shape beef mixture into 4 patties slightly larger than the buns. Cover and chill.

3. Preheat broiler. Place burgers on wire rack on prepared baking sheet. Broil 6 inches from heat source for 4 to 5 minutes per side for medium.

4. Spread toasted onion roll with Blue Cheese Butter. Place burger on roll bottom; top with lettuce, tomato, and onion. Add top of roll.

Chili Fountain Fries

Prep 5 minutes   **Broil** 8 minutes   **Makes** 4 servings

1   **bag (28-ounce) frozen steak fries, thawed, *Ore-Ida*®**
2   **tablespoons canola oil, *Wesson*®**
1   **tablespoon chili seasoning, *McCormick*®**
     Barbecue sauce, *Heinz*®

1. Preheat broiler. Place frozen fries on a foil-lined baking sheet.

2. Toss fries with oil and chili seasoning.

3. Broil fries for 8 to 12 minutes or until crispy and light brown, turning once. Serve hot with barbecue sauce for dipping.

Pretzel-Crusted Chicken

Prep 10 minutes   **Bake** 10 minutes   **Makes** 4 servings

4   cups unsalted tiny pretzels, crushed, *Laura Scudder's®*
4   6-ounce boneless, skinless chicken breast halves,
         cut into 1-inch-thick strips
¾   cup honey Dijon mustard, *French's®*
3   tablespoons organic chicken broth, *Swanson®*
1½   teaspoons dried Italian seasoning, *McCormick®*

1. Preheat oven to 375 degrees F. Line a baking sheet with foil; set aside. Place crushed pretzels in a pie plate; set aside.

2. Brush both sides of chicken pieces with ¼ cup of the honey mustard. Press chicken into crushed pretzels to coat. Place on the prepared baking sheet. Bake chicken in preheated oven about 10 minutes or until chicken is no longer pink.

3. Meanwhile, in a small microwave-safe bowl, combine the remaining ½ cup honey mustard, chicken broth, and Italian seasoning. Microwave on high heat setting (100 percent power) about 1 minute or until heated through. Serve with chicken.

Bacon and Scallion Potato Salad

Start to Finish 10 minutes   **Makes** 4 servings

1   package (16-ounce) precooked rosemary and garlic potatoes,
         Reser's®
⅓   cup mayonnaise, *Hellmann's®* or *Best Foods®*
¼   cup real bacon pieces, *Hormel®* (plus more for garnish,
         optional)
2   scallions (green onions), finely chopped (plus more for garnish,
         optional)
1   teaspoon dried tarragon, crushed, *McCormick®*
1   teaspoon bottled crushed garlic, *Christopher Ranch®*
1   teaspoon Dijon mustard, *Grey Poupon®*
1   teaspoon balsamic vinegar

1. Place potatoes in a microwave-safe bowl. Cover with plastic wrap; microwave on high heat setting (100 percent power) for 5 to 7 minutes.

2. In a medium bowl, combine mayonnaise, the ¼ cup bacon pieces, the 2 finely chopped scallions, the tarragon, garlic, mustard, and vinegar. Add cooked potatoes and toss to combine. Garnish with bacon pieces and chopped scallion (optional). Serve warm or chilled.

Smothered Chicken

Prep 15 minutes   **Cook** 28 minutes   **Makes** 4 servings

3½	pounds cut-up chicken
1	packet (5-ounce) fry coating, *Dixie Fry*®
2	tablespoons salt-free chicken seasoning, divided, *McCormick*® *Grill Mates*®
	Canola oil
2	jars (12 ounces each) roasted chicken gravy, *Franco American*®
1	teaspoon bottled crushed garlic, *Christopher Ranch*®

1. Cut away excess skin and fat from chicken pieces. Rinse with cold water; do not pat dry. In a shallow bowl, stir together fry coating and 1 tablespoon of the chicken seasoning. Dredge chicken pieces in coating mixture and shake off excess.

2. In a large straight-sided pan, heat ½ inch oil over medium-high heat. Oil is ready for frying when a drop of water splatters when dropped in (350 degrees F). Place a few pieces of coated chicken in oil (oil temperature will drop; maintain temperature at 325 degrees F). Fry chicken for 4 to 5 minutes per side or until chicken is golden brown. Remove chicken from pan; drain on a paper towel-lined plate. Repeat process with remaining chicken pieces.

3. In a medium bowl, stir together gravy, remaining chicken seasoning, and crushed garlic. Place chicken in large saucepan. Pour gravy over chicken and bring to a boil over medium heat. Reduce heat, cover, and simmer for 20 minutes. Serve hot.

Cajun Mashed Potatoes

Prep 5 minutes   **Cook** 5 minutes   **Makes** 4 servings

1	container (24-ounce) mashed potatoes, *Country Crock*®
¼	cup buttermilk
2	teaspoons Cajun seasoning, *McCormick*®

1. Uncover the container of mashed potatoes and microwave on high heat setting (100 percent power) for 5 to 6 minutes, stirring once. Transfer mashed potatoes to a medium bowl. Add buttermilk and Cajun seasoning. Stir thoroughly. Serve hot.

BBQ Brisket with Guinness® Mop Sauce

Prep 15 minutes **Grill** 3½ hours **Stand** 10 minutes **Makes** 12 servings

1	6-pound beef brisket
15	whole peeled garlic cloves, *Global Farms®*
2	tablespoons Montreal steak seasoning, *McCormick® Grill Mates®*
2	teaspoons gumbo filé, *Zatarain's®*
1	packet (1.31-ounce) sloppy joe mix, *McCormick®*
2	bottles (12 ounces each) stout, *Guinness®*
1	cup or more apple cider, *Tree Top®*
2	sweet onions, sliced
2	cups barbecue sauce, *KC Masterpiece®*

1. Soak 1 cup *hickory or oak wood chips* in water for at least 1 hour; drain. Set up grill for indirect cooking over medium heat (no direct heat source under brisket; see page 17).

2. Cut small slits all over brisket and insert garlic cloves. In a small bowl, combine steak seasoning, gumbo filé, and sloppy joe mix. Rub seasoning mixture into brisket and place in foil baking pan. Pour stout over top. Add enough apple cider to cover brisket halfway. Top with onions. Cover with heavy-duty foil.

3. Place on hot grill over drip pan. Cover grill and cook for 2½ hours. If using charcoal, add 10 briquettes to each pile of coals every hour.

4. Remove brisket and foil pan from grill. Add wood chips to smoke box if using gas grill or place chips onto hot coals if using charcoal. Remove brisket from braising liquid and place directly on grill grate over drip pan. Reserve onions and braising liquid.

5. To make mop sauce, combine 2 cups of the braising liquid with the barbecue sauce. Baste brisket thoroughly with mop sauce. Cover grill. Cook for 1 hour more, turning and basting brisket with sauce every 20 minutes. Transfer brisket to cutting board and let stand for 10 minutes. Thinly slice beef against the grain. Serve with sweet onions and mop sauce on the side.

Herbed Pork Roast and Cranberry-Pine Nut Chutney

Prep 5 minutes   **Cook** 1 hour 15 minutes   **Stand** 5 minutes
Makes 4 servings

FOR PORK ROAST:
2½	pounds boneless pork loin roast, rinsed and patted dry
	Salt and ground black pepper
2	tablespoons herbes de Provence, *McCormick®*
1	teaspoon onion powder, *McCormick®*
1	tablespoon bottled crushed garlic, *Christopher Ranch®*
1	tablespoon lemon juice, *ReaLemon®*

FOR CHUTNEY:
1	can (16-ounce) whole cranberry sauce, *Ocean Spray®*
⅓	cup pine nuts, lightly toasted
1	teaspoon lemon juice, *ReaLemon®*
1	teaspoon herbes de Provence, *McCormick®*
¼	teaspoon bottled crushed garlic, *Christopher Ranch®*

1. Preheat oven to 450 degrees F. For Pork Roast, season pork roast with salt and pepper. In a small bowl, stir together herbes de Provence, onion powder, garlic, and lemon juice. Rub over pork roast and place roast in shallow roasting pan. Place roast in preheated oven and reduce heat to 325 degrees F. Roast about 30 minutes per pound or until internal temperature reaches 165 degrees F. (Roast will continue to cook up to 170 degrees F out of the oven.) Let pork roast rest for 5 to 10 minutes before slicing.

2. To make the Chutney, in a medium bowl, combine cranberry sauce, pine nuts, lemon juice, herbes de Provence, and garlic; stir thoroughly. Serve chutney at room temperature with sliced pork.

TIP: Herbes de Provence is a blend of dry herbs most commonly used in southern France. It usually contains basil, fennel seeds, lavender, marjoram, rosemary, sage, summer savory, and thyme.

Apricot-Glazed Baby Back Ribs

Start to Finish 20 minutes   **Makes** 4 servings

1   jar (18-ounce) apricot preserves, *Smucker's*®
¼   cup spicy Thai chili sauce, *Thai Kitchen*®
2   packages (26 ounces each) fully cooked baby back ribs

1. Preheat broiler. Line a baking sheet with foil; set aside. For glaze, in a medium saucepan, combine preserves and chili sauce over medium heat. Cook for 2 to 4 minutes or until heated through; set aside.

2. Remove ribs from packages. If any excess sauce from the package remains on ribs, wipe off. Place ribs, meaty sides up, on prepared baking sheet. Broil 6 to 8 inches from the heat for 6 minutes. Turn ribs; brush glaze over back sides of ribs. Broil for 4 minutes. Turn; brush with glaze. Broil for 2 minutes more.

3. Remove ribs from broiler; generously brush both sides with glaze. Cut into serving-size (3 or 4 bones) pieces. Serve with remaining glaze on the side.

Cauliflower Gratin

Start to Finish 15 minutes   **Makes** 4 servings

1   can (10¾-ounce) condensed cheddar cheese soup, *Campbell's*®
1   package (10-ounce) frozen cauliflower florets, thawed, *Pictsweet*®
¼   teaspoon cayenne pepper, *McCormick*®
¼   teaspoon salt
½   cup shredded Mexican cheese blend, *Sargento*®
2   tablespoons grated Parmesan cheese, *DiGiorno*®
2   tablespoons Italian-style bread crumbs, *Progresso*®
1   teaspoon extra virgin olive oil, *Bertolli*®

1. Preheat broiler. In a microwave-safe, broiler-safe dish, combine soup, cauliflower, cayenne pepper, and salt. Stir in Mexican cheese blend. Cover with plastic wrap; microwave on high heat setting (100 percent power) for 6 minutes. In a small bowl, combine Parmesan cheese, bread crumbs, and olive oil. Spoon bread crumb mixture over cauliflower mixture. Broil 6 inches from heat for 1 to 2 minutes or until top is golden brown. Serve hot.

Creole Short Ribs

Prep 15 minutes **Cook** 2½ hours **Makes** 6 servings

1½	cups all-purpose flour
2	tablespoons blackened seasoning, *Old Bay*®
4½	pounds meaty beef short ribs, rinsed and patted dry
2	tablespoons canola oil
1	can (14.5-ounce) diced tomatoes with green bell peppers, celery, and onion, *Hunt's*®
1	can (14-ounce) reduced-sodium beef broth, *Swanson*®
2	ribs celery, finely chopped
1	cup frozen chopped onion, *Ore-Ida*®
1	cup frozen chopped green bell pepper, *Pictsweet*®
1	tablespoon bottled crushed garlic, *Christopher Ranch*®

1. In a small bowl, combine flour and blackened seasoning. Dredge short ribs in flour mixture.

2. In a large straight-sided, oven-proof skillet with lid, heat oil over medium-high heat. Brown ribs on all sides in hot oil. Remove ribs from skillet and drain off fat. Add diced tomatoes, broth, celery, onion, green pepper, and garlic. Bring to a boil over medium-high heat, scraping brown bits from the bottom of skillet.

3. Preheat oven to 350 degrees F. Return ribs to skillet and spoon sauce over top. Return to a boil and tightly cover. Place skillet in preheated oven and bake for 2 to 2½ hours or until ribs are tender.

Red Rice

Prep 10 minutes **Cook** 35 minutes **Makes** 6 servings

2	tablespoons butter
½	pound diced ham, *Farmland*®
2	ribs celery, finely chopped
1	cup frozen chopped onion, *Ore-Ida*®
1	cup frozen chopped green bell pepper, *Pictsweet*®
1	can (14.5-ounce) diced tomatoes with green bell peppers, celery, and onion, *Hunt's*®
1	jar (14-ounce) pasta sauce, *Prego*®
1½	cups reduced-sodium chicken broth, *Swanson*®
1	teaspoon salt
4	dashes or more hot sauce, *Tabasco*®
1½	cups uncooked converted long grain rice, *Uncle Ben's*®

1. In a large skillet, melt butter over medium-high heat. Add ham, celery, onion, and green pepper. Cook and stir for about 5 minutes or until celery is soft. Add tomatoes, pasta sauce, broth, salt, and hot sauce. Stir in rice until evenly distributed. Bring to a boil. Cover and simmer about 30 minutes or until all liquid is absorbed.

Mini Chicken Pot Pies

Prep 15 minutes **Cook** 20 minutes **Bake** 25 minutes
Makes 12 side dish portions or appetizers

Who wouldn't take quick comfort in these petite pies stuffed with herbed vegetables and tender bites of white meat chicken? A scaled-down version of the kind Mom made, these minis feature frozen vegetables, canned chicken breast, and ready-made phyllo dough. Each pie is baked in an espresso cup—a cute contemporary twist that perks up any occasion.

⅓	cup chicken broth, *Swanson*®
2	cans (10 ounces each) chicken breast, drained, *Hormel*®
8	ounces frozen mixed vegetables (corn, peas, carrots)
½	can (10¾-ounce) condensed cream of celery soup, *Campbell's*®
1	tablespoon garlic herb seasoning blend, *McCormick*®
	Ground black pepper
½	stick (¼ cup) butter, melted
5	sheets phyllo dough, *Athens Foods*®

1. Preheat oven to 375 degrees F. In a medium saucepan, heat broth over medium heat. Add chicken and frozen vegetables; simmer for 15 minutes. Add soup and seasoning blend; cook for another 5 minutes. Season to taste with pepper. Set aside.

2. Arrange 12 oven-safe espresso (demitasse) cups 2 inches apart on a baking sheet lined with parchment paper. Fill each cup with 1 heaping tablespoon of the chicken mixture.

3. Brush melted butter over each sheet of phyllo dough; cut each sheet into 3-inch squares. Top each cup with 5 phyllo squares; fold ends toward sides of cups.

4. Bake in preheated oven about 25 minutes or until phyllo turns golden brown and sheets puff up slightly. Serve warm.

NOTE: To reheat pot pies, place chilled cups on a baking sheet; loosely cover with parchment paper or foil. Bake at 300 degrees F for 10 minutes.

Spaghetti With Garlic Meat Sauce

Prep 10 minutes **Cook** 25 minutes **Makes** 4 to 6 servings

Anyone who samples this homey dish will swear the recipe has been lovingly passed down for generations. Only you'll know it started with you—and a jar of Newman's Own® marinara sauce. A glass of robust red wine gives the sauce its rich flavor. The alcohol in the wine evaporates with cooking, making this dish a family-friendly choice.

¼	cup olive oil, *Bertolli*®
½	stick (¼ cup) butter
2	tablespoons minced fresh garlic
1	package (8-ounce) sliced fresh mushrooms
1	jar (6.5-ounce) peeled garlic cloves, *Christopher Ranch*®
1½	pounds lean ground beef
1	jar (26-ounce) mushroom marinara sauce, *Newman's Own*®
⅔	cup red wine (Merlot or Cabernet)
2	tablespoons Italian seasoning, *McCormick*®
1	box (16-ounce) spaghetti
	Grated Parmesan cheese

1. In a large skillet, heat olive oil and butter over medium heat. When butter melts, add minced garlic; cook and stir for 20 seconds. Add mushrooms and peeled garlic cloves; cook and stir for 3 minutes. Add beef and cook until browned. Add marinara sauce, wine, and Italian seasoning. Stir to combine. Cover skillet. Reduce heat to low and simmer for 15 minutes to combine flavors.

2. Meanwhile, cook spaghetti in a large pot of boiling salted water until al dente (8 to 10 minutes). Drain. Toss hot spaghetti with the sauce. Top with grated Parmesan cheese.

Chocolaty Chili

Prep 15 minutes **Cook** 4 to 6 hours (Low) **Makes** 6 servings

1½   pounds ground pork
2   cans (15 ounces each) pinto beans, rinsed and drained,
        Bush's®
1   jar (16-ounce) chipotle salsa, *Pace®*
1¼   cups red wine (such as Merlot)
1   cup frozen chopped onion, *Ore-Ida®*
1   can (4-ounce) diced mild green chile peppers,
        La Victoria®
3   tablespoons unsweetened cocoa powder, *Hershey's®*
        (plus more for garnish, optional)
3   tablespoons packed brown sugar, *C&H®*
3   tablespoons tomato paste, *Hunt's®*
1   packet (1.25-ounce) chipotle taco seasoning mix,
        Ortega®
1   teaspoon ground cinnamon, *McCormick®*
     Sour cream, *Knudsen®* (optional)
     Chopped scallions (green onions) (optional)

1. In a large skillet, cook and stir ground pork over high heat until browned, breaking up clumps. Drain off fat.

2. In a 4- to 5-quart slow cooker, stir together pork, beans, salsa, wine, onion, chile peppers, the 3 tablespoons cocoa powder, brown sugar, tomato paste, taco seasoning mix, and cinnamon until combined. Cover and cook on low heat setting for 4 to 6 hours.

3. Spoon into bowls. Garnish each serving with sour cream, scallions, and additional cocoa powder (optional).

White Chili

Prep 15 minutes **Cook** 6 to 8 hours (Low) **Makes** 8 servings

2   pounds boneless, skinless chicken breast halves,
        cut into ½-inch pieces
2   cans (15 ounces each) cannellini beans, rinsed and drained,
        Progresso®
1   can (15-ounce) cream-style corn, *Green Giant®*
2   cans (4 ounces each) diced mild green chile peppers,
        La Victoria®
1   cup frozen chopped onion, *Ore-Ida®*
1   cup reduced-sodium chicken broth, *Swanson®*
2   packets (1.25 ounces each) white chicken chili seasoning mix,
        McCormick®
     Shredded cheddar cheese, *Kraft®* (optional)
     Chopped green bell pepper (optional)

1. In a 4-quart slow cooker, stir together chicken, beans, corn, chile peppers, onion, chicken broth, and chili seasoning mix until combined. Cover and cook on low heat setting for 6 to 8 hours.

2. Spoon into bowls. Garnish each serving with cheese and chopped green pepper (optional).

Chicken With Roasted Garlic Pizza

Prep 20 minutes **Bake** 12 minutes **Makes** 4 servings

	Olive oil cooking spray, *Pam®*
1	package (6.5-ounce) pizza crust mix, *Betty Crocker®*
2	teaspoons salt-free chicken seasoning, *McCormick®*
½	cup hot water
¾	cup organic four cheese pasta sauce, *Muir Glen®*
¼	cup fat-free Caesar salad dressing, *Girard's®*
½	cup shredded low-fat mozzarella cheese, *Precious®*
1	tablespoon thinly sliced bottled roasted garlic cloves, *Christopher Ranch®*
1	package (7-ounce) chunk chicken breast meat, rinsed and drained, *Tyson®*
1	tablespoon finely chopped flat-leaf parsley

1. Preheat oven to 450 degrees F. Lightly coat a baking sheet with cooking spray; set aside.

2. In a medium bowl, combine pizza crust mix and chicken seasoning. Stir in hot water until mixture is well moistened. Beat 20 times to form dough. Cover and let rest for 5 to 10 minutes.

3. Meanwhile, in a small bowl, stir together pasta sauce and salad dressing; set aside.

4. Using floured fingers, press dough into a 12-inch circle on prepared baking sheet. Top with pasta sauce mixture, leaving a 1-inch border. Sprinkle with mozzarella cheese and garlic. Add chicken and parsley.

5. Bake pizza in preheated oven for 12 to 17 minutes or until crust is golden brown.

BBQ Turkey Pizza

Prep 20 minutes   **Bake** 12 minutes   **Makes** 4 servings

	Olive oil cooking spray, *Pam*®
1	package (6.5-ounce) pizza crust mix, ***Betty Crocker***®
2	tablespoons cornmeal
½	cup hot water
1	cup diced cooked turkey breast
⅓	cup barbecue sauce, *Sweet Baby Ray's*®
2	tablespoons chopped red onion
¼	cup shredded part-skim mozzarella cheese, *Precious*®
2	tablespoons finely chopped fresh cilantro
1	tablespoon shredded Gouda cheese

1. Preheat oven to 450 degrees F. Coat a large baking sheet with cooking spray; set aside.

2. In a medium bowl, combine pizza crust mix and cornmeal. Stir in hot water until mixture is well moistened. Beat 20 times to form dough. Cover and let rest for 5 to 10 minutes.

3. Meanwhile, coat a small saucepan with cooking spray; heat over medium-high heat. Add turkey and 1 tablespoon of the barbecue sauce. Cook and stir for 4 to 6 minutes. Remove from heat; set aside.

4. Divide dough into 4 portions. Using floured fingers, press each dough portion into a 5-inch circle on prepared baking sheet. Spread the remaining barbecue sauce evenly over dough rounds, leaving a ½-inch border. Top with turkey and onion. Sprinkle with mozzarella cheese, cilantro, and Gouda cheese.

5. Bake pizza in preheated oven for 12 to 15 minutes or until crust is golden brown.

Quick Weeknight Meals

Cooking during the work week can be downright daunting, even for those who look forward to doing it. Cooking both relaxes and stimulates me, helping me unwind after a busy day. But some days, I don't have the energy to spend one second more than I have to in the kitchen. This chapter is cooking at its quickest—everything you need to feed yourself and your loved ones all week long.

The Recipes

Blackberry and Herb Filet Mignon

Prep 5 minutes   **Marinate:** 6 to 8 hours   **Stand:** 30 minutes
Cook 6 minutes   **Makes** 4 servings

⅓	cup cognac
3	tablespoons black and raspberry vinegar, *Kozlowski Farms®*
3	tablespoons olive oil, *Bertolli®*
1	packet (1.06-ounce) herb marinade mix, *McCormick® Grill Mates®*
1	tablespoon herbes de Provence, *McCormick®*
1	cup frozen blackberries, thawed
4	(8 ounces each) beef filet mignon medallions
3	tablespoons butter
	Fresh blackberries (optional)

1. In large zip-top plastic bag, combine cognac, vinegar, olive oil, marinade mix, and herbes de Provence. Add thawed frozen blackberries; massage bag until ingredients are well combined and marinade mix is dissolved. Add filet mignon medallions to bag. Squeeze air out of bag; seal. Marinate in refrigerator for 6 to 8 hours.

2. Remove bag from refrigerator 30 minutes before cooking. Remove medallions from marinade; discard marinade. In heavy-bottom skillet, melt butter over medium-high heat. Sear medallions in hot butter for 3 to 5 minutes per side. Garnish with fresh blackberries (optional). Serve hot.

Roquefort Cheese Chips

Prep 10 minutes   **Cook** 15 minutes   **Makes** 4 servings

A creamy potato gratin becomes pleasingly sharp when crunchy kettle chips are topped with Roquefort, a pungent blue cheese. Serve these with Blackberry and Herb Filet Mignon for an elegant meal.

1	bag (5-ounce) lightly salted potato chips, *Cape Cod Kettle Chips®*
½	cup canned white sauce, *Aunt Penny's®*
¼	cup cream cheese, *Philadelphia®*
2	tablespoons crumbled Roquefort cheese
1	tablespoon half-and-half
¼	cup blue cheese crumbles, *Athenos®*

1. Preheat oven to 350 degrees F. Place potato chips on baking sheet. Bake in preheated oven for 15 minutes.

2. In a small saucepan, combine white sauce, cream cheese, Roquefort cheese, and half-and-half. Cook over medium heat until cheese melts, stirring constantly. Remove from heat.

3. Drizzle cheese sauce over hot chips. Sprinkle blue cheese crumbles over the top.

Rib-Eye Steaks with Cognac-Peppercorn Sauce

Start to Finish 20 minutes   **Makes** 4 servings

4	beef rib-eye steaks
	Freshly ground black pepper
1	tablespoon au jus gravy mix, *Lawry's*®
1	cup reduced-sodium beef broth, *Swanson*®
¼	cup cognac
1	packet (1-ounce) peppercorn sauce mix, *Knorr*®

1. Preheat broiler. Line a baking sheet with foil. Sprinkle steaks with black pepper and au jus gravy mix. Place on prepared baking sheet; broil steaks 4 to 6 inches from heat source for 5 minutes per side.

2. For cognac-peppercorn sauce, in a medium saucepan, whisk together beef broth, cognac, and peppercorn sauce mix. Bring to a boil over medium-high heat, stirring constantly. Reduce heat and simmer for 2 minutes. Drizzle hot steaks with cognac-peppercorn sauce.

Creamy Cheesy Potatoes and Broccoli

Start to Finish 10 minutes   **Makes** 4 servings

2	tablespoons extra virgin olive oil, *Bertolli*®
1	package (16-ounce) precooked and diced red potatoes, *Reser's*®
1	teaspoon garlic salt, *Lawry's*®
1½	cups frozen chopped broccoli, thawed, *Birds Eye*®
1	can (10.5-ounce) white sauce, *Aunt Penny's*®
¾	cup finely shredded mild cheddar cheese, *Kraft*®

1. In a large skillet, heat oil over medium-high heat. Add potatoes and garlic salt. Cook and stir for 4 minutes. Stir in broccoli.

2. Reduce heat and stir in white sauce and cheese. Heat through, stirring often until cheese melts. Serve immediately.

Steak Diane

Prep 5 minutes   **Cook** 6 minutes   **Makes** 4 servings

4	(3 ounces each) beef filet mignon medallions
1	teaspoon Montreal steak seasoning, *McCormick® Grill Mates®*
2	tablespoons butter
1	cup fresh sliced mushrooms
1	teaspoon bottled crushed garlic, *Christopher Ranch®*
¼	cup cognac
¼	cup heavy cream
¼	cup reduced-sodium beef broth, *Swanson®*
1	tablespoon steak sauce, *A1®*
1	tablespoon finely chopped fresh chives

1. Season both sides of filets with steak seasoning. In a large skillet, melt butter over medium-high heat. Add filets and cook for 2 minutes on one side. Turn and cook for 1 minute more. Add mushrooms and garlic and cook for 2 minutes, stirring constantly. Remove filets and set aside on a plate.

2. Remove skillet from stovetop. Tip skillet away from you and add cognac. With a "clicker" (long lighter), ignite cognac, keeping skillet tipped away from you at all times. When flame has burned out, return skillet to stovetop. Stir in cream, beef broth, and steak sauce. Stir thoroughly and bring sauce to a simmer.

3 . Return filets and any accumulated juices to skillet. Coat with sauce and warm through. Stir in chives. Place filets on warm plates. Spoon sauce and mushrooms over filets.

Delmonico Potatoes

Prep 8 minutes   **Bake** 30 minutes   **Makes** 4 servings

	Butter
½	cup bread crumbs, *Progresso®*
½	cup grated Parmesan cheese, *DiGiorno®*
2	tablespoons butter, melted
1	bag (16-ounce) cooked diced potatoes, *Reser's®*
2	cans (10.5 ounces each) white sauce, *Aunt Penny's®*
⅛	teaspoon ground nutmeg, *McCormick®*
¼	teaspoon ground black pepper
½	teaspoon salt

1. Preheat oven to 350 degrees F. Coat a shallow 1-quart baking dish with butter and set aside. In a small bowl, thoroughly combine bread crumbs, Parmesan cheese, and melted butter.

2. In a large bowl, combine remaining ingredients and stir thoroughly. Transfer to prepared baking dish. Cover with bread crumb mixture. Bake in preheated oven for 30 to 35 minutes.

Mini Burgers On Toasted Disks

Prep 20 minutes **Bake** 19 minutes **Broil:** 5 minutes **Stand:** 7 minutes
Makes 32 burgers

8	thin slices white bread
	Olive oil nonstick cooking spray, *Pam*®
1	pound lean ground beef
1	egg, lightly beaten
2	tablespoons Worcestershire sauce, *Lea & Perrins*®
1	packet (1-ounce) pot roast seasoning, *Lawry's*®
	Ketchup and/or mustard

1. Preheat oven to 400 degrees F. Using a 1¾-inch round pastry cutter, cut 32 circles out of bread slices. Arrange circles on a baking sheet and spray lightly with cooking spray. Bake circles in preheated oven about 7 minutes or until toasted. Cool completely.

2. In a large bowl, combine beef, egg, Worcestershire sauce, and pot roast seasoning. Form thirty-two 1-inch meatballs using 1 tablespoon of meat mixture per ball. Place meatballs 1 inch apart on a broiler pan. Using your finger, gently poke an indentation in each meatball.

3. Bake for 12 minutes. Turn on broiler; broil for 5 minutes. Remove from oven. Let stand on baking sheet for 7 minutes; place on toasted bread circles. Fill each burger indentation with ketchup and/or mustard. Serve warm.

Poker Potato Chips

Prep 15 minutes **Chill** 20 minutes **Cook** 15 minutes **Makes** 6 to 8 servings

1	cup all-purpose flour
4	packets (0.6-ounce each) roasted garlic dressing mix, *Good Seasons*®
2	medium sweet potatoes
2	large red skin potatoes
	Vegetable oil, for deep-frying
	Salt and ground black pepper

1. In a large zip-top plastic bag, combine flour and dressing mix; set aside. Rinse potatoes and pat dry with paper towels. Using a mandoline slicer, thinly slice potatoes into round disks. Starting with sweet potatoes, add about half of the slices to the seasoned flour. Seal bag and shake. Arrange slices on a baking sheet; repeat with remaining potatoes. Chill seasoned potatoes about 20 minutes.

2. In a large, heavy-bottomed Dutch oven, add enough oil to rise a little less than halfway up the sides of the pot. Heat oil to 375 degrees F. Add a small batch of the potatoes; fry until crisp. Remove with slotted spoon and drain on paper towels. Season to taste with salt and pepper. Repeat with remaining potato slices.

Coney Island Chili Dogs

Prep 15 minutes **Cook** 30 minutes **Makes** 8 servings

In college, my best friend Colleen and I would hop in the car to get chili dogs and root beer floats at least three nights a week. My version delivers the same fun on the run but uses higher-quality ingredients, like lean ground beef. (You can always substitute ground turkey or ground chicken, if desired, to be even more healthful.) Pair the dogs with frozen onion rings, baked piping hot, and Orange Smoothies (recipe, below) for a flash-back diner dinner.

1	pound 90-percent-lean ground beef
1	bottle (12-ounce) chili sauce, *Heinz®*
½	cup water
1	packet (1.48-ounce) chili seasoning, *Lawry's®*
1	teaspoon Worcestershire sauce, *Lea & Perrins®*
1	tablespoon yellow mustard, *French's®*
½	teaspoon onion powder, *McCormick®*
8	beef hot dogs
8	hot dog buns, split
	Shredded cheddar cheese, *Kraft®*
	Chopped white onion

1. In a large saucepan, brown ground beef over medium heat. Add chili sauce, the water, chili seasoning, Worcestershire sauce, mustard, and onion powder. Bring to boil. Lower heat and simmer for 30 minutes.

2. Meanwhile, cook hot dogs according to package instructions.

3. Place hot dogs in buns; top with chili, cheddar cheese, and chopped onion.

Orange Smoothie

Prep 5 minutes **Makes** 2 servings

1	can (16-ounce) frozen orange juice concentrate
1	packet (1-ounce) sugar-free, fat-free vanilla pudding mix, *Jell-O®*
1	container (4-ounce) orange cream yogurt, *Yoplait®*
1	cup low-fat milk
3	cups ice cubes

1. In a blender, combine orange juice concentrate, pudding mix, yogurt, milk, and ice cubes. Cover and blend until smooth. Divide between 2 glasses.

Pan-Seared Rosemary Pork Chops

Start to Finish 20 minutes   **Makes** 4 servings

- 1½   pounds boneless center-cut pork chops
         Salt and ground black pepper
- ⅓   cup Italian-style bread crumbs, *Progresso*®
- 1   tablespoon finely chopped fresh rosemary
- 2   tablespoons extra virgin olive oil, *Bertolli*®
         Fresh rosemary sprigs (optional)

1. Season pork chops with salt and pepper; set aside.

2. In a small bowl, combine bread crumbs and rosemary. Spread mixture on a plate. Press both sides of chops into bread crumb mixture to coat; set aside.

3. In a large skillet, heat olive oil over medium-high heat. Add chops to hot oil; cook for 4 to 6 minutes per side or until cooked through (160 degrees F). Garnish with rosemary sprigs (optional).

Sweet Potato and Apple Saute

Start to Finish 20 minutes   **Makes** 4 servings

- 2   tablespoons unsalted butter
- 2   medium Golden Delicious apples, diced (do not peel)
- 1   medium onion, diced
- 2   cans (15 ounces each) sweet potatoes, drained and diced, *Princella*®
- ½   cup apple juice, *Tree Top*®
- 1½   teaspoons pumpkin pie spice, *McCormick*®
- 1   teaspoon cider vinegar, *Heinz*®
- ¼   teaspoon kosher salt

1. In a large skillet, melt butter over medium-high heat. Add apples and onion to skillet; cook and stir about 5 minutes or until tender.

2. Stir in diced sweet potatoes, apple juice, pumpkin pie spice, vinegar, and salt. Bring mixture to a boil; reduce heat. Simmer about 10 minutes or until most of the liquid has evaporated. Serve hot.

Planked Pork Tenderloin

Prep 15 minutes   **Soak:** 1 hour (plank)   **Grill** 18 minutes
Stand 5 minutes   **Makes** 4 servings

FOR APPLE-SAGE GLAZE:
½	cup frozen apple juice concentrate, *Tree Top®*
2	tablespoons packed brown sugar, *C&H®*
1	tablespoon cider vinegar, *Heinz®*
1	teaspoon bottled crushed garlic, *Gourmet Garden®*
½	teaspoon dried whole sage leaves
¼	teaspoon pumpkin pie spice, *McCormick®*
	Pinch red pepper flakes, *McCormick®*

FOR SEASONED PORK:
1½	pounds pork tenderloin, trimmed
2	teaspoons Montreal steak seasoning, *McCormick® Grill Mates®*
	Fresh sage (optional)

1. Soak a *hickory grilling plank* in water for 1 hour. Set up grill for direct cooking over medium-high heat (see page 17). For Apple-Sage Glaze, in a saucepan, combine juice concentrate, brown sugar, vinegar, garlic, dried sage, pumpkin pie spice, and red pepper flakes. Bring to a boil over medium-high heat. Reduce to simmer, stirring constantly until sugar dissolves; set aside.

2. For Seasoned Pork, sprinkle pork with steak seasoning. Place soaked plank on hot grill; cover grill for 3 minutes, turning plank every minute. Place pork on plank; brush with glaze. Cover grill. Cook for 10 minutes, brushing with glaze every 5 minutes. Cook for 8 to 10 minutes more or until slightly pink in center and juices run clear (155 degrees F). Remove pork from grill; let stand for 5 minutes. Meanwhile, return remaining glaze to boiling. Slice pork. Serve hot drizzled with hot Apple-Sage Glaze. Top with fresh sage (optional).

Sweet Potato Pone

Prep 10 minutes   **Bake** 50 minutes   **Makes** 6 servings

	Nonstick cooking spray, *Pam®*
2	cans (15 ounces each) sweet potatoes, drained, *Princella®*
1½	cups packed brown sugar, *C&H®*
1	stick (½ cup) butter, melted
½	cup baking mix, *Bisquick®*
¼	cup robust molasses, *Mother's®*
¼	cup evaporated milk, *Carnation®*
2	teaspoons pumpkin pie spice, *McCormick®*
½	cup shredded, sweetened coconut, *Baker's®*
½	cup raisins, *Sun-Maid®*

1. Preheat oven to 350 degrees F. Lightly spray a 2-quart casserole dish with cooking spray; set aside. In a large bowl, beat sweet potatoes, brown sugar, and melted butter with an electric mixer until mostly smooth. Add baking mix, molasses, milk, and pumpkin pie spice; beat until well mixed. Stir in coconut and raisins.

2. Pour mixture into prepared casserole dish and bake in preheated oven for 50 to 60 minutes or until tester comes out clean.

Chicken with Peanut Curry Sauce

Start to Finish 20 minutes **Makes** 4 servings

FOR CHICKEN AND VEGETABLES:
2 tablespoons canola oil, *Wesson*®
1½ pounds boneless, skinless chicken breast halves, cut into 1-inch pieces
Salt and ground black pepper
2 cups loose-pack frozen cut green beans, *C&W*®
2 cups loose-pack frozen pepper strips, *C&W*®

FOR PEANUT CURRY SAUCE:
1½ cups light coconut milk, *A Taste of Thai*®
½ cup reduced-sodium chicken broth, *Swanson*®
⅓ cup chunky peanut butter, *Laura Scudder's*®
2 tablespoons packed brown sugar
2 tablespoons lime juice, *ReaLime*®
1 tablespoon red curry paste, *Thai Kitchen*®

1. For Chicken and Vegetables, in a large skillet, heat canola oil over medium-high heat. Sprinkle chicken pieces with salt and pepper. Add chicken to hot oil; cook about 5 minutes or until cooked through, stirring occasionally. Add frozen green beans and pepper strips; cook and stir for 3 minutes more.

2. Meanwhile, for Peanut Curry Sauce, in a medium bowl, whisk together coconut milk, broth, peanut butter, brown sugar, lime juice, and red curry paste. Pour over chicken and vegetables, stirring to combine. Bring to a boil, stirring occasionally. Reduce heat; simmer for 10 minutes.

Coconut Rice

Start to Finish 20 minutes **Makes** 4 servings

2 cups quick-cooking rice, *Uncle Ben's*®
1 cup reduced-sodium chicken broth, *Swanson*®
¾ cup light coconut milk, *A Taste of Thai*®
1 tablespoon bottled lime juice, *ReaLime*®
¼ cup flaked coconut, toasted,* *Baker's*®

1. In a medium saucepan, combine rice, chicken broth, coconut milk, and lime juice. Bring to a boil over medium-high heat. Remove from heat; cover. Let stand for 7 to 9 minutes. Fluff rice with fork and stir in toasted coconut. Serve hot.

*NOTE: To toast coconut, seeds, or nuts, place in a dry skillet over medium-low heat and stir occasionally until golden brown.

Key Lime Grilled Chicken

Prep 10 minutes   Grill 36 minutes   Makes 4 servings

1	stick (½ cup) butter
¼	cup key lime juice, *Nellie & Joe's®*
¼	cup chili sauce, *Heinz®*
2	teaspoons All-Purpose Poultry Sprinkle (right)
4	pounds meaty chicken pieces
1	tablespoon All-Purpose Poultry Sprinkle (right)

1. Set up grill for direct cooking over medium heat (see page 17). Oil grate when ready to start cooking.

2. For key lime sauce, in a small saucepan, melt butter over medium heat. Stir in lime juice, chili sauce, and the 2 teaspoons All-Purpose Poultry Sprinkle. Cook 1 minute. Remove from heat; set aside.

3. Season chicken pieces with the 1 tablespoon All-Purpose Poultry Sprinkle. Place chicken on hot, oiled grill and cook for 18 to 22 minutes per side or until chicken is no longer pink and juices run clear (170 degrees F for breast halves; 180 degrees F for thighs and drumsticks), basting with key lime sauce every few minutes until last 2 minutes of cooking. Discard any remaining sauce.

ALL PURPOSE POULTRY SPRINKLE: In an airtight container, combine 2 tablespoons garlic salt, *Lawry's®*; 2 tablespoons citrus-herb seasoning, *Spice Islands®*; 2 teaspoons poultry seasoning, *McCormick®*; and ⅛ teaspoon cayenne pepper, *McCormick®*. Cover; store for up to 4 months.

Baja-Style Corn

Start to Finish 15 minutes   Makes 4 servings

Frozen corn goes from boring to extraordinary with the additions of canned tomatoes, fresh cilantro, and lime juice. Although it's great with Key Lime Grilled Chicken, use it as a quick side to complement any Tex-Mex main dish.

2	tablespoons butter
2	cups loose-pack frozen whole-kernel corn, *C&W®*
1	can (10-ounce) diced tomatoes, *Ro-Tel® Original*
¼	cup chopped fresh cilantro
1	tablespoon lime juice, *ReaLime®*
	Fresh cilantro leaves (optional)

1. In a large skillet, melt butter over medium-high heat. Add frozen corn to hot butter; cook for 4 to 5 minutes. Add diced tomatoes and bring to a simmer.

2. Remove from heat and stir in chopped cilantro and lime juice. Garnish with cilantro leaves (optional). Serve hot.

Chicken and Mushrooms in Creamy Tarragon Sauce

Start to Finish 20 minutes **Makes** 4 servings

2	tablespoons extra virgin olive oil, *Bertolli®*
1½	pounds boneless, skinless chicken breasts, cut into bite-size pieces
1	package (8-ounce) fresh sliced mushrooms
1	can (10-ounce) condensed cream of mushroom soup, *Campbell's®*
½	cup white wine (Chardonnay)
3	tablespoons chopped fresh tarragon
1	teaspoon salt-free lemon pepper, *McCormick®*
1	teaspoon bottled crushed garlic, *Christopher Ranch®*

1. In a large skillet, heat oil over medium-high heat. Add chicken and mushrooms. Cook and stir for 8 to 10 minutes or until chicken is cooked through.

2. Stir in soup, wine, tarragon, lemon pepper, and garlic. Bring to a boil. Reduce heat and simmer for 5 minutes. Serve hot.

Nutty Herbed Rice

Start to Finish 10 minutes **Makes** 4 servings

2	packages (8.8 ounces each) whole grain brown rice *Uncle Ben's® Ready Rice*
2	tablespoons butter
⅓	cup chopped nut topping, *Diamond®*
¼	cup fresh chopped herbs (such as parsley, thyme, and marjoram)

1. Microwave rice according to package directions.

2. In medium skillet, melt butter over medium-high heat. Add nut topping and cook for 30 seconds. Stir in rice and herbs. Serve immediately.

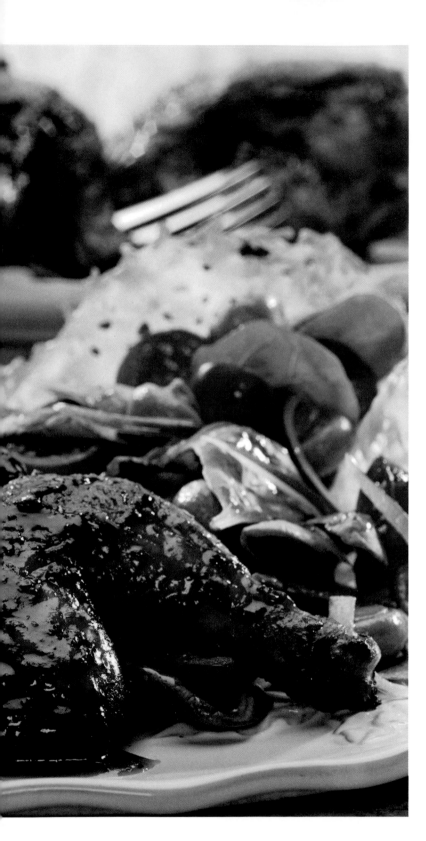

Sweet and Spicy Game Hens

Prep 10 minutes   **Marinate** 2 to 8 hours   **Roast** 40 minutes
Makes 4 servings

¼	cup frozen pineapple juice concentrate, thawed
1	tablespoon Jamaican jerk seasoning blend, *McCormick® Gourmet Collection®*
2	tablespoons canola oil, *Wesson®*
1	teaspoon salt
¼	teaspoon ground black pepper
2	Cornish game hens, halved, rinsed, and patted dry

1. In a small bowl, combine juice concentrate, seasoning blend, oil, salt, and pepper. Place hens in a large zip-top bag. Add marinade; seal bag. Turn bag to coat hens. Marinate in refrigerator for 2 to 8 hours, turning bag occasionally.

2. Preheat oven to 400 degrees F. Remove hens from the marinade and place them, breast sides up, in a roasting pan. Pour the remaining marinade over the hens. Roast in preheated oven for 40 to 45 minutes or until golden.

Mushroom Salad In Cheese Crisps

Prep 15 minutes   **Bake** 15 minutes   **Makes** 4 servings

	Olive oil nonstick cooking spray, *Pam®*
1	container (7-ounce) shredded Parmesan, Romano, and Asiago cheese blend, *Kraft®*
1½	cups baby spinach leaves
1	jar (4.5-ounce) whole mushrooms, *Green Giant®*
1	cup halved cherry tomatoes
⅓	cup thinly sliced red onion
¼	cup bottled Italian dressing

1. Preheat oven to 425 degrees F. Line baking sheet with parchment paper; spray paper with cooking spray. Place ½ cup of the shredded cheese on baking sheet and shape into a circle about 5 inches in diameter. Form a second circle on other half of baking sheet. Bake in preheated oven about 5 minutes or until cheese is golden around edges. Using a wide spatula, turn cheese rounds over. Bake about 2 minutes more or until deep golden around edges and set in the center. Using the spatula, carefully remove rounds and drape them over a large rolling pin suspended like a bridge between 2 tall cans. Let cool. Repeat with remaining cheese to make 2 more rounds.

2. In a large bowl, combine spinach, mushrooms, tomatoes, and onion. Add dressing; toss to combine. To serve, place a cheese crisp on each of 4 salad plates, then top evenly with salad.

Tropical Salmon

Prep 15 minutes   **Cook** 20 minutes   **Makes** 2 servings

When I moved to Los Angeles from Wisconsin, I rented a room in a house from two German men and a Portuguese woman. One of the men was a private chef for the rich and famous and shared many of his secret recipes with me. This was one of his favorites, and now I'm happy to be sharing it with you. It's perfect for a romantic evening and will make you look brilliant.

FOR TROPICAL RICE:
1	bag (2-cup) white rice, *Uncle Ben's Boil-in-Bag Rice*®
¼	cup dried tropical fruit mix, *Sunsweet Fruitlings*®
¼	cup dry-roasted peanuts, chopped, *Planters*®

FOR SALMON AND CHIVE SAUCE:
2	tablespoons tartar sauce, *Kraft*®
2	tablespoons sour cream
2	tablespoons fresh lime juice
1	tablespoon Dijon mustard, *French's*®
2	teaspoons chopped fresh chives
1	skinless salmon fillet (12-ounce), cut crosswise into ten ½-inch slices
	Fresh dill (optional)

1. For Tropical Rice, prepare rice according to package instructions. Transfer rice to serving bowl. Stir in dried fruit. Cover and let stand until serving time.

2. Meanwhile, for Chive Sauce, in a small bowl, mix tartar sauce, sour cream, lime juice, mustard, and chives. Cover Chive Sauce and refrigerate until serving time.

3. For Salmon, preheat broiler. Divide salmon slices between 2 broilerproof glass or ceramic plates, placing salmon on one-half of each plate. Place plates under broiler and cook until salmon is pale pink and flaky (about 1 minute), watching salmon carefully so it does not overcook.

4. Using potholders, carefully remove hot plates. Spoon Chive Sauce on top of salmon. Stir peanuts into rice; serve with salmon. Garnish with fresh dill (optional).

Niçoise on a Roll

Prep 10 minutes **Makes** 2 servings

1	can (6-ounce) tuna, oil packed, drained
2	eggs, hard-cooked, peeled, and chopped
3	tablespoons mayonnaise, *Hellmann's®* or *Best Foods®*
1	tablespoon capers
10	niçoise olives, pitted
1	teaspoon fines herbes, *Spice Islands®*
	Salt and ground black pepper
2	round potato buns
2	Bibb lettuce leaves
6	slices roma tomato
¼	red onion, peeled and thinly sliced into rings

1. In a medium bowl, combine tuna, eggs, mayonnaise, capers, olives, fines herbes, and salt and pepper to taste. Mix thoroughly.

2. Open potato buns and place one lettuce leaf on the bottom half of each bun. Divide tuna mixture between the 2 sandwiches. Top each with 3 tomato slices and half of the red onion rings.

Greek Garlic Fries

Start to Finish 10 minutes **Makes** 4 servings

½	26-ounce bag frozen "fast food" fries (13 ounces total), *Ore-Ida®*
2	tablespoons extra virgin olive oil, *Bertolli®*
1½	teaspoons bottled crushed garlic, *Christopher Ranch®*
1	teaspoon Greek seasoning, *Spice Islands®*
	Premade tzatziki or gyro dressing

1. Preheat broiler. On a baking sheet, toss together fries, olive oil, garlic, and Greek seasoning. Arrange fries in a single layer.

2. Broil 6 inches from heat source for 5 to 8 minutes. Serve fries hot with tzatziki for dipping.

Almond-Crusted Trout

Start to Finish 20 minutes   **Makes** 4 servings

⅓   cup all-purpose flour
2   large eggs, lightly beaten
2   tablespoons water
¾   cup ground almonds,* *Planters*®
½   cup panko (Japanese-style) bread crumbs
1   tablespoon shredded orange zest
3   tablespoons olive oil, *Bertolli*®
1½   pounds fresh trout fillets
¼   cup orange-flavored liqueur, *Grand Marnier*®
1¼   cups orange juice, *Minute Maid*®
1   package (1.8-ounce) white sauce mix, *Knorr*®
    Salt and ground black pepper

1. Place flour in a shallow bowl; set aside. In a second shallow bowl, beat together eggs and the water. In a third shallow bowl, combine almonds, panko bread crumbs, and orange zest.

2. In a large skillet, heat olive oil over medium-high heat. Meanwhile, dredge trout in flour; shake off excess. Dip in egg mixture. Coat with almond mixture. Fry trout in hot oil for 2 to 3 minutes per side or until fish flakes easily when tested with a fork. Transfer to plate; keep warm.

3. For orange sauce, reduce heat to medium; add liqueur to skillet, scraping up browned bits from bottom. Add orange juice; whisk in white sauce mix. Simmer for 2 to 3 minutes or until mixture thickens. Season with salt and pepper. Serve trout with orange sauce.

*NOTE: For uniform pieces, grind the almonds in a blender.

Orange Couscous with Mint

Start to Finish 15 minutes   **Makes** 4 servings

1¾   cups reduced-sodium chicken broth, *Swanson*®
¼   cup frozen orange juice concentrate, *Minute Maid*®
1   tablespoon orange olive oil, *O Olive Oil*®
1½   teaspoons salt
1   box (10-ounce) couscous, *Near East*®
⅓   cup chopped fresh mint
¼   cup chopped fresh flat-leaf parsley

1. In a medium saucepan, combine broth, orange juice concentrate, olive oil, and salt; bring to a boil over medium-high heat. Stir in couscous. Cover; remove from heat. Let stand for 5 minutes. To serve, fluff couscous with a fork and stir in mint and parsley.

Gold and Green Salad

Start to Finish 15 minutes **Makes** 4 servings

¼	cup light mayonnaise, *Hellmann's® or Best Foods®*
¼	cup fat-free sour cream, *Knudsen®*
1	tablespoon lemon juice, *ReaLemon®*
½	teaspoon reduced-sodium soy sauce, *Kikkoman®*
4	cups spring salad mix, *Fresh Express®*
12	refrigerated mango slices, drained, *Ready Pac®*
1	avocado, sliced into 12 slices
12	slices cucumber (optional)
¼	cup bias-sliced scallions (green onions)

1. For dressing, in a small bowl, stir together mayonnaise, sour cream, lemon juice, and soy sauce; set aside.

2. For salad, divide salad mix among 4 chilled salad plates. Divide mango, avocado, and cucumber slices (optional) among plates. Spoon dressing over salads; sprinkle with scallions.

Sweet and Spicy Slaw

Prep 10 minutes **Chill** 1 hour **Makes** 6 servings

1	package (12-ounce) broccoli slaw (or 4 cups coleslaw mix), *The Produce Stand®*
¼	cup chopped red onion
⅔	cup fat-free plain yogurt, *Horizon Organic®*
¼	cup honey, *Sue Bee®*
2	tablespoons cider vinegar, *Heinz®*
2	tablespoons canned chopped jalapeño chile peppers, drained, *Ortega®*
	Salt and ground black pepper

1. In a large bowl, combine broccoli slaw and red onion; set aside.

2. In a small bowl, stir together yogurt, honey, vinegar, and chile peppers. Pour over broccoli slaw mixture, tossing to combine. Season with salt and black pepper. Chill in the refrigerator for 1 hour before serving.

Ravioli Balsamico

Start to Finish 10 minutes   **Makes** 4 servings

14	ounces refrigerated four cheese ravioli, about 1½ (9-ounce) packages, *Buitoni*®
1¼	cups light balsamic vinaigrette, *Newman's Own*®
¼	cup julienne cut sun-dried tomatoes, chopped, *California*®
½	cup chopped walnuts, *Diamond*®
2	tablespoons butter, cold

1. In a large pot of boiling salted water, cook ravioli according to package directions. Meanwhile, in a large skillet, bring vinaigrette to a boil over medium-high heat. Add sun-dried tomatoes and walnuts. Reduce heat and simmer for 2 to 3 minutes. Whisk in butter until sauce is smooth and shiny.

2. Drain pasta. Add to vinaigrette mixture and heat through.

Roasted Asparagus With Portobello Mushrooms

Start to Finish 20 minutes   **Makes** 4 servings

1	pound asparagus, trimmed and bottoms peeled
1	package (6-ounce) sliced portobello mushrooms, cut into 2-inch pieces
2	tablespoons extra virgin olive oil, *Bertolli*®
½	teaspoon salt
¼	teaspoon ground black pepper
⅔	cup olive bruschetta topping, *Delallo*®

1. Preheat oven to 400 degrees F. Line a baking sheet with foil. Place asparagus and portobello mushrooms on prepared baking sheet. Drizzle with olive oil and season with salt and pepper. Sprinkle with bruschetta topping.

2. Roast in preheated oven for 10 to 15 minutes or until asparagus reaches desired tenderness. Serve hot.

Sherried Mushrooms-and-Onion Penne

Start to Finish 25 minutes **Makes** 6 servings

12	ounces penne pasta, *Barilla® Plus*
1	tablespoon extra virgin olive oil, *Bertolli®*
1	red onion, quartered and thinly sliced
2	packages (8 ounces each) sliced fresh mushrooms
¼	cup sherry, *Christian Brothers®*
2	teaspoons fines herbes, *Spice Islands®*
½	cup reduced-sodium beef broth, *Swanson®*
⅓	cup light sour cream, *Horizon Organic®*
	Chopped fresh parsley (optional)

1. In a large pot of boiling salted water, cook pasta according to package directions. Drain well; return pasta to hot pot. Cover; keep warm.

2. Meanwhile, in a large nonstick skillet, heat oil over medium-high heat. Add onion; cook and stir for 8 to 10 minutes or until cooked down and translucent. Add mushrooms; cook and stir for 10 minutes more. Stir in sherry and fines herbes. Cook until liquid is evaporated.

3. In a small bowl, combine beef broth and sour cream. Stir into mixture in skillet; cook for 4 to 5 minutes or until heated through. Toss mixture with hot cooked pasta. Garnish with parsley (optional).

Spicy Hoisin Tuna Steaks

Prep 20 minutes **Soak** 1 hour (plank) **Grill** 8 minutes **Makes** 4 servings

FOR SPICY HOISIN SAUCE:

½	cup hoisin sauce, *Lee Kum Kee®*
2	tablespoons rice vinegar, *Marukan®*
1	tablespoon soy sauce, *Kikkoman®*
2	teaspoons chile blend, *Gourmet Garden®*
1	teaspoon bottled crushed garlic, *Gourmet Garden®*
1	teaspoon bottled minced ginger, *Gourmet Garden®*

FOR TUNA STEAKS:

4	6-ounce tuna steaks
4	teaspoons sesame seeds

1. Soak a *cedar grilling plank* in water for at least 1 hour. Set up grill for direct cooking over medium-high heat (see page 17). For Spicy Hoisin Sauce, in a small saucepan, combine the hoisin sauce, vinegar, soy sauce, chile blend, garlic, and ginger. Bring to a boil; reduce heat. Simmer for 5 minutes.

2. For Tuna Steaks, place soaked plank on hot grill; cover grill for 3 minutes, turning plank every minute. Measure out ⅓ cup of Spicy Hoisin Sauce; brush over fish. Sprinkle with sesame seeds. Place fish on plank; cover grill. Cook for 8 to 12 minutes or until fish flakes easily when tested with a fork. Serve tuna hot with remaining Spicy Hoisin Sauce.

Around the World

Chalupas, pizzas, stir-fries—ethnic cuisine is some of America's most popular food. In the originating countries, each dish is prepared with unrestrained passion and a lust for living—and cooking. I've found a way to duplicate those flavor without spending all day in the kitchen.

The Recipes

Guacamole

Start to Finish 10 minutes   **Makes** 8 servings

2	**large Hass avocados**
2	**tablespoons medium salsa, *Pace*®**
1	**tablespoon sour cream**
1	**tablespoon jalapeño juice (from jarred jalapeños) (optional)**
	Salt

1. Peel avocados and remove pits. Place in a bowl and mash. Stir in salsa and sour cream. Add jalapeño juice (optional). Add salt to taste. Serve with Spicy Corn Chips (below).

Mesquite Salsa

Start to Finish 5 minutes   **Makes** 8 servings

1	**jar (24-ounce) chunky salsa, *Pace*®**
⅓	**cup chopped fresh cilantro**
3	**green onions, chopped**
2	**teaspoons mesquite marinade mix, *McCormick*® *Grill Mates*®**

1. In a medium bowl, combine salsa, cilantro, green onions, and marinade mix. Serve with Spicy Corn Chips (below).

Spicy Corn Chips

Prep 3 minutes per batch   **Bake** 5 minutes per batch   **Makes** 8 servings

1	**bag (1 pound 12 ounces) restaurant-style tortilla chips, *Mission*®**
	Nonstick cooking spray, *Pam*®
1	**packet (1.25-ounce) Tex-Mex chili seasoning, *McCormick*®**

1. Preheat oven to 350 degrees F. Working in batches, spread a single layer of chips on a baking sheet. Very lightly coat with nonstick spray. Lightly sprinkle with chili seasoning. Bake for 5 minutes. Repeat until all chips are seasoned and baked. Serve with Guacamole and Mesquite Salsa (above).

Las Chalupas

Prep 15 minutes **Cook** 25 minutes **Makes** 4 to 6 servings

1	**pound ground beef**
1	**package (1.25-ounce) taco seasoning mix, *Ortega*®**
⅔	**cup salsa, *Pace*®**
¼	**cup jalapeño juice**
¼	**cup canola oil, *Wesson*®**
4	**to 6 flour tortillas (8 inch), *Mission*®**
½	**cup shredded cheese blend**
	Assorted toppings (such as shredded lettuce, chopped tomatoes, sliced olives, purchased guacamole, and sour cream)

1. In a large skillet, brown beef over medium heat. Add taco seasoning, salsa, and jalapeño juice. Add a little water if mixture is too dry. Reduce heat to low and simmer for 10 minutes.

2. In another large skillet, heat oil over medium-high heat. Fry tortillas flat until crispy on both sides. Place tortillas on individual ovenproof plates. Cover each tortilla with meat mixture, then sprinkle cheese over top. Broil 6 inches from heat about 2 minutes or until cheese melts. Remove plates; top cheese with shredded lettuce, tomatoes, and olives. Place spoonfuls of guacamole and sour cream on chalupas.

Chorizo Taquitos

Prep 15 minutes **Cook** 25 minutes **Makes** 12 pieces

1	**package (16-ounce, bulk) beef chorizo sausage, casing removed**
1	**cup medium chunky salsa, drained, *Pace*®**
1	**cup shredded mild cheddar cheese, *Kraft*®**
6	**fajita-size (8-inch) flour tortillas, *Mission*®**
1	**cup purchased guacamole**
¼	**cup sour cream**

1. Preheat oven to 400 degrees F. Line a baking sheet with aluminum foil. In a large skillet, cook and stir sausage over medium heat about 6 minutes or until brown. Drain fat from cooked sausage; discard. Set sausage aside to cool. Stir salsa and cheese into sausage in skillet.

2. Place 1 tortilla on a clean work surface. Spoon ¼ cup of the sausage mixture down tortilla center. Fold tortilla in half, then roll up. Secure with toothpicks. Place on prepared baking sheet. Repeat with remaining tortillas and filling. Bake for 18 minutes or until filling is hot and tortillas are crisp and golden brown. Cut taquitos in half crosswise. Serve hot with guacamole and sour cream.

Carnitas Tacos

Start to Finish 10 minutes   **Makes** 4 servings

1	container (17-ounce) precooked pork roast, *Hormel*®
¼	cup enchilada sauce, *Las Palmas*®
1	teaspoon Mexican seasoning, *The Spice Hunter*®
8	(6-inch) white corn tortillas, *Mission*®
⅓	cup chopped onions, *Ready Pac*®
2	tablespoons chopped fresh cilantro
1	lime, cut into wedges
	Shredded lettuce
	Chopped tomatoes (optional)

1. Remove pork roast from package; set aside. In a medium microwave-safe bowl, combine enchilada sauce and Mexican seasoning. Add pork roast. Cover with plastic wrap; microwave on high heat setting (100 percent power) for 4 minutes. Remove and set aside.

2. Place tortillas on a microwave-safe plate. Cover with moist paper towel; microwave on high heat setting (100 percent power) for 1 minute. Meanwhile, use a fork to shred pork in bowl. Add onion and cilantro. Stir to combine. Divide pork mixture among heated tortillas. Serve tacos with lime, lettuce, and tomatoes (optional).

Green Chile Pintos

Start to Finish 10 minutes   **Makes** 4 servings

1	can (15-ounce) pinto beans, drained, *S&W*®
1	can (10-ounce) Mexican diced tomatoes, drained, *Ro-Tel*®
1	can (4-ounce) diced green chiles, *Ortega*®
1	tablespoon tequila, *Jose Cuervo*®
2	teaspoons Mexican seasoning, *The Spice Hunter*®
½	cup Mexican cheese blend, *Sargento*®

1. In a medium saucepan, combine pinto beans, diced tomatoes, green chiles, tequila, and Mexican seasoning. Cook over medium-high heat about 4 minutes or until heated through.

2. Spoon pinto beans into 4 bowls. Top each serving with cheese.

Black Bean Quesadilla

Prep 5 minutes **Cook** 15 minutes **Makes** 2 servings

2   flour tortillas (10 inch), *Mission®*
1   cup canned refried low-fat black beans, *Rosarito®*
1   cup chunky salsa, *Pace®*
1   cup Mexican-style shredded cheese, *Kraft®*
½   cup purchased guacamole
2   tablespoons sour cream
    Cilantro sprigs (optional)

1. Preheat oven to 400 degrees F. Line a baking sheet with aluminum foil. Lay one tortilla on a clean work surface. Spread the beans evenly over the tortilla. Spoon ¾ cup of the salsa over the beans, then sprinkle with the cheese. Top with the second tortilla.

2. Place the quesadilla on prepared baking sheet. Bake for 15 minutes or until the cheese is melted and the top is crisp and brown. Meanwhile, in a small bowl, swirl together the guacamole and sour cream together. Cut the quesadilla into 4 equal portions and transfer to a plate. Serve with the guacamole mixture and remaining ¼ cup of salsa. Garnish with cilantro (optional).

Best Black Beans

Start to Finish 20 minutes **Makes** 4 servings

1   can (15-ounce) no-salt-added organic black beans, rinsed and drained, *Eden®*
1   can (10-ounce) diced tomatoes with chiles in sauce, *Ro-Tel®*
½   cup frozen chopped onions, *Ore-Ida®*
¼   cup finely chopped fresh cilantro
1   tablespoon lime juice, *ReaLime®*
1   teaspoon crushed garlic, *Christopher Ranch®*

1. In a medium saucepan, combine beans, tomatoes, onions, cilantro, lime juice, and garlic. Bring to a boil over medium-high heat; reduce heat to low. Simmer for 10 minutes.

Broccoli, Shrimp, and Chicken Quesadilla

Prep 15 minutes **Cook** 6 minutes **Makes** 4 servings

Butter
12   soft taco-size flour tortillas, *Mission*®
½   cup jalapeño cream cheese, *Philadelphia*®
⅓   pound cooked bay shrimp
1   cup cooked chopped broccoli, *Birds Eye*®
½   cup premade guacamole, *Calavo*®
1   package (6-ounce) cooked Southwest chicken strips, *Tyson*®
2   cups shredded Jack cheese, *Kraft*®
   Chunky salsa, *Newman's Own*® (optional)

1. Lightly butter both sides of 4 flour tortillas. In a large nonstick skillet, toast both sides of tortillas over medium-high heat; set aside.

2. Spread 2 tablespoons of cream cheese on one side of 4 more tortillas. Top each with one-quarter of shrimp and broccoli. Top each with one of the toasted tortillas. Spread 2 tablespoons guacamole on each of the toasted tortillas. Arrange one-quarter of chicken strips over guacamole and top with ½ cup shredded cheese. Place remaining tortillas on each quesadilla club.

3. Lightly butter top tortilla. Reheat skillet over medium to medium-high heat. Place quesadilla club, butter side down, in skillet and cook 3 to 5 minutes or until golden brown and cheese has melted. While quesadilla club is cooking, lightly butter top tortilla. Using tongs, turn quesadilla club and cook an additional 3 to 5 minutes. Repeat with remaining quesadilla clubs. Cut into wedges and serve with chunky salsa (optional).

Halibut Salsa Tacos

Prep 4 servings   **Chill** 30 minutes   **Grill** 8 minutes   **Makes** 4 servings

1	**pound halibut**
1	**packet (1-ounce) hot taco seasoning, *Lawry's*®**
2	**cups mild chunky salsa, *Newman's Own*®**
1	**cup frozen peach slices, chopped and thawed, *Dole*®**
1	**teaspoon ground allspice, *McCormick*®**
8	**yellow corn tortillas, warmed, *Mission*®**
1	**package (8-ounce) coleslaw mix, *Ready Pac*®**

1. Rub halibut with taco seasoning. Marinate in the refrigerator for 30 minutes.

2. Set up grill for direct cooking over medium heat (see page 17). Oil grate when ready to start cooking. Place halibut on hot, oiled grill. Cover grill; cook for 4 minutes per side. Let cool. Cut into bite-size pieces.

3. In a medium bowl, combine salsa, peaches, and allspice. Put halibut pieces in warm tortillas; spoon on coleslaw. Top with salsa mixture. Serve warm.

Avocado Shrimp

Start to Finish 10 minutes   **Makes** 4 servings

8	**ounces cooked, peeled, and deveined bay or other shrimp**
½	**cup refrigerated pico de gallo salsa**
2	**tablespoons bottled lime juice, *ReaLime*®**
2	**tablespoons finely chopped fresh cilantro**
1	**avocado, diced**
	Salt and ground black pepper

1. In a medium bowl, combine shrimp, salsa, lime juice, and cilantro. Let stand for 5 to 10 minutes.

2. Add avocado; toss to combine. Season to taste with salt and pepper.

Tortilla Soup with Grilled Chicken

Prep 10 minutes   **Cook** 15 minutes   **Males** 4 to 6 servings

2   **tablespoons corn oil**
1   **cup frozen diced onions, *Ore-Ida*®**
1   **carton (32-ounce) chicken broth, *Swanson*®**
1   **can (14.5-ounce) diced tomatoes with roasted garlic,**
      Contadina*®*
1   **can (4-ounce) diced green chiles, drained, *Ortega*®**
¼   **cup lime juice, *ReaLime*®**
2   **cups shredded grilled chicken breast**
      Salt and ground black pepper
2   **cups broken tortilla chips**
      Chopped avocado, cilantro, and green onions

1. In a large saucepan, heat oil over medium-high heat. Add onions and cook for 3 minutes, stirring occasionally. Add broth, tomatoes, chiles, and lime juice. Bring to boil; reduce heat and simmer 5 minutes. Stir in chicken and cook about 2 minutes or until just heated through. Season to taste with salt and pepper.

2. Ladle soup into bowls. Top each with tortilla chips. Serve with avocado, cilantro, and green onions.

Chilled Avocado Soup

Start to Finish 20 minutes   **Makes** 4 servings

1½   **cups vegetable broth, *Swanson*®**
2   **containers (12 ounces each) purchased guacamole, *Calavo*®**
1   **can (4-ounce) diced green chiles, *Ortega*®**
2   **tablespoons lemon juice, *ReaLemon*®**
2   **tablespoons garlic salt, *Lawry's*®**
2   **tablespoons fresh chopped cilantro**
4   **tablespoons premade salsa**
4   **tablespoons sour cream**
      Mild hot sauce, *Tabasco*® (optional)

1. In a blender, combine broth, guacamole, green chiles, lemon juice, garlic salt, and cilantro. Blend until smooth. Chill in freezer for 15 minutes.

2. Divide among 4 serving bowls. Top each with one tablespoon salsa and one tablespoon sour cream. Serve with mild hot sauce (optional).

Mexican Pizzas

Prep 15 minutes   **Microwave** 4 minutes   **Grill** 4 minutes   **Makes** 4 servings

FOR SAUCE:
¼	cup salsa, *Pace*®
¼	cup sour cream

FOR PIZZA:
4	garlic-herb wraps, *Mission*® (or any 10-inch tortillas)
2	cups shredded Mexican cheese blend, *Kraft*®
1	can (16-ounce) refried black beans, *Rosarita*®
1	package (18-ounce) precooked ground beef for tacos, *Old El Paso*®
½	red onion, diced
2	cups shredded lettuce
1	tomato, diced
	Nacho sliced jalapeños, *Embasa*® (or sliced pickled jalapeños) (optional)

1. Set up grill for direct cooking over medium heat (see page 17). Oil grate when ready to start cooking.

2. In a small bowl, combine salsa and sour cream; set aside.

3. Lay out 2 garlic-herb wraps; sprinkle with cheese blend. Top with remaining wraps; set aside.

4. In a microwave-safe bowl, microwave refried black beans on high heat setting (100 percent power) for 4 to 6 minutes or until heated through, stirring twice.

5. Using a cookie sheet, place cheese-filled wraps on hot, oiled grill. Cook for 2 minutes; turn over. Divide refried beans between cheese-filled wraps. Spread evenly over the tops of the pizzas, leaving a ½-inch border. Top beans with taco meat and onion. Cover grill; cook 2 minutes. Using the cookie sheet, remove pizza from grill.

6. Top with lettuce and tomato; drizzle with salsa-sour cream mixture. Garnish with sliced jalapeños (optional). Serve hot.

Beef Fajitas Corona®

Prep 20 minutes   **Cook** 8 to 10 hours (Low)   **Makes** 6 servings

2½   pounds beef round steaks
2   packets (1.27 ounces each) fajita seasoning mix, *Lawry's*®
2   medium red bell peppers, sliced into ½-inch strips
1   medium green bell pepper, sliced into ½-inch strips
1   medium onion, thickly sliced
½   cup beer, *Corona*®
     Warmed flour tortillas, *Mission*® (optional)

1. Sprinkle steak pieces with one packet of the fajita seasoning mix. Roll steak pieces from short ends and secure with 100-percent-cotton kitchen string; set aside.

2. In a 5-quart slow cooker, toss together bell pepper strips, onion, and remaining packet of fajita seasoning mix. Place rolled steaks on top of vegetables. Pour in beer.

3. Cover and cook on low heat setting for 8 to 10 hours.

4. Transfer steaks to a cutting board; slice. Using a slotted spoon, transfer vegetables to a serving bowl. Serve steak slices with vegetables in warmed tortillas (optional).

Arroz con Pollo

Prep 15 minutes   **Cook** 2 hours (High)   **Makes** 6 servings

1½   pounds boneless, skinless chicken breast halves, cut into bite-size pieces
3   cups reduced-sodium chicken broth, *Swanson*®
1   can (14.5-ounce) diced tomatoes with green chiles, *S&W*®
2   bags (5 ounces each) saffron yellow rice, *Mahatma*®
1   cup frozen chopped onion, *Ore-Ida*®
1   cup dry sherry, *Christian Brothers*®
½   cup pimiento-stuffed green olives, sliced, *Early California*®

1. In a 4- to 5-quart slow cooker, stir together the chicken, chicken broth, undrained tomatoes, rice, onion, sherry, and olives until thoroughly combined.

2. Cover and cook on high heat setting for 2 hours or until chicken is cooked. (Rice should be slightly wet.)

Chipotle Java-Rubbed Tenderloin

Prep 10 minutes   **Grill** 40 minutes   **Stand** 35 minutes
Chill 2 hours   **Makes** 4 servings

1 ½	pounds center-cut beef tenderloin roast, trimmed of fat and silver skin
1	packet (1.13-ounce) chipotle pepper marinade mix, *McCormick® Grill Mates®*
½	cup instant coffee crystals, *Folgers®*
½	teaspoon ground cinnamon, *McCormick®*

1. Tie tenderloin roast with butcher's string to hold roast together (tuck any thin ends under for a uniform thickness). In a small bowl, combine marinade mix, coffee crystals, and cinnamon. Rub into tenderloin. Wrap in plastic wrap; chill in refrigerator for 2 to 4 hours.

2. Set up grill for direct cooking over medium heat (see page 17). Oil grate when ready to start cooking. Let meat stand at room temperature for 30 to 40 minutes.

3. Place tenderloin on hot, oiled grill. Cook about 40 minutes for medium (150 degrees F), rolling roast a quarter turn every 10 minutes. Remove from grill; let stand for 5 to 10 minutes. Slice tenderloin in ½-inch-thick slices. Serve immediately.

Shrimp and Jicama Ceviche

Prep 10 minutes   **Chill** 4 hours   **Makes** 4 servings

8	ounces fresh shrimp, peeled and deveined
1	avocado, peeled, pitted, and cut into chunks
1	cup diced peeled jicama
¾	cup thick and chunky salsa, *Ortega*®
¼	cup freshly squeezed lime juice
	Cilantro sprigs and lime wedges, for garnish
	Tortilla chips

1. In a large bowl, combine shrimp, avocado, jicama, salsa, and lime juice. Chill for 4 to 6 hours or until shrimp are opaque.

2. Spoon equal amounts of shrimp mixture into 4 stemmed glasses or small bowls. Garnish with cilantro sprigs and lime wedges. Serve with tortilla chips.

Chile Relleno Bake

Prep 5 minutes   **Cook** 45 minutes   **Makes** 8 servings

This meatless casserole is a hit at The Oaks Spa in Ojai, California. My version uses corn muffin mix and a Mexican cheese combo to make it easy for every day. To cut back on calories, use low-fat cheese and milk.

	Nonstick cooking spray, *Pam*®
6	eggs
3	cups milk
1	box (8.5-ounce) corn muffin mix, *Jiffy*®
1	can (7-ounce) diced green chiles, *La Victoria*®
2	packages (8 ounces each) shredded Mexican-style cheese, *Kraft*®
1	teaspoon salt

1. Preheat oven to 350 degrees F. Lightly spray 9×13-inch baking dish with cooking spray. In a large bowl, whisk together eggs and milk. Stir in milk, muffin mix, green chiles, cheese, and salt. Pour egg mixture into prepared baking dish.

2. Bake for 45 to 50 minutes or until puffed and golden brown.

Italian Baked Pork Chops

Prep 5 minutes **Bake** 10 minutes **Makes** 4 servings

1	tablespoon Dijon mustard, *French's®*
1	tablespoon extra virgin olive oil, *Bertolli®*
½	teaspoon Italian seasoning, *McCormick®*
4	pork center loin chops (6 ounces each)
	Salt and ground black pepper
½	cup shredded Parmesan cheese, *Kraft®*

1. Preheat oven to 400 degrees F. Line baking sheet with kitchen parchment. Set aside.

2. In a small bowl, whisk together mustard, oil, and Italian seasoning. Season the pork chops with salt and pepper, then brush both sides of chops with mustard mixture. Press Parmesan into both sides of chops.

3. Place chops on prepared baking sheet. Bake about 10 minutes or until just cooked through.

Bread Salad

Prep 10 minutes **Makes** 6 servings

2	medium tomatoes, chopped
1	yellow bell pepper, stemmed, seeded, and sliced
½	cucumber, halved lengthwise, seeded, and sliced
½	small red onion, thinly sliced
1	tablespoon capers, rinsed, *Star®*
½	cup extra virgin olive oil, *Bertolli®*
¼	cup red wine vinegar, *Star®*
	Salt and ground black pepper
2	cups garlic and herb croutons, *Marie Callender's®*

1. In a large bowl, combine tomatoes, pepper, cucumber, onion, and capers. In a small bowl, whisk together oil and vinegar. Season to taste with salt and pepper. Pour over vegetables and toss to combine.

2. Spread croutons in a single layer on a large platter. Spoon the vegetables evenly over croutons. Pour any remaining liquid in bowl over all.

Ziti with Spicy Ragout

Prep 25 minutes   **Cook** 2 to 4 hours (Low)   **Makes** 6 servings

1	pound dried ziti pasta
1¼	pounds bulk hot Italian sausage
1	jar (26-ounce) spicy red pepper pasta sauce, *Classico*®
2	cups shredded Italian cheese blend, *Kraft*®
1	cup red wine (Merlot)
	Shredded Parmesan cheese, *Kraft*® (optional)

1. In a large pot of salted, boiling water, cook ziti about 10 minutes or just until al dente. Drain and transfer to a 4- to 5-quart slow cooker.

2. In a large skillet, cook and stir sausage until browned over medium-high heat, breaking up clumps. Transfer to slow cooker. Stir in pasta sauce, Italian cheese blend, and wine.

3. Cover and cook on low heat setting for 2 to 4 hours. Serve with shredded Parmesan cheese (optional).

Italian Bread Soup

Prep 10 minutes   **Cook** 4 to 6 hours (High)   **Makes** 4 servings

2	cans (14 ounces each) reduced-sodium chicken broth, *Swanson*®
4	cans (14.5 ounces each) organic fire-roasted diced tomatoes, *Muir Glen*®
3	cups Caesar-style croutons
1	cup frozen chopped onion, *Ore-Ida*®
1	packet (0.7-ounce) Italian salad dressing mix, *Good Seasons*®
	Salt and ground black pepper
	Grated Parmesan cheese, *DiGiorno*® (optional)
	Shredded fresh basil (optional)

1. In a 4-quart slow cooker, combine chicken broth, undrained tomatoes, croutons, onion, and salad dressing mix. Cover and cook on high heat setting for 4 to 6 hours. Season with salt and pepper. Serve with Parmesan cheese (optional) and fresh basil (optional).

Italian Fondue

Prep 5 minutes **Cook** 10 minutes **Makes** 6 servings

I love to make this fondue and serve it in individual cups or bowls for each person. When entertaining, serve alongside crusty dinner rolls for an extra special touch. They're adorable, delicious, unique, and your guests will be amazed at your creative attention to detail.

2	tablespoons butter
2	tablespoons finely chopped fresh sage
2	tablespoons all-purpose flour, *Pillsbury*®
1¼	cups dry white wine, *Vendage*®
1	jar (16-ounce) Alfredo sauce, *Classico*®
1	package (8-ounce) shredded Six-Cheese Italian Blend (mozzarella, smoked provolone, Parmesan, Romano, fontina, and Asiago cheeses), *Sargento*®
	Assorted dippers, such as crusty Italian bread cubes, quartered figs, and cooked potato cubes

1. In a large heavy saucepan, melt butter over medium heat. Add sage and cook about 2 minutes or until butter is golden brown.

2. Whisk in flour and cook for 1 minute. Whisk in wine and simmer for 2 minutes. Whisk in Alfredo sauce. Gradually add cheese, whisking until cheese melts and mixture is smooth.

3. Transfer mixture to a fondue pot, chafing dish, or ceramic bowl. Serve with dippers.

Ravioli with Sun-Dried Tomatoes

Prep 5 minutes **Cook** 10 minutes **Makes** 4 servings

Browning butter brings out a subtle nuttiness that complements the heart-healthy walnuts and releases an irresistibly sweet perfume. Summery sun-dried tomatoes give it just the right squish of juiciness.

1	package (16-ounce) mozzarella and herb double-stuffed ravioli, *Buitoni*®
1	stick (½ cup) butter
2	teaspoons Italian salad dressing mix, *Good Seasons*®
¼	cup walnut pieces, *Planters*®
⅓	cup sun-dried tomatoes, oil packed, drained, and julienned

1. Bring a large pot of salted water to a boil. Add ravioli and cook for 8 to 9 minutes or until they are al dente.

2. Meanwhile, in a small saucepan, melt butter over medium to high heat. Cook butter until golden brown and bubbling. Add Italian dressing mix, walnut pieces, and sun-dried tomatoes and heat through.

3. Use a colander to drain ravioli. Toss ravioli with sauce.

Prosciutto and Goat Cheese Pizza

Prep 6 minutes   **Bake** 12 minutes   **Makes** 2 servings

I am in love with this pizza! It's delicious, and once you put the first bite in your mouth, you'll be in love with it too! It's simple, quick, and fun to make.

1	fully baked thin pizza crust (10-ounce), *Boboli®*
½	cup marinara sauce, *Boboli®*
1	cup shredded mozzarella cheese, *Kraft®*
1	package (3-ounce) thinly sliced prosciutto (deli section), *Citterio®*
1	ounce soft fresh goat cheese, coarsely crumbled
2	tablespoons chopped fresh basil

1. Preheat oven to 425 degrees F.

2. Lay pizza crust on an aluminum foil-covered pizza pan or cookie sheet. Spread sauce evenly over pizza crust. Sprinkle mozzarella cheese over crust, leaving a 1-inch border around edge. Arrange prosciutto on top of cheese. Sprinkle goat cheese over prosciutto.

3. Bake about 12 minutes or until prosciutto is crisp and cheeses are melted. Sprinkle fresh basil over pizza. Cut into 6 slices and serve.

Fig and Prosciutto Crostata

Prep 15 minutes   **Bake** 15 minutes   **Makes** 6 to 8 servings

1	box (11-ounce) piecrust mix, *Betty Crocker®*
2	teaspoons salt-free citrus herb seasoning, *Spice Islands®*
⅓	cup plus 1 tablespoon cold water
½	brick (4-ounce) cream cheese, softened, *Philadelphia®*
1	jar (10-ounce, about ¾ cup) fig preserves, *St. Dalfour®*
1	package (3-ounce) prosciutto, cut into ½-inch strips
1	egg
	Fresh thyme leaves (optional)

1. Preheat oven to 425 degrees F. In a medium bowl, stir together piecrust mix, citrus herb seasoning, and ⅓ cup water until moistened. Stir 20 times until dough ball forms. Let rest 5 minutes.

2. On a lightly floured surface, flatten ball into a disk and roll into 15-inch circle. Fold in half to transfer to pizza stone or baking sheet, then unfold.

3. Spread cream cheese over piecrust, leaving a 1-inch border, and top with fig preserves. Fold border over fig preserves. Top with prosciutto strips. Lightly beat egg with 1 tablespoon of water, and use a pastry brush to brush edge of crust with egg wash.

4. Bake for 15 to 18 minutes or until crust is golden brown. Garnish with fresh thyme (optional). Cut into 6 to 8 pieces and serve.

Wasabi Chicken

Start to Finish 20 minutes   **Makes** 4 servings

Fiery wasabi is Japanese horseradish. Tempered with ginger, its tangy hot mustard taste adds spark to mellow chicken breasts. Serve it with Four Pea Stir-Fry to deliver the signature flavors of Asian cooking—sweet, sour, spicy, and salty.

2	teaspoons wasabi powder, *Eden®*
1	tablespoon hot water
1	tablespoon canola oil
1	teaspoon minced ginger, *Christopher Ranch®*
4	boneless, skinless thin-cut chicken fillets, rinsed and patted dry
½	cup sake, *Gekkeikan®*
1	can (10.5-ounce) white sauce, *Aunt Penny's®*

1. In a small bowl, combine wasabi powder and hot water. Let sit for 5 minutes to make a paste. Meanwhile, in a large skillet, heat oil and ginger over medium-high heat. Add chicken and cook 3 to 4 minutes per side or until cooked through. Remove chicken from skillet.

2. Remove skillet from heat and carefully add sake. Deglaze by scraping bits from bottom of pan. Return skillet to heat and add wasabi paste; stir and heat until dissolved. Stir in white sauce and heat through. Return chicken to pan and heat through. Serve chicken immediately with wasabi sauce.

Four Pea Stir-Fry

Start to Finish 10 minutes   **Makes** 4 servings

1	tablespoon canola oil
1	teaspoon sesame seed oil
1	teaspoon crushed garlic, *Christopher Ranch®*
1	cup frozen snow peas, thawed, *C&W®*
1	cup frozen sugar snaps, thawed, *C&W®*
1	cup frozen early peas, thawed, *C&W®*
¼	cup wasabi peas, lightly crushed, *Hapi®*
1	tablespoon diced pimientos, *Dromedary®*
2	tablespoons stir-fry sauce, *Kikkoman®*

1. In a large skillet, heat canola oil and sesame seed oil over medium-high heat.

2. Stir in garlic. Add all peas and pimientos. Cook and stir about 5 minutes or until peas and pimientos are tender. Stir in stir-fry sauce and serve.

Tandoori Chicken Thighs

Prep 10 minutes   **Marinate** 2 hours   **Stand** 30 minutes   **Grill** 36 minutes
Makes 4 servings

8	chicken thighs
1½	cups plain yogurt, *Dannon®*
2	teaspoons garam masala*, *Spice Hunter®*
2	teaspoons paprika
1	teaspoon minced ginger, *Christopher Ranch®*
1	teaspoon crushed garlic, *Christopher Ranch®*

1. Rinse chicken thighs with cold water and pat dry.

2. In a large bowl, combine yogurt, garam masala, paprika, ginger, and garlic; stir until smooth. Add chicken; toss to coat. Cover with plastic wrap and marinate in the refrigerator at least 2 hours, preferably overnight.

3. Set up grill for direct cooking over medium heat (see page 17). Oil grate when ready to start cooking. Remove chicken from refrigerator; let stand at room temperature about 30 minutes.

4. Place chicken on hot, oiled grill. Cook for 18 to 22 minutes per side or until internal temperature reaches 180 degrees F. Serve hot.

*****NOTE:** Garam masala is a blend of aromatic spices used in Indian cooking. It can be found in the spice section of the grocery store.

Teriyaki Chicken Noodles

Start to Finish 20 minutes   **Makes** 4 servings

6	ounces somen noodles
2	tablespoons canola oil, *Wesson*®
1½	pounds chicken tenders, cut into bite-size pieces
1	bag (6-ounce) prewashed baby spinach, *Fresh Express*®
1	cup loose-pack frozen carrot slices, thawed, *C&W*®
½	cup teriyaki sauce, *Kikkoman*®
½	cup reduced-sodium chicken broth, *Swanson*®
1	teaspoon bottled crushed garlic, *Christopher Ranch*®
1	teaspoon bottled minced ginger, *Christopher Ranch*®

1. In a large pot of boiling salted water, cook noodles for 3 minutes. Drain; rinse with cold water. Drain well; set aside.

2. Meanwhile, in a large skillet, heat canola oil over medium-high heat. Add chicken to hot oil; cook and stir about 7 minutes or until cooked through.

3. Add spinach, thawed carrots, teriyaki sauce, chicken broth, garlic, and ginger to skillet. Stir to combine; simmer over medium heat for 5 minutes. Add cooked noodles and toss to combine.

Sugar Snap Peas with Red Pepper

Start to Finish 10 minutes   **Makes** 4 servings

1	bag (14-ounce) loose-pack frozen sugar snap peas, *C&W*®
¼	cup roasted red bell pepper, cut into thin strips, *Delallo*®
1	teaspoon dark sesame oil
2	teaspoons sesame seeds

1. In a microwave-safe bowl, combine the frozen snap peas, red bell pepper, and sesame oil. Cover with plastic wrap; microwave on high heat setting (100 percent power) for 6 to 7 minutes, stirring halfway through cooking time.

2. Toss with sesame seeds. Serve hot.

Cashew Chicken

Prep 15 minutes   **Cook** 5 minutes   **Makes** 6 servings

¾	cup stir-fry sauce, *Kikkoman*®
3	teaspoons chopped ginger, *Christopher Ranch*®
2	tablespoons plus 1 teaspoon brown sugar, *C&H*®
2	tablespoons vegetable oil
1¼	pounds chicken breast tenders, cut into bite-sized pieces
1	package (8-ounce) sliced mushrooms
1	cup frozen chopped green bell peppers, thawed, *Pictsweet*®
¼	cup scallions, sliced diagonally (plus more for garnish, optional)
1	can (8-ounce) sliced water chestnuts, *Polar*®
1	teaspoon red pepper flakes, *McCormick*®
1½	cups cashews, *Planters*®

1. In a small bowl, combine stir-fry sauce, ginger, and brown sugar. In a large skillet, heat oil over medium-high heat. Add chicken pieces. Cook and stir for 3 to 5 minutes or until just cooked. Add mushrooms, green bell pepper, and scallions. Cook and stir for 2 to 3 minutes or until tender.

2. Add stir-fry sauce mixture, water chestnuts, and red pepper flakes. Stir thoroughly. Remove skillet from heat; stir in cashews. Garnish with *scallions* (optional). Serve hot.

Broccoli Rabe with Black Bean Sauce

Prep 10 minutes   **Cook** 7 minutes   **Makes** 4 servings

1	pound broccoli rabe, rinsed and trimmed
½	cup black bean garlic sauce, *Lee Kum Kee*®
2	tablespoons honey, *SueBee*®
1	teaspoon sesame seed oil, *Dynasty*®

1. In microwave-safe bowl, combine broccoli and ¼ cup *water*. Cover with wet paper towel. Microwave on high heat setting (100 percent power) for 6 to 8 minutes or until tender but crisp. Remove bowl from microwave; drain water.

2. Immediately stir in black bean sauce, honey and oil; toss to coat and serve warm.

Asian Pork Burgers

Prep 15 minutes   **Grill** 8 minutes   **Makes** 4 servings

FOR BURGERS:
1½   pounds ground pork
3   scallions (green onions), finely chopped
2   tablespoons stir-fry seasoning mix, *Sun Bird*®
2   tablespoons sesame seeds
1   teaspoon toasted sesame oil

FOR WASABI AÏOLI:
½   cup All-Purpose Burger Aïoli (below)
1½   teaspoons premade wasabi,* *S&B*®

4   sesame hamburger buns, toasted
      Shredded lettuce and sliced onion

1. For burgers, in a large bowl, combine ground pork, scallions, seasoning mix, sesame seeds, and sesame oil. Mix thoroughly. Form into 4 patties slightly larger than buns.

2. For Wasabi Aïoli, in a small bowl, thoroughly combine All-Purpose Burger Aïoli and wasabi. Set up grill for direct cooking over high heat (see page 17). Oil grate when ready to start cooking. Place patties on hot, oiled grill. Cook for 4 to 5 minutes per side for medium (160 degrees F). Serve hot on toasted buns with lettuce, onion, and Wasabi Aïoli.

ALL-PURPOSE BURGER AÏOLI: In a large bowl, combine 1 cup mayonnaise, ¼ cup lemon juice, 2 tablespoons minced garlic, and 1 tablespoon Dijon mustard. Store leftovers in an airtight container in the refrigerator for up to 2 weeks.

***TIP:** If you can't find premade wasabi, instead mix wasabi powder with a little water. Wasabi powder is available from McCormick® and is sold in the spice section of the supermarket.

Beef and Vegetable Stir-Fry

Prep 15 minutes   **Cook** 15 minutes   **Makes** 6 servings

2	tablespoons vegetable oil, *Wesson*®
½	pound boneless top sirloin steak, thinly sliced
½	cup onion, sliced into strips
1	tablespoon bottled minced garlic, *McCormick*®
1	tablespoon minced ginger
1	bag (12-ounce) fresh vegetable stir-fry mix
1	package (6-ounce) frozen sliced mushrooms, *PictSweet*®
1	can (8-ounce) sliced water chestnuts, *Geisha*®
1	red bell pepper, sliced into strips
2	tablespoons oyster sauce, *Dynasty*®
1	packet (1-ounce) stir-fry seasoning mix, *Kikkoman*® (dissolved in 2 tablespoons of water)
½	teaspoon red pepper flakes

1. In a large skillet or wok, heat 1 tablespoon of the oil over high heat. Add beef and stir-fry for 3 minutes. Remove from skillet.

2. Add the remaining 1 tablespoon oil to pan. Add onion, garlic, and ginger; stir-fry for 1 minute. Add mixed vegetables and stir-fry for 3 minutes. Add mushrooms, water chestnuts, and red bell pepper. Stir-fry for another 3 minutes. Return beef to pan and stir in oyster sauce, seasoning mix, and pepper flakes; stir-fry for 3 more minutes. Serve with steamed rice.

White-Chocolate Fortune Cookies

Prep 20 minutes   **Cook** 20 minutes   **Makes** 12 cookies

1	cup white dipping chocolate, *Baker's*®
12	fortune cookies
	Decorating sugar

1. Line a baking sheet with waxed paper or plastic wrap. In a small microwave-safe bowl, microwave white dipping chocolate on medium heat setting (50 percent power) for 1 to 2 minutes or until melted, stirring every 30 seconds. Dip one side of each fortune cookie into melted white chocolate. Sprinkle with decorating sugar. Place onto baking sheet to cool.

Thai Grilled Beef Salad

Prep 20 minutes   **Grill** 10 minutes   **Stand** 25 minutes   **Marinate** 1 hour
Makes 4 servings

1	1½-pound beef flank steak
¾	cup dry sherry, *Christian Brothers*®
¼	cup canola oil, *Wesson*®
¼	cup soy sauce, *Kikkoman*®
1	fresh red chile pepper, finely chopped
2	tablespoons Thai seasoning, *Spice Islands*®
2	tablespoons lime juice, *ReaLime*®

FOR SESAME SALAD DRESSING:

¼	cup soy sauce, *Kikkoman*®
3	tablespoons lime juice, *ReaLime*®
2	tablespoons sherry vinegar
2	tablespoons toasted sesame oil
1	tablespoon Thai seasoning, *Spice Island*®

FOR SALAD:

12	cups butter lettuce salad mix, *Fresh Express*®
16	cherry tomatoes, halved, *Nature Sweet*®
1	cucumber, sliced
	Chopped fresh cilantro (optional)
	Chopped fresh mint (optional)

1. Place steak in a large zip-top bag and add the sherry, canola oil, ¼ cup soy sauce, red chile, the 2 tablespoons Thai seasoning, and the 2 tablespoons lime juice. Squeeze air out of bag; seal. Gently massage bag to combine. Marinate in refrigerator for 1 to 3 hours.

2. For Sesame Salad Dressing, in a medium bowl, whisk together ¼ cup soy sauce, the 3 tablespoons lime juice, vinegar, sesame oil, and the 1 tablespoon Thai seasoning. Set aside until ready to serve.

3. Set up grill for direct cooking over high heat (see page 17). Oil grate when ready to start cooking. Let steak stand at room temperature for 20 to 30 minutes. Remove steak from marinade; discard marinade.

4. Place steak on hot, oiled grill and cook for 5 to 8 minutes per side for medium (160 degrees F). Transfer steak to a platter and let stand for 5 minutes before slicing thinly across the grain.

5. For salads, divide salad mix, tomatoes, and cucumber among four chilled plates. Arrange steak slices on top and drizzle with Sesame Salad Dressing. Top with chopped cilantro (optional) and mint (optional).

One-Dish Dinners

When you hear "casserole," you think family. My friend Hilary grew up with great cooking. She took her mother's recipes off to college and has been quick-cooking ever since. Now she's the mom. With two daughters in grade school and her husband, AJ, busy in his own home office, juggling two careers, two kids, and three meals a day is everyday life in the Lentini household. Casseroles make life manageable, helping you serve heartwarming dishes like Tamale Pie and Lasagna, just like Mom used to make. Jazz up the ingredients and feisty Jambalaya Bake and sumptuous Crab Enchilada Suizas cook colorfully for company. The question isn't "What's for dinner?" The question is "What did you do today?" These one-dish dinners do the work, so you can spend time with those you care most about.

The Recipes

Turkey Pot Pie with Pepper Biscuit Topping

Prep 20 minutes **Bake** 75 minutes **Makes** 6 servings

1	pound boneless, skinless turkey breast, cut into bite-size pieces
2	cans (10.75 ounces each) condensed cream of chicken soup, *Campbell's*®
1	large red potato, diced
½	package (16-ounce) frozen loose-pack mixed vegetables (carrots, corn, peas, green beans), thawed, *C&W*®
1	cup frozen chopped onion, *Ore-Ida*®
1	teaspoon salt-free chicken seasoning, *McCormick*®
1	can (16-ounce) refrigerated biscuits, *Pillsbury Grands!*®
1	tablespoon butter, melted
¾	teaspoon ground black pepper

1. Preheat oven to 350 degrees F. Line a baking sheet with aluminum foil; set aside. In a large bowl, stir together turkey, soup, potato, mixed vegetables, onion, and chicken seasoning until thoroughly combined. Transfer to a 2½-quart casserole. Cover with aluminum foil and place on prepared baking sheet.

2. Bake for 1 hour or until hot and bubbly. Remove from oven; remove foil. Gently stir mixture to evenly distribute heat.

3. Arrange 6 biscuits* on top of casserole. Brush tops of biscuits with melted butter. Sprinkle with pepper. Return casserole to oven. Bake for 15 to 18 minutes more or until biscuits have risen and are golden brown.

***NOTE:** Place the extra biscuits in a pie plate and bake alongside the casserole for 15 to 18 minutes or until biscuits have risen and are golden brown. Serve with casserole or cool on a wire rack to use at another meal.

Jambalaya Bake

Prep 15 minutes **Bake** 70 minutes **Makes** 6 servings

1	pound boneless, skinless chicken breast halves, cut into 1-inch pieces
1	can (14.5-ounce) diced tomatoes with onion, celery, and bell pepper, *Hunt's*®
1	can (14-ounce) reduced-sodium chicken broth, *Swanson*®
8	ounces hot Louisiana sausage, cut into 1-inch pieces, *Farmer John*®
1	box (8-ounce) jambalaya mix, *Zatarain's*®

1. Preheat oven to 350 degrees F.

2. In a 2-quart casserole, stir together chicken, undrained tomatoes, chicken broth, sausage, and jambalaya mix until thoroughly combined. Cover with aluminum foil. Bake for 70 to 85 minutes.

Tex-Mex Turkey Casserole

Prep 15 minutes **Bake** 30 minutes **Makes** 6 servings

1¼ pounds uncooked ground turkey
1   packet (1.25-ounce) Tex-Mex chili seasoning mix, *McCormick®*
1   can (15-ounce) reduced-sodium black beans, rinsed and drained, *S&W®*
1   can (11-ounce) mexicorn, *Green Giant®*
1   can (10.75-ounce) condensed creamy ranchero tomato soup, *Campbell's®*
1   can (4-ounce) diced green chile peppers, drained, *La Victoria®*
1   cup crushed tortilla chips, *Tostitos®*
1   cup shredded Mexican cheese blend, *Kraft®*
⅓   cup sliced black olives, drained, *Early California®*
⅓   cup jalapeño chile pepper slices, drained, *Ortega®*
    Sour cream, *Knudsen®* (optional)
    Salsa (optional)

1. Preheat oven to 350 degrees F.

2. In a large skillet, cook and stir turkey with chili seasoning mix over medium-high heat until turkey is browned, breaking up clumps. Drain off fat. Stir in beans, mexicorn, soup, and green chile peppers. Divide mixture among six 8-ounce casseroles.*

3. Cover with crushed tortilla chips and cheese. Sprinkle with olives and jalapeño pepper slices.

4. Bake about 30 minutes or until hot. Serve with sour cream (optional) and salsa (optional).

*NOTE: If you don't have individual casseroles, spoon the mixture into a 2-quart casserole. Preheat oven to 350 degrees F. Cover with crushed tortilla chips and cheese. Sprinkle with olives and jalapeño pepper slices. Bake for 45 to 50 minutes or until hot. Serve as above.

Turkey Day Casserole

Prep 15 minutes **Bake** 30 minutes **Makes** 6 servings

1   container (24-ounce) mashed potatoes, *Country Crock®*
1   pound uncooked ground turkey
1   box (6-ounce) stuffing for turkey, *Stove Top®*
1   can (16-ounce) whole cranberry sauce, *Ocean Spray®*
2   jars (12 ounces each) homestyle turkey gravy, *Heinz®*
2   tablespoons butter, cut into small pieces

1. Preheat oven to 350 degrees F.

2. In container, microwave the mashed potatoes, uncovered, on high heat setting (100 percent power) for 1 minute. Stir to break up potatoes; set aside.

3. In a medium saucepan, cook and stir turkey over medium-high heat until turkey is browned, breaking up clumps. Drain off fat; set aside.

4. In the bottom of a 2½-quart casserole Spread dry stuffing mix. Top with cranberry sauce. Layer turkey and 1 jar of the gravy. Spread mashed potatoes evenly over layers in casserole. Dot with butter pieces. Bake for 30 to 40 minutes or until hot.

5. Heat remaining gravy according to directions. Serve with casserole.

King Ranch-Style Casseroles

Prep 25 minutes   **Bake** 25 minutes   **Makes** 8 servings

	Olive oil cooking spray, *Pam®*
8	6-inch yellow corn tortillas, *Mission®*
1	cup organic chicken broth, *Swanson®* (optional)
1	cup frozen chopped onions, *Ore-Ida®*
1	cup frozen chopped green bell peppers, *Pictsweet®*
2	tablespoons organic chicken broth, *Swanson®*
1½	teaspoons crushed garlic, *Christopher Ranch®*
1	pound boneless, skinless turkey breast, cut into bite-size pieces
1	package (8-ounce) presliced fresh mushrooms
2	cups plain fat-free yogurt, *Horizon Organic®*
1	can (15-ounce) artichoke hearts in water, drained and chopped, *Maria®*
1	can (14.5-ounce) organic diced tomatoes, drained, *Muir Glen®*
3	tablespoons quick-mixing flour, *Wondra®*
2	tablespoons low-sodium chili seasoning, *McCormick®*
1½	cups organic shredded Jack cheese, *Horizon Organic®*
½	cup crushed baked tortilla chips, *Guiltless® Gourmet*

1. Preheat oven to 350 degrees F. Coat eight 10-ounce casseroles with cooking spray; set aside. If desired, place tortillas in a pie plate with the 1 cup chicken broth to soften.

2. In a microwave-safe bowl, combine onions, peppers, the 2 tablespoons chicken broth, and garlic. Cover and microwave on high heat setting (100 percent power) for 5 minutes; set aside.

3. Coat a large nonstick skillet with cooking spray. Heat over medium-high heat; add turkey pieces and mushrooms. Cook and stir for 7 to 9 minutes or until turkey is no longer pink. Stir in onion mixture, yogurt, artichokes, tomatoes, flour, and chili seasoning. Bring to a boil; reduce heat. Simmer for 5 minutes.

4. Meanwhile, line each prepared casserole with a tortilla. Divide turkey mixture evenly among casseroles. Sprinkle with cheese and crushed tortilla chips.

5. Bake about 25 minutes for individual casseroles or until mixture is hot and bubbly.

Chicken Tetrazzini

Prep 25 minutes **Bake** 30 minutes **Makes** 6 servings

3	tablespoons butter
1	package (8-ounce) presliced fresh mushrooms
1	teaspoon bottled chopped garlic, *Christopher Ranch*®
1	can (14-ounce) reduced-sodium chicken broth, *Swanson*®
1	packet (1.8-ounce) white sauce mix, *Knorr*®
½	cup half-and-half
2	tablespoons sherry, *Christian Brothers*®
1	cup shredded Swiss cheese, *Kraft*®
4	ounces dried spaghetti, broken in half, *Barilla*®
2	cups cooked chicken white meat, cubed
¼	cup grated Parmesan cheese, *DiGiorno*®

1. Preheat oven to 325 degrees F. Lightly butter a 2-quart casserole with some of the butter; set aside.

2. In a large saucepan, melt remaining butter over medium heat. Add mushrooms and garlic. Cook and stir until mushrooms are soft. Transfer to a medium bowl; set aside.

3. In same saucepan, whisk together chicken broth and sauce mix. Bring to a boil over high heat. Reduce heat. Add half-and-half and sherry. Stir in Swiss cheese. Cook and stir until cheese is melted.

4. Add dried spaghetti to saucepan. Cook for 8 to 10 minutes over low heat or until spaghetti is al dente, stirring occasionally. Remove from heat. Stir in chicken and mushroom mixture.

5. Transfer chicken mixture to prepared casserole. Sprinkle with Parmesan cheese. Bake about 30 minutes or until hot.

Sweet Potato Shepherd's Pie

Prep 15 minutes **Bake** 45 minutes **Makes** 6 servings

1   container (23-ounce) mashed sweet potatoes, *Country Crock®*
1½ pounds pork tenderloin, cut into 1-inch pieces
     Salt and ground black pepper
1   package (16-ounce) frozen petite mixed vegetables, *C&W®*
1   can (10.75-ounce) condensed cream of mushroom soup with roasted garlic, *Campbell's®*
2   teaspoons salt-free garlic-and-herb seasoning, *McCormick®*

1. Preheat oven to 350 degrees F.

2. In container, microwave the mashed potatoes, uncovered, on high heat setting (100 percent power) for 2 minutes. Stir to break up potatoes; set aside.

3. Sprinkle pork with salt and pepper. In a 2½-quart casserole, stir together pork, vegetables, soup, and garlic-and-herb seasoning until thoroughly combined. Spread sweet potatoes evenly over pork mixture. Bake for 45 to 55 minutes or until hot and bubbly.

NOTE: For a fancier presentation, use a pastry bag or zip-top plastic bag with a corner snipped off to pipe the sweet potatoes in a lattice design on top of the pork mixture.

Scalloped Ham and Potatoes

Prep 10 minutes **Bake** 1 hour **Makes** 6 servings

1½ pounds frozen shredded potatoes, *Ore-Ida®*
½   pound diced ham, *Farmland®*
1   cup frozen chopped onion, *Ore-Ida®*
1   package (8-ounce) crumbled sharp cheddar cheese, *Kraft®*
2   cans (10.75 ounces each) condensed cream of mushroom soup, *Campbell's®*
1   cup heavy cream
½   cup grated Parmesan cheese, *DiGiorno®*

1. Preheat oven to 350 degrees F.

2. In a 2½- to 3-quart casserole dish, layer half of the potatoes, half of the ham, half of the onion, and half of the cheese. Spread 1 can of soup evenly over layers. Repeat layers once more. Top with remaining can of soup.

3. Pour cream over layers, tipping the casserole back and forth to allow cream to soak in. Sprinkle with Parmesan cheese. Bake for 1 hour or until hot and bubbly.

Tamale Pie

Prep 20 minutes Bake 50 minutes Makes 4 servings

1	pound ground beef
1	can (10-ounce) diced tomatoes and green chiles, drained, *Ro-Tel®*
1	cup chunky salsa verde, *La Victoria®*
1	package (8.5-ounce) corn muffin mix, *Jiffy®*
1	cup cream-style corn, *C&W®*
1	can (2.25-ounce) sliced black olives, drained, *Early California®*
1	cup shredded Mexican cheese blend, *Kraft®*

1. Preheat oven to 350 degrees F. In a saucepan, cook and stir ground beef over medium heat until browned, breaking up clumps. Drain off fat. Stir in tomatoes and salsa. Transfer meat mixture to a 1½-quart casserole

2. In a bowl, stir together muffin mix and corn until combined. Spread over mixture in casserole. Sprinkle with olives. Bake for 45 to 50 minutes or until bubbly. (If edges start to brown, cover with foil.) Top with cheese. Bake for 5 minutes more or until cheese is melted.

Lasagna

Prep 20 minutes Bake 30 minutes Makes 6 to 8 servings

1	package (16-ounce) lasagna noodles
1½	pounds ground beef
1	medium yellow onion, finely chopped
2	cans (10¾-ounces each) condensed tomato soup, *Campbell's®*
2	tablespoons apple cider vinegar, *Heinz®*
1	tablespoon dried oregano, *McCormick®*
1	teaspoon bottled minced garlic, *McCormick®*
1	container (16-ounce) small-curd cottage cheese
1	package (8-ounce) shredded mozzarella cheese, *Sargento®*

1. Preheat oven to 350 degrees F. Cook noodles according to package directions. Drain.

2. While noodles are cooking, in a large skillet, cook and stir ground beef over medium heat until browned, breaking up clumps. Drain off fat. Add onion, tomato soup, vinegar, oregano, and garlic. Simmer for 20 minutes.

3. Lay noodles lengthwise across bottom of a greased 9×13-inch baking dish. Spread a layer of cottage cheese over noodles. Add a layer of meat mixture, then cover with mozzarella cheese. Repeat for three layers. Finish with a layer of cheese. Bake about 30 minutes or until bubbly and cheese is golden.

Taco Lasagna

Prep 15 minutes **Cook** 1 hour **Stand** 10 minutes **Makes** 12 servings

1	pound lean ground beef
¾	cup water
1	packet (1.25-ounce) reduced-sodium taco seasoning, *McCormick®*
1	can (4-ounce) diced green chiles, *Ortega®*
1	cup frozen chopped onion, *Ore-Ida®*
1	container (16-ounce) ricotta cheese, *Precious®*
2	eggs, lightly beaten
¼	cup chopped fresh cilantro (plus more for garnish, optional)
1	tablespoon Mexican seasoning, *McCormick®*
1	can (28-ounce) crushed tomatoes, *Progresso®*
1	jar (16-ounce) chunky salsa, *Newman's Own®*
1	box (16-ounce) curly lasagna noodles, cooked according to package directions, *Anthony's®*
3	cups shredded Mexican cheese blend, *Kraft®*

1. In medium skillet, cook and stir ground beef over medium heat until browned, breaking up clumps. Drain off fat. Add the ¾ cup water, taco seasoning, green chiles, and onion. Bring to a boil. Reduce heat and simmer, uncovered, for 5 minutes.

2. In a medium bowl, stir together ricotta cheese, eggs, cilantro, and Mexican seasoning. In a second medium bowl, stir together tomatoes and salsa.

3. Preheat oven to 400 degrees F. In a deep 9×13-inch baking dish, spread one-quarter of sauce on bottom of dish. Add a layer of lasagna noodles. Top with one-half of ricotta mixture, one-half ground beef, 1 cup shredded cheese, one-quarter sauce, and another layer of lasagna noodles. Repeat layers with remaining ingredients. Top final layer with just noodles, sauce, and cheese.

4. Cover with aluminum foil and bake for 45 minutes. Remove foil and bake 15 minutes more. Remove from oven. Let stand for 10 minutes before serving.

Crab Enchilada Suizas

Prep 10 minutes **Cook** 30 minutes **Makes** 6 servings

	Nonstick cooking spray, *Pam*®
1	can (28-ounce) green enchilada sauce, *Las Palmas*®
3	cans (6 ounces each) lump crabmeat, *Crown Prince*®
3	cups shredded pepper Jack cheese, divided, *Tillamook*®
1	cup sour cream
½	cup frozen chopped onion, *Ore-Ida*®
1	can (4-ounce) diced green chiles, *Ortega*®
½	cup canola oil or corn oil
12	corn tortillas, *Mission*®
	Mexican crema (optional)

1. Preheat oven to 350 degrees F. Lightly spray 9×13-inch baking dish with cooking spray. Spread 1 cup enchilada sauce on bottom of dish; set aside. In large bowl, stir together crab, 2 cups of the shredded cheese, sour cream, onion, and chiles.

2. In a medium skillet, heat oil over medium-high heat until a drop of water sizzles when dripped into oil. Lightly fry tortillas, one at a time, about 5 seconds each side (leaving them pliable). Use tongs to remove from pan and drain on paper towels.

3. Working in batches of 3 or 4, dip tortillas into enchilada sauce. Fill each dipped tortilla with ¼ cup of the crab mixture and roll. Place in prepared baking dish. Repeat to make 12 enchiladas. Spoon any remaining sauce over top of enchiladas and sprinkle with remaining cheese.

4. Bake for 30 to 35 minutes. Drizzle with Mexican crema (optional) and serve hot.

Clam Chowder

Prep 10 minutes   **Cook** 25 minutes   **Makes** 3 servings

1	tablespoon butter
½	onion, minced
3	tablespoons dry vermouth
1	can (6.5-ounce) chopped clams in juice, *Snow's*®
1	cup heavy cream
	Salt and ground white pepper
	Sugar
1	can (10.75-ounce) cream of potato soup, *Campbell's*®
½	teaspoon truffle oil (optional)
	Sourdough bread bowls (optional)
	Brioche croutons (optional)
	Chopped parsley leaves (optional)

1. In a medium saucepan melt butter over medium heat. Add onion; cook and stir until tender. Stir in vermouth. Bring to a simmer and allow vermouth to reduce slightly.

2. Strain clams, reserving juice. Add clam juice to pan. Bring to a simmer and allow juice to reduce slightly. Add cream; reduce by half. Season to taste with salt, pepper, and sugar. Add potato soup. Bring to a simmer.

3. Add clams and cook until just heated through. Add truffle oil (optional). Serve in sourdough bowls. Top with croutons (optional) and chopped parsley (optional).

Southwestern Turkey Chili and Corn Bread

Canned chili and stew carried me through my college years. I put it in omelets, poured it over biscuits, and sometimes would eat it right out of the can. It was hearty, satisfying, and affordable. At the time I didn't even think about what the meat content might be—thank goodness, because I would have starved! But here's a way to tantalize your taste buds with an all-time favorite using vegetarian-like products and your own fresh meat. This chili is fantastic every day and fabulous for football Sundays.

Prep 5 minutes **Cook** 25 minutes **Makes** 2 servings

FOR CORN BREAD:
Nonstick vegetable cooking spray, *Pam*®
1   can (11-ounce) mexicorn, *Green Giant*®
1   egg
1   package (8.5-ounce) corn muffin mix, *Jiffy*®

FOR CHILI:
10   ounces lean ground turkey, crumbled
1   tablespoon all-purpose flour, *Pillsbury*®
1   tablespoon olive oil, *Bertolli*®
1   can (15.5-ounce) spicy black beans,
     S&W Regional Recipe: San Antonio Beans®
1   can (14.5-ounce) stewed tomatoes, Mexican recipe style, *S&W*®

1. Preheat oven to 400 degrees F. Spray a 8×8-inch baking pan with nonstick spray.

2. Drain liquid from mexicorn, reserving 2 tablespoons liquid. In a medium bowl, stir together the reserved 2 tablespoons liquid and egg. Stir in mexicorn. Add corn muffin mix; stir just until combined.

3. Transfer mixture to prepared pan. Bake about 20 minutes or until a toothpick inserted into center of corn bread comes out clean.

4. Meanwhile, in a large zip-top plastic bag, toss turkey with flour until flour is absorbed into meat. In a wide 2-quart pot, heat oil over medium heat. Cook and stir the turkey about 5 minutes or until browned.

5. Add the black beans and tomatoes. Simmer over medium-low heat about 8 minutes more or until chili is slightly thick. To serve, spoon chili into soup bowls. Serve hot with corn bread.

Chicken and Dumplings

Prep 15 minutes   **Cook** 50 minutes   **Makes** 8 servings

2	whole (2-pound) store-bought deli roasted chickens
2	tablespoons vegetable oil
1	package (7-ounce) chopped onions, *Ready Pac®*
1	container (14-ounce) carrot sticks, chopped, *Ready Pac®*
1	container (14-ounce) celery sticks, chopped, *Ready Pac®*
6	cans (14 ounces each) reduced-sodium chicken broth, *Swanson®*
2	teaspoons poultry seasoning, *McCormick®*
1	teaspoon salt
½	teaspoon ground black pepper
	All-purpose flour, for dusting
1	container (16.3-ounce) refrigerated buttermilk biscuit dough, *Pillsbury® Grands!®*
1	can (10.5-ounce) condensed chicken gravy, *Campbell's®*

1. Remove skin and bones from chickens. Shred cooked chicken into large pieces; set aside.

2. In a large heavy pot or Dutch oven, heat oil over medium heat. Add onions, carrots, and celery. Cook about 10 minutes or until soft.

3. Add broth, poultry seasoning, salt, pepper. Stir in chicken. Bring to a boil. Reduce heat and simmer for 30 minutes.

4. While stew simmers, prepare dumplings. On a lightly floured surface, roll each biscuit ¼ inch thick. With a pizza cutter, cut biscuits into 1-inch-wide strips. Set aside.

5. Skim off any fat that has risen to surface of soup. Stir in chicken gravy. Stir in dumplings, a few at a time. Cover with a tight-fitting lid and simmer for 10 minutes more. To serve, ladle into bowls and serve hot.

Beefy Stew

Prep 10 minutes **Cook** 35 minutes **Makes** 4 servings

When making stew, I like to use canned vegetable soup and then add my own choice of fresh meat to it. To me, it tastes much better than ordinary canned stew and it's fresher. This stew recipe makes a wonderfully hearty meal. Double or triple the recipe and keep it in the fridge—it makes great leftovers!

1½	pounds beef cube steak, cut into 1-inch pieces
	Salt and ground black pepper
2	tablespoons all-purpose flour, *Pillsbury*®
¼	cup vegetable oil, *Wesson*®
1	can (14-ounce) reduced-sodium beef broth, *Swanson*®
1	jar (24-ounce) country vegetable soup, *Campbell's*®
1	sheet frozen puff pastry, thawed, cut into four 4-inch rounds, *Pepperidge Farm*®

1. Sprinkle beef with salt and pepper. In a large bowl, toss beef with flour to coat. In a large heavy saucepan, heat oil over medium-high heat. Add a third of the beef to oil; cook and stir about 5 minutes or until browned. Using a slotted spoon, transfer beef to bowl. Repeat with remaining beef.

2. Add beef broth. Bring to a simmer, stirring to loosen browned bits on bottom. Return all beef and any accumulated juices to casserole. Add soup and simmer, uncovered, about 15 minutes or until liquid thickens slightly and beef is tender.

3. Meanwhile, position rack in center of oven and preheat oven to 425 degrees F.

4. On a large heavy baking sheet, arrange puff pastry rounds. Bake pastry rounds about 12 minutes or until puffed, golden brown, and cooked through.

5. To serve, ladle into bowls. Top each with a warm puff pastry round and serve warm.

Gumbo Ya-Ya

Prep 10 minutes **Cook** 30 minutes **Makes** 8 servings

4	cups water
1	bag (16-ounce) frozen okra and tomatoes, *Pictsweet®*
1	bag (16-ounce) frozen veggie crumbles (soy protein), *Morningstar Farms®*
2	ribs celery, chopped
1	cup frozen chopped onions, *Ore-Ida®*
1	cup frozen crowder peas, *Pictsweet®*
½	cup frozen chopped green bell peppers, *Pictsweet®*
2	teaspoons salt-free herb seasoning blend, *Spice Hunter®*
1	teaspoon black and red pepper blend, *McCormick®*
1	can (15-ounce) organic Cajun beans and rice, *Eden®*

1. In a small stockpot, combine water, okra and tomatoes, veggie crumbles, celery, onions, crowder peas, bell peppers, herb seasoning blend, and pepper blend.

2. Bring to a boil over high heat; reduce heat. Cover and simmer for 20 to 25 minutes or until vegetables are tender.

3. Stir in beans and rice; simmer for 10 to 15 minutes more.

Mediterranean Chili

Prep 15 minutes **Cook** 30 minutes **Makes** 6 servings

1	tablespoon canola oil, *Wesson*®
2	small zucchini, finely chopped
2	small yellow summer squash, finely chopped
1	cup frozen chopped onions, *Ore-Ida*®
1	package (12-ounce) frozen veggie crumbles (soy protein), *Morningstar Farms*®
1	packet (1.25-ounce) low-sodium taco seasoning mix, *McCormick*®
2	cans (15 ounces each) no-salt-added organic kidney beans, rinsed and drained, *Eden*®
1	can (14.5-ounce) diced tomatoes with basil and garlic, *Muir Glen*®
2	cups fat-free vegetable broth, *Health Valley*®
¼	cup red wine vinegar
1	teaspoon hot pepper sauce, *Tabasco*®

1. In a medium saucepan, heat oil over medium-high heat. Add zucchini, summer squash, and onions. Cook and stir until tender. Stir in veggie crumbles and taco seasoning mix.

2. Stir in beans, tomatoes, vegetable broth, vinegar, and hot pepper sauce. Bring to a boil; reduce heat. Simmer for 30 minutes. Serve with *Parmesan cheese* (optional).

Beer Brats and Kraut

Prep 5 minutes **Cook** 10 minutes **Makes** 6 servings

3	bottles (12 ounces each) dark beer
6	brats
1	jar (25-ounce) sauerkraut, *Bubbies*®
6	sesame brat buns or hot dog buns
	Dijon mustard or yellow mustard, *French's*®

1. In a large saucepan, heat beer over medium heat. Add brats and sauerkraut. Simmer for 10 minutes.

2. With tongs, remove brats from beer and place 1 in each bun. Using a slotted spoon, spoon sauerkraut over brats. Drizzle mustard on top.

One-Dish Dinners | 159

Gumbo for a Crowd

Start to Finish 1¾ hours   **Makes** 25 servings

3	pounds boneless, skinless chicken breast halves
3	pounds boneless, skinless chicken thighs
2	tablespoons Cajun seasoning, *McCormick*®
2	tablespoons or more vegetable oil, *Wesson*®
2	sticks (1 cup) butter
6	bags (12 ounces each) frozen seasoning blend (chopped onions, peppers, celery) thawed, *Pictsweet*®
2	bags (16 ounces each) frozen cut okra, thawed, *Pictsweet*®
2	tablespoons crushed garlic, *Gourmet Garden*®
3	packages (12 ounces each) beef hot links, cut into ¼-inch-thick rounds, *Hillshire Farm*®
2	packages (16 ounces each) beef smoked sausages, cut into ¼-inch-thick rounds, *Hillshire Farm*®
6	cans (49 ounces each) reduced-sodium chicken broth, *Swanson*®
6	cups water
4	boxes (7 ounces each) gumbo mix with rice, *Zatarain's*®
3	bay leaves
4	pounds frozen peeled and deveined large shrimp, thawed
6	pounds frozen crab legs, thawed
	Salt and ground black pepper
¼	cup gumbo filé powder,* *Zatarain's*®
	Hot cooked white rice
	Louisiana-style hot sauce, *Crystal*®

1. Cut chicken into bite-size pieces. In a large bowl, toss chicken with Cajun seasoning. In a large, deep skillet, heat oil over medium heat. Cook chicken, working in batches, until chicken is browned on both sides. Remove from skillet; set aside.

2. Wipe out skillet. Return to skillet to medium heat; melt butter. Add seasoning blend, okra, and garlic. Cook, stirring frequently, until completely heated through. Remove skillet from heat; set aside.

3. Set a 30- to 34-quart turkey fryer on medium heat setting. Add beef hot links and smoked sausages to fryer. Cook, stirring occasionally, until meat is lightly browned and juices are released. Add chicken and vegetable mixture and stir to combine.

4. Add chicken broth, the water, gumbo mix, and bay leaves. Stir to thoroughly combine. Bring to a boil; reduce heat. Simmer for 1 hour. Add the shrimp and crab legs. Simmer about 15 minutes more or until shrimp and crab are opaque and cooked through. During the last 5 minutes of cooking, season to taste with salt and pepper. Stir in filé powder. Serve hot with rice and Louisiana-style hot sauce.

***TIP:** Filé powder is made from ground, dried leaves of the sassafras tree. It has become an integral part of Creole cooking and is used to thicken and flavor gumbos and other Creole dishes. Filé powder can be found in the spice section of the supermarket.

Light and Healthy Meals

The older I get, the more health conscious I become and the more I find myself having to constantly balance my love for good food with my desire to be fit. When it comes to eating, many people are of the "no fat, no point" persuasion. That's what I thought, until I came up with these light, luscious recipes that say good riddance to bad habits—and look great doing it!

From full-flavored salads and wraps to rich and satisfying pasta and meat dishes, this chapter introduces food with a new attitude. A fit and trim version of more sinful concoctions, every recipe uses a creative mix of ingredients, seasonings, and savvy substitutions to maximize flavor and taste and minimize fat and calories. Whether you're watching cholesterol, salt, sugar, or simply your waistline, they're a hassle-free way to achieve a healthy new you.

The Recipes

Cilantro-Pesto Chicken

Prep 10 minutes   **Broil** 12 minutes   **Makes** 4 servings

1 ¼	**cups chopped fresh cilantro (about 1 bunch)**
¼	**cup reduced-sodium chicken broth, *Swanson*®**
2	**tablespoons walnuts, toasted**
2	**teaspoons extra virgin olive oil, *Bertolli*®**
½	**teaspoon crushed garlic, *Christopher Ranch*®**
½	**teaspoon lemon juice, *ReaLemon*®**
4	**6-ounce boneless, skinless chicken breast halves**
2	**tablespoons extra virgin olive oil, *Bertolli*®**
2	**teaspoons salt-free lemon-pepper seasoning, *McCormick*®**
	Salt (optional)
	Broiled or grilled sweet bell pepper strips and/or onion wedges (optional)

1. For pesto, in a blender, combine cilantro, chicken broth, walnuts, the 2 teaspoons olive oil, garlic, and lemon juice. Cover and pulse until well combined, scraping down sides of blender. Set aside.

2. Preheat broiler. Brush both sides of chicken pieces with the 2 tablespoons olive oil and sprinkle with lemon-pepper seasoning and salt (optional).

3. Broil chicken 4 to 5 inches from heat for 6 to 8 minutes per side or until chicken is no longer pink (165 degrees F).

4. Top hot chicken pieces with pesto. Serve with bell peppers and/or onions (optional).

Per serving 307 cal., 14 g total fat (2 g sat. fat), 98 mg chol.

Provençal Turkey Breast

Prep 10 minutes **Bake** 1 hour **Stand** 5 minutes **Makes** 6 servings

Low-fat protein foods such as turkey white meat are even better baked. To add a wonderfully earthy flavor, slit pockets in turkey and insert garlic cloves and rub with pungent herbes de Provence and Dijon mustard.

	Olive oil cooking spray, *Pam®*
1	2-pound boneless, skinless turkey breast
10	roasted whole garlic cloves, *Christopher Ranch®*
¼	cup Dijon mustard, *Grey Poupon®*
1	tablespoon herbes de Provence, *McCormick®*
1	tablespoon extra virgin olive oil, *Bertolli®*
1	organic lemon, thinly sliced
18	garlic-stuffed green olives, *Mezzetta®*
	Fresh thyme sprigs (optional)

1. Preheat oven to 350 degrees F. Lightly coat a 9×13-inch baking dish with cooking spray; set aside.

2. With a paring knife, cut 10 slits randomly into turkey breast and insert a roasted garlic clove into each slit; set aside. In a small bowl, stir together mustard, herbes de Provence, and oil; set aside.

3. Cover bottom of prepared baking dish with a layer of lemon slices. Arrange olives evenly over lemon slices. Top with turkey, making sure some olives are beneath turkey. Spread mustard mixture evenly over top of turkey.

4. Bake turkey in for 60 to 70 minutes or until turkey is no longer pink (165 degrees F). Place baking dish on a wire rack. Cover with foil to keep warm. Let stand 5 to 10 minutes before slicing. Garnish with thyme (optional).

Per serving 221 cal., 4 g total fat (1 g sat. fat), 94 mg chol.

Turkey-and-Red Bean Gumbo

Start to Finish 40 minutes   **Makes** 8 servings

   Olive oil cooking spray, *Pam®*
2 pounds boneless, skinless turkey breast, cut into bite-size pieces
6 cups organic reduced-sodium chicken broth, *Pacific Foods®*
1 can (15-ounce) no-salt-added organic kidney beans, rinsed and drained, *Eden®*
1 can (14.5-ounce) diced tomatoes with onion, celery, and bell pepper, *Hunt's®*
1 package (6.4-ounce) Cajun red beans and rice, *Knorr® or Lipton®*

1. Coat a large nonstick skillet with cooking spray; heat over medium-high heat. Add turkey pieces; cook and stir for 8 to 10 minutes or until no longer pink.

2. Place turkey in a 4-quart pot. Stir in chicken broth, beans, tomatoes, and red beans and rice. Bring to a boil over high heat; reduce heat to low. Cover and simmer for 25 minutes.

NOTE: Gumbo may also be cooked in a 4-quart slow cooker. Do not cook turkey in skillet. Combine all ingredients in a 4- to 5-quart slow cooker. Cover and cook on low heat setting for 6 to 8 hours.

Per serving 234 cal., 2 g total fat (1 g sat. fat), 70 mg chol.

Red Beans-and-Rice Salad

Start to Finish 25 minutes   **Makes** 6 servings

1 can (14-ounce) organic chicken broth, *Swanson®*
1 box (6.2-ounce) quick-cooking long grain and wild rice, *Uncle Ben's®*
1 can (15-ounce) no-salt-added organic kidney beans, rinsed and drained, *Eden®*
1 cup chopped sweet onion
2 ribs celery, chopped
1 jar (4-ounce) chopped pimientos, drained, *Dromedary®*
¼ cup light balsamic vinegar salad dressing, *Newman's Own®*

1. In small saucepan, combine chicken broth and rice with seasoning packet. Bring to a boil over high heat; reduce heat. Cover and simmer for 5 minutes. Remove from heat. Fluff with fork and spread on a baking sheet to cool.

2. In a large bowl, combine cooled rice, beans, onion, celery, pimientos, and salad dressing. Toss thoroughly. Serve at once or cover and chill in the refrigerator for up to 24 hours.

Per serving 194 cal., 2 g total fat (0 g sat. fat), 1 mg chol.

Pork Marsala

Start to Finish 30 minutes **Makes** 4 servings

1	pound pork tenderloin
1	tablespoon dried Italian seasoning, *McCormick®*
	Olive oil cooking spray, *Pam®*
¼	cup Marsala wine
2	cups presliced fresh mushrooms
½	tablespoon chopped garlic, *Christopher Ranch®*
½	cup organic chicken broth, *Swanson®*
¼	cup light roasted garlic balsamic salad dressing, *Bernstein's®*
	Hot cooked spaghetti, *Barilla® Plus* (optional)
	Fresh oregano sprigs (optional)

1. Trim any fat and silver skin from pork. Slice into 8 pieces. Using the smooth side of a meat mallet or a small pot, pound pork pieces to a ½-inch thickness. Sprinkle both sides of pork pieces with Italian seasoning.

2. Coat a large skillet with cooking spray; heat over medium-high heat. Add pork; cook for 2 to 3 minutes per side or until cooked through. Transfer the pork to a platter; cover with aluminum foil to keep warm.

3. Add Marsala wine to skillet and deglaze by scraping bits from bottom of skillet. Add mushrooms and garlic. Cook and stir on medium-high heat for 2 minutes. Add chicken broth and salad dressing; bring to a boil over high heat. Cook until mushrooms are tender. Reduce heat and return pork to skillet. Simmer for 3 to 4 minutes or until heated through.

4. Serve with hot cooked spaghetti (optional) and oregano (optional).

Per serving 187 cal., 6 g total fat (2 g sat. fat), 73 mg chol.

Crab Louie Salad

Start to Finish 15 minutes   **Makes** 4 servings

2	cans (6 ounces each) lump crabmeat, drained, *Geisha®*, or 12 ounces fresh crabmeat
⅓	cup bacon and tomato twist mayonnaise, *Best Foods®*
¼	cup sweet pickle relish, *Del Monte®*
1	medium head green leaf lettuce, chopped
1	medium head iceberg lettuce, chopped
1	small green bell pepper, sliced into ¼-inch rings
1	medium cucumber, sliced ¼ inch thick
1	tomato, sliced into 8 wedges
½	cup (½ of a 6-ounce can) ripe olives (whole and pitted), drained, *Lindsay®*
2	hard-boiled eggs, quartered lengthwise

1. In a medium bowl, combine crabmeat, mayonnaise, and relish. Set aside.

2. On a large chilled platter or in a chilled bowl, combine the two types of lettuce. Spoon the crabmeat mixture into the center. Arrange the remaining ingredients around the crabmeat mixture.

Per serving 332 cal., 19 g total fat (3 g sat fat), 3 mg chol.

Lobster Wraps

Prep 15 minutes   **Chill** 1 hour   **Makes** 4 to 6 servings

1	package (8-ounce) imitation lobster nuggets, *Louis Kemp®*
1	avocado, peeled, pitted, and diced
1	cup diced, seeded tomato
¼	cup pepita-cilantro Caesar dressing, *El Torito®*
4	cups salad mix, *Ready Pac®*
2	jalapeño-cilantro tortillas (12-inch), *Mission®*

1. In a medium bowl, combine lobster, avocado, tomato, and dressing. Pile equal amounts of salad mix on tortillas, spreading to within 1 inch of edges. Top with lobster mixture.

2. Roll tortillas up tightly and wrap in plastic wrap. Chill for at least 1 hour. Remove plastic wrap. If desired, slice into 1-inch rounds.

Per serving 307 cal., 17 g total fat (2 g sat fat), 17 mg chol.

Vegetables with Lemon Sauce

Prep 10 minutes   **Cook** 15 minutes   **Makes** 8 servings

12	small red potatoes, cut into quarters
1	large green or red bell pepper, cut into ¼-inch rings
2	cups broccoli florets
1	can (10.75-ounce) cream of broccoli soup (98% fat-free), *Campbell's*®
½	cup low-fat mayonnaise, *Best Foods*®
4	green onions, finely chopped
1	tablespoon fresh lemon juice, or *ReaLemon*®
¼	teaspoon dried thyme leaves, crushed, *McCormick*®

1. In a saucepan, combine potatoes with water to cover. Bring to boil. Cover, reduce heat, and simmer 10 minutes. Add pepper and broccoli. Cook 5 minutes more or until vegetables are tender.

2. In second saucepan, combine soup, mayonnaise, onions, lemon juice, and thyme. Heat through and serve over vegetables.

Per serving 126 cal., 6 g total fat (1 g sat fat), 7 mg chol.

Mango-Marinated Swordfish and Salsa

Prep 15 minutes   **Marinate** 1 hour   **Cook** 10 minutes   **Makes** 4 servings

4	swordfish steaks (6 to 8 ounces each)

FOR MARINADE:

¼	cup mango nectar
1	tablespoon canola oil, *Wesson*®
2	tablespoons balsamic vinegar
1	teaspoon ground ginger, *McCormick*®
1	teaspoon ground black pepper
1	teaspoon red pepper flakes, *McCormick*®
¼	teaspoon ground nutmeg, *McCormick*®

FOR SALSA:

1	can (15.25-ounce) tropical fruit salad, drained, *Dole*®
1	green onion, finely chopped
½	lime, juiced
1	small jalapeño, membrane removed, seeded, and minced
1	tablespoon finely chopped fresh cilantro
	Salt
1	tablespoon canola oil, *Wesson*®

1. Place swordfish steaks in a large zip-top plastic bag.

2. For marinade, add mango nectar, the 1 tablespoon oil, vinegar, ginger, pepper, pepper flakes, and nutmeg. Squeeze out air and seal. Gently massage bag to combine ingredients. Marinate in the refrigerator for 1 hour, turning bag occasionally.

3. For salsa, chop up drained fruit. In a medium bowl, combine fruit, green onion, lime juice, jalapeño, cilantro, and salt . Cover and chill in the refrigerator while fish marinates.

4. In a large skillet, heat the 1 tablespoon oil over medium-high heat. Cook fish about 5 minutes per side or until fish flakes easily when tested with a fork. Serve topped with salsa.

Per serving 329 cal., 14 g total fat (2 g sat fat), 66 mg chol.

Broiled Salmon with Creamy Horseradish

Prep 15 minutes **Broil** 8 minutes **Makes** 4 servings

Cream sauces have been the downfall of many a diet, but fat-free sour cream and heart-healthy olive oil keep calories in line. A 1-pound fillet will feed four when the fish is as rich as salmon.

1	pound fresh or frozen salmon fillets
	Olive oil cooking spray, *Pam*®
½	cup fat-free sour cream, *Horizon Organic*®
2	tablespoons prepared horseradish, *Morehouse*®
1	teaspoon Worcestershire sauce, *Lea & Perrins*®
2	teaspoons extra virgin olive oil, *Bertolli*®
1½	teaspoons salt-free lemon-pepper seasoning, *McCormick*®

1. Thaw fish, if frozen. Preheat broiler. Rinse fish under cold water and pat dry with paper towels. Cut into 4 serving-size portions. Lightly coat a baking sheet with cooking spray; set aside.

2. In a small bowl, stir together sour cream, horseradish, and Worcestershire sauce. Cover and chill in the refrigerator until ready to serve.

3. Brush fish with olive oil; sprinkle with lemon-pepper seasoning. Place on prepared baking sheet.

4. Broil fish 4 to 6 inches from heat for 4 to 6 minutes per side or until fish flakes easily when tested with a fork. Do not overcook. Serve with sour cream mixture.

Per serving 257 cal., 15 g total fat (3 g sat. fat), 69 mg chol.

Ale-Poached Halibut

Prep 10 minutes   **Cook** 8 minutes   **Makes** 2 servings

2	halibut fillets, about 1 inch thick (6 to 8 ounces each)
	Water
1	bottle (12-ounce) ale-style beer
2	teaspoons seafood seasoning, *Old Bay*®
½	lemon, juiced
1	teaspoon salt
10	whole peppercorns, *McCormick*®

1. Place the fish in poacher or a skillet with 4-inch sides. Add enough water to cover fish. Remove fish from water and set aside.

2. Add beer, seafood seasoning, lemon juice, salt, and peppercorns to pan. Bring to boil. Reduce heat to simmer. Return fish to pan and poach about 8 minutes or until fish flakes easily when tested with a fork.

Per serving 275 cal., 5 g total fat (1 g sat fat), 54 mg chol.

Apple Rice Pilaf with Toasted Almonds

Prep 5 minutes   **Cook** 10 minutes   **Stand** 5 minutes   **Makes** 6 servings

1	tablespoon butter
¼	onion, finely chopped
¼	Golden Delicious apple, finely chopped
2	cups apple juice
2	cups long grain instant rice, *Uncle Ben's*®
¼	cup slivered almonds, toasted

1. In a medium saucepan, melt butter over medium heat. Add onion and apple. Cook and stir until soft. Add apple juice. Bring to boil. Stir in rice.

2. Cover and remove saucepan from heat. Let stand for 5 minutes. Stir in almonds.

Per serving 222 cal., 5 g total fat (1 g sat fat), 5 mg chol

Citrus Snapper with Orange Relish

Prep 15 minutes **Marinate** 30 minutes **Stand** 30 minutes
Grill 8 minutes **Makes** 4 servings

1	pound fresh or frozen red snapper fillets
1	can (8.4-ounce) mandarin oranges in juice, *Dole*®
2	tablespoons frozen limeade concentrate, thawed, *Minute Maid*®
1	teaspoon salt-free citrus-herb seasoning, *Spice Islands*®
1	cup roasted bell peppers, chopped, *Mezzetta*®
1	tablespoon chopped fresh cilantro
1	teaspoon chopped scallion (green onion)
1	teaspoon lime juice, *ReaLime*®
	Salt and ground black pepper
	Scallions (green onions), slivered (optional)

1. Thaw fish, if frozen. Remove bones and cut into 4 serving-size portions. Place fish in a large zip-top plastic bag. Drain oranges, reserving juice. Set oranges aside.

2. For marinade, in a small bowl, combine reserved juice, limeade concentrate, and citrus-herb seasoning. Pour into bag with fish. Squeeze air from bag and seal. Gently massage bag to combine ingredients. Marinate in the refrigerator for 30 to 60 minutes.

3. Set up grill for direct cooking over medium-high heat (see page 17). Remove fish from the refrigerator 30 minutes before grilling. Oil grate when ready to start cooking.

4. For relish, chop oranges. In a medium bowl combine chopped oranges, bell peppers, cilantro, chopped scallion, and lime juice. Season with salt and black pepper; set aside.

5. Remove fish from zip-top bag; discard marinade. Place fish on hot, oiled grill. Cook for 4 to 6 minutes per side or until fish flakes easily when tested with a fork. Do not overcook. Serve with relish. Garnish with slivered scallions (optional).

Per serving 163 cal., 1 g total fat (0 g sat. fat), 41 mg chol.

Blackened Cajun Catfish

Prep 10 minutes   **Cook** 15 minutes   **Makes** 4 servings

1½	tablespoons extra virgin olive oil, *Bertolli®*
2	cloves garlic, smashed
2	tablespoons Cajun seasoning, *McCormick®*
1	teaspoon poultry seasoning, *McCormick®*
1	pound catfish fillets
½	cup white wine
2	tablespoons fresh lemon juice, or *ReaLemon®*
1	teaspoon butter

1. In a large skillet, heat oil over medium-low heat. Add garlic cloves and cook until golden brown. Remove; discard garlic cloves. Remove skillet from heat. In a small bowl, combine Cajun and poultry seasonings; set aside. Rinse fish and pat dry with paper towels. Sprinkle both sides of fish with seasoning mix.

2. Return skillet to medium-high heat. When oil is hot, add fish, presentation side (the side against the bone) down. Cook fish for 5 minutes per side or until fish flakes easily when tested with a fork. Transfer fish to a plate.

3. Deglaze pan with white wine and lemon juice. Bring to boil. Reduce heat and simmer for 2 minutes. Swirl butter into sauce. Pour over fish.

Per serving 245 cal., 15 g total fat (4 g sat fat), 56 mg chol.

Dirty Rice

Prep 10 minutes   **Cook** 30 minutes   **Makes** 4 servings

1	tablespoon extra virgin olive oil, *Bertolli®*
¼	cup finely diced onion
¼	cup finely diced celery
½	green bell pepper, finely diced
2⅓	cups reduced-sodium chicken broth, *Swanson®*
¾	teaspoon poultry seasoning, *McCormick®*
1	box (6-ounce) long grain and wild rice mix, *Uncle Ben's®*

1. In a medium skillet, heat oil over medium heat. Add onion, celery, and pepper to hot oil. Cook until vegetables are soft but not brown.

2. Add broth and poultry seasoning; bring to boil. Add rice and seasoning packet. Cover, reduce heat to low, and simmer for 25 minutes. Fluff with fork and serve.

Per serving 198 cal., 4 g total fat (1 g sat fat), 10mg chol.

Whole Grain Portobello Bake

Prep 15 minutes   **Bake** 1 hour 45 minutes   **Makes** 6 servings

	Olive oil cooking spray, *Pam*®
1	package (6-ounce) fresh portobello mushrooms, sliced
1	can (15-ounce) no-salt-added organic navy beans, rinsed and drained, *Eden*®
1	can (15-ounce) artichoke hearts in water, drained and quartered, *Maria*®
1	can (14.5-ounce) fire-roasted diced tomatoes, *Muir Glen*®
1	cup frozen chopped onions, *Ore-Ida*®
1	cup whole grain rice blend, *Rice Selects*®
2	teaspoons dried Italian seasoning, *McCormick*®
1	teaspoon crushed garlic, *Christopher Ranch*®
2	cups vegetable broth, *Health Valley*®

1. Preheat oven to 375 degrees F. Lightly coat a 2½-quart casserole with cooking spray; set aside.

2. In a large bowl, combine mushrooms, beans, artichoke hearts, tomatoes, onions, rice blend, Italian seasoning, and garlic. Transfer to prepared casserole. Pour in vegetable broth. Cover with aluminum foil.

3. Bake casserole for 1 hour and 45 minutes or until liquid is absorbed.

Per serving 239 cal., 3 g total fat (0 g sat. fat), 14 mg chol.

Moroccan Stew

Prep 10 minutes   **Cook** 30 minutes   **Stand** 5 minutes   **Makes** 4 servings

1	container (32-ounce) vegetable broth, *Health Valley*®
1	box (5.7-ounce) curry-flavored couscous, *Near East*®
1	bag (12-ounce) frozen broccoli, cauliflower, and carrots, *Birds Eye*®
1	can (15-ounce) organic garbanzo beans, rinsed and drained, *Eden*®
1	can (14.5-ounce) organic diced tomatoes, *Muir Glen*®
1	cup dried apricots, *Sun-Maid*®
½	cup frozen chopped onions, *Ore-Ida*®
1	tablespoon lemon juice, *ReaLemon*®
2	teaspoons crushed garlic, *Christopher Ranch*®
1	teaspoon ground cinnamon, *McCormick*®
¼	teaspoon cayenne pepper, *McCormick*®

1. In a large pot, combine vegetable broth, curry packet from the couscous, frozen vegetables, beans, tomatoes, apricots, onions, lemon juice, garlic, cinnamon, and cayenne pepper.

2. Bring to a boil over medium-high heat; reduce heat. Simmer for 30 minutes. Stir in couscous. Cover and remove from heat. Let stand for 5 minutes.

Per serving 407 cal., 3 g total fat (0 g sat. fat), 10 mg chol.

Sun-Dried Tomato Primavera

Start to Finish 35 minutes **Makes** 6 servings

12	ounces rotini pasta, *Barilla® Plus*
½	pound asparagus, trimmed and cut into 1-inch pieces
1	zucchini, halved lengthwise and sliced
1	yellow summer squash, halved lengthwise and sliced
2	teaspoons extra virgin olive oil, *Bertolli®*
1	jar (25.5-ounce) organic Italian herb pasta sauce, *Muir Glen®*
1½	cups frozen bell pepper strips, *C&W®*
¼	cup oil-pack sun-dried tomatoes, drained and chopped, *Alessi®*
½	cup organic chicken broth, *Swanson®*
¼	cup finely chopped fresh mint
¼	cup finely chopped fresh basil
1	tablespoon balsamic vinegar
	Salt and ground black pepper
	Shredded Parmesan cheese, *Kraft®* (optional)

1. Preheat oven to 400 degrees F. In a large pot of boiling salted water, cook pasta according to package directions. Drain well; return pasta to hot pot. Cover; keep warm.

2. In a medium bowl, combine asparagus, zucchini, yellow summer squash, and olive oil, tossing to coat vegetables. Spread in a single layer on a baking sheet. Roast for 10 minutes; set aside.

3. In a large skillet, combine pasta sauce, bell peppers, and tomatoes. Bring to a low boil. Stir in roasted vegetables, chicken broth, mint, basil, and vinegar; reduce heat. Simmer about 10 minutes or until thickened. Season to taste with salt and black pepper. Serve over hot cooked pasta. Sprinkle with Parmesan cheese (optional).

Per serving 295 cal., 4 g total fat (0 g sat. fat), 0 mg chol.

Angel Hair with Rosa Sauce

Start to Finish 25 minutes **Makes** 6 servings

12	ounces angel hair pasta, *Barilla® Plus*
1	can (12-ounce) fat-free evaporated milk, *Carnation®*
1	tablespoon all-purpose flour
2	cups organic spicy tomato pasta sauce, *Muir Glen®*
2	ounces prosciutto, finely chopped
¼	cup finely chopped fresh basil
1	tablespoon sherry vinegar

1. In a large pot of boiling salted water, cook pasta according to package directions. Drain; return pasta to pot. Cover; keep warm.

2. Meanwhile, in a saucepan, combine evaporated milk and flour. Bring to a simmer over medium-high heat until mixture thickens, whisking constantly. Once thickened and bubbling, cook for 1 minute. Stir in pasta sauce, prosciutto, chopped basil, and vinegar. Bring to a boil; reduce heat. Simmer for 10 minutes. Toss with hot cooked pasta. Garnish with *fresh basil leaves* (optional).

Per serving 332 cal., 5 g total fat (1 g sat. fat), 7 mg chol.

Angel Hair with Clam Sauce

Start to Finish 25 minutes **Makes** 6 servings

12	ounces angel hair pasta, *Barilla® Plus*
1	cup frozen chopped onions, *Ore-Ida®*
1	cup Chardonnay or other white wine
1	teaspoon crushed garlic, *Christopher Ranch®*
1	jar (25.5-ounce) organic spicy tomato pasta sauce, *Muir Glen®*
2	cans (6.5 ounces each) chopped clams, drained, *Snow's®*
¼	teaspoon red pepper flakes, *McCormick®*

1. Cook pasta according to package directions. Drain; return pasta to pot. Keep warm. In a skillet, combine onions, wine, and garlic. Bring to boil over medium-high heat. Cook until liquid is reduced to ¼ cup. Stir in sauce, clams, and pepper flakes. Bring to a boil. Simmer for 5 to 10 minutes or until sauce has thickened. Serve over pasta. Top with *finely chopped fresh oregano* (optional).

Per serving 417 cal., 7 g total fat (1 g sat. fat), 41 mg chol.

Grilling Greats

Grilling is one of our grand old American traditions, a throwback to the time when cowboys huddled around the campfire and grilled slabs of beef over fragrant embers. The smell was an invitation to relax, socialize, and enjoy life. It still is. During the week, we work hard, but when the weekend comes, we're ready to grill and chill. No matter what time of year you fire up the grill, these down-home delights are the best of carefree cooking. Served plain or fancy, with saucy sides and kick-back cocktails, it's All-American food at its simplest.

The Recipes

Peppercorn Steaks

Prep 10 minutes   **Marinate** 2 hours   **Grill** 12 minutes
Stand 25 minutes   **Makes** 4 servings

4	1-inch-thick New York beef strip steaks
1½	cups olive oil-and-vinegar salad dressing, *Newman's Own®*
¼	cup chopped fresh flat-leaf parsley
¼	cup pink peppercorns, *Spice Hunter®*
1	tablespoon Montreal steak seasoning, *McCormick® Grill Mates®*

1. Place steaks in a zip-top bag. Add salad dressing, parsley, peppercorns, and seasoning. Squeeze out air and seal. Massage bag. Marinate in the refrigerator for 2 hours. Set up grill for direct cooking over high heat (see page 17). Oil grate when ready to start cooking. Let steaks stand at room temperature for 20 minutes. Remove from marinade; discard marinade. Place steaks on hot, oiled grill; cook for 6 to 8 minutes per side for medium (160 degrees F). Let stand for 5 minutes.

Talk-of-the-Town New York Strip

Prep 10 minutes   **Marinate** 1 hour   **Stand** 25 minutes
Grill 12 minutes   **Makes** 4 servings

4	New York strip steaks
¾	cup dry sherry, *Christian Brothers®*
¼	cup canola oil, *Wesson®*
¼	cup soy sauce, *Kikkoman®*
2	tablespoons lime juice, *ReaLime®*
2	tablespoons Thai seasoning, *Spice Islands®*

1. Put steaks in a large zip-top plastic bag. Add dry sherry, oil, soy sauce, lime juice, and Thai seasoning. Squeeze out air and seal. Gently massage bag to combine ingredients. Marinate in the refrigerator for 1 to 3 hours.

2. Set up grill for direct cooking over high heat (see page 17). Oil grate when ready to start cooking. Remove steaks from refrigerator; let stand at room temperature for 20 to 30 minutes. Remove steaks from marinade; discard marinade. Place steaks on hot, oiled gril; cook for 6 to 8 minutes per side for medium doneness (160 degrees F). Transfer steaks to platter. Let stand for 5 minutes before serving.

Red Wine T-Bone Steaks

Prep 40 minutes   **Marinate** 2 hours   **Grill** 10 minutes
Stand 25 minutes   **Makes** 4 servings

4	¾-inch-thick beef T-bone steaks
1½	cups red wine
4½	teaspoons salt-free garlic-herb seasoning, *McCormick®*
1	tablespoon Montreal steak seasoning, *McCormick® Grill Mates®*

FOR RED WINE BUTTER:

1	cup red wine
⅓	cup finely chopped shallots
1	tablespoon frozen orange juice concentrate, *Minute Maid®*
1	teaspoon crushed garlic, finely chopped, *Gourmet Garden®*
½	cup (1 stick) butter, softened

1. Place steaks in a large zip-top plastic bag. Add the 1½ cups wine, the garlic-herb seasoning, and steak seasoning. Squeeze out air and seal. Gently massage bag to combine ingredients. Marinate in the refrigerator for 2 to 4 hours.

2. For Red Wine Butter, in a saucepan, combine the 1 cup wine, the shallots, orange juice concentrate, and garlic. Reduce mixture over medium-high heat to ¼ cup; cool completely. Work reduction into butter with a fork; form into a log. Wrap with plastic wrap. Chill until firm.

3. Set up grill for direct cooking over high heat (see page 17). Oil grate when ready to start cooking. Let steaks stand at room temperature for 20 to 30 minutes. Remove steaks from marinade; discard marinade. Place steaks on hot, oiled grill and cook for 5 to 7 minutes per side for medium (160 degrees F). Transfer steaks to a platter; let stand for 5 minutes before serving. Serve with slices of Red Wine Butter.

Italian Beef

Prep 10 minutes **Marinate** 1 hour **Stand** 30 minutes **Grill** 12 minutes
Makes 6 servings

Organic pasta sauce, garlic, and red wine turn ordinary flank steak into an extraordinary eating experience. Marinate extra-lean meat to tenderize it and lock in flavor. Magnifico!

1½	pounds beef flank steak
1½	cups organic tomato basil pasta sauce, *Muir Glen*®
½	cup light Italian salad dressing, *Newman's Own*®
1	tablespoon chopped garlic, *Christopher Ranch*®
¼	cup red wine (Chianti)
1	teaspoon dried Italian seasoning, *McCormick*®
	Grilled green and/or red bell pepper wedges (optional)
	Grilled onion slices (optional)

1. Place steak in a large zip-top plastic bag. Add ½ cup of the pasta sauce, salad dressing, and garlic. Squeeze out air and seal. Gently massage bag to combine ingredients. Marinate in the refrigerator for 1 to 8 hours.

2. Set up grill for direct cooking over high heat (see page 17). Remove steak from the refrigerator 30 minutes before cooking. Oil grate when ready to start cooking.

3. Remove steak from zip-top bag; discard marinade. Place steak on hot, oiled grill. Cook for 6 to 7 minutes per side.

4. Meanwhile, for sauce, in a small saucepan, combine remaining pasta sauce, wine, and Italian seasoning. Bring to a boil over medium-high heat. Serve with steak. Serve steak with grilled peppers and onions (optional).

Tri-Tip Steak with Mango-Red Pepper Salsa

Prep 20 minutes   **Marinate** 2 hours   **Stand** 25 minutes   **Grill** 1 hour
Makes 4 servings

1	2½-pound beef tri-tip steak
1	can (11.5-ounce) mango nectar, *Kern's®*
½	cup chopped fresh cilantro
¼	cup diced canned jalapeño chile peppers, *Ortega®*
¼	cup lime juice, *ReaLime®*
¼	cup canola oil, *Wesson®*
1	tablespoon Jamaican jerk seasoning, *McCormick®*

FOR MANGO-RED PEPPER SALSA:

1	jar (12-ounce) roasted red bell peppers, diced fine, *Delallo®*
8	ounces frozen mango chunks, diced small, *Dole®*
¼	cup chopped fresh cilantro
2	tablespoons lime juice, *ReaLime®*
1	fresh jalapeño chile pepper, finely chopped
¼	teaspoon salt

1. Place steak in a large zip-top plastic bag. Add the mango nectar, the ½ cup cilantro, the canned chile peppers, the ¼ cup lime juice, canola oil, and the jerk seasoning. Squeeze out air and seal. Gently massage bag to combine ingredients. Marinate in the refrigerator for 2 to 4 hours.

2. For Mango-Red Pepper Salsa, in a medium bowl, combine roasted peppers, mango, the ¼ cup cilantro, the 2 tablespoons lime juice, the fresh chile pepper, and the salt. Set aside until ready to serve.

3. Set up grill for indirect cooking over medium-high heat (no direct heat source under steak; see page 17). Oil grate when ready to start cooking. Let steak stand at room temperature for 20 to 30 minutes.

4. Remove steak from marinade; discard marinade. Place steak on hot, oiled grill. Cover grill and cook for 30 to 35 minutes per side for medium (145 to 150 degrees F).

5. Transfer steak to a platter and let stand for 5 to 10 minutes before thinly slicing across the grain. Serve warm with Mango-Red Pepper Salsa.

Adobo Beef

Prep 10 minutes **Marinate** 4 hours **Stand** 30 minutes
Grill 10 minutes **Makes** 4 servings

1	can (7-ounce) chipotle peppers in adobo sauce, *Embasa®*
4	4-ounce beef tenderloin steaks
1	cup organic beef broth, *Swanson®*
¼	cup tequila, *José Cuervo®*
2	tablespoons frozen orange juice concentrate, thawed, *Minute Maid®*
1	tablespoon salt-free Mexican seasoning, *Spice Hunter®*
½	cup organic tomato sauce, *Muir Glen®*
½	teaspoon salt-free Mexican seasoning, *Spice Hunter®*
	Fresh cilantro leaves (optional)
	Black-eyed peas* (optional)

1. Drain chipotle peppers, reserving 3 tablespoons of the adobo sauce. Chop enough pepper to make 1 tablespoon. Reserve remaining chipotle peppers and adobo sauce for another use.

2. Place steaks in a large zip-top plastic bag. Add combine ¾ cup of the beef broth, tequila, orange juice concentrate, the 1 tablespoon Mexican seasoning, chopped chipotle pepper, and 2 tablespoons of the reserved adobo sauce. Squeeze out air and seal. Gently massage bag to combine ingredients. Marinate in the refrigerator for 4 to 8 hours.

3. Set up grill for direct cooking over high heat (see page 17). Remove steaks from the refrigerator 30 minutes before cooking. Oil grate when ready to start cooking.

4. Remove steaks from zip-top bag; discard marinade. Place steaks on hot, oiled grill. Cook for 5 to 6 minutes per side for medium (160 degrees F).

5. For sauce, in a microwave-safe bowl, combine tomato sauce, the ½ teaspoon Mexican seasoning, the remaining ¼ cup beef broth, and the remaining 1 tablespoon adobo sauce. Cover and microwave on high heat setting (100 percent power) for 1½ minutes. Spoon over steaks. Garnish with cilantro (optional). Serve with black-eyed peas (optional).

***NOTE:** For an easy side dish, heat canned black-eyed peas with chopped celery and chopped carrot.

Chipotle Steak with Tequila Sauce

Prep 10 minutes **Marinate** 6 to 8 hours **Cook** 45 minutes **Makes** 4 servings

Colleen and I met at college in Wisconsin and have been like sisters ever since. With three kids and an "I'll try anything" attitude, she's always up for something new—like this bold-flavored steak that pays tribute to her husband Bill's Texas roots. The smoky chipotle marinade and lime tequila sauce have a real sassy Southwestern twang—just like Bill. Try this recipe and you'll be smiling from ear to ear—just like I do every time I think of Colleen.

FOR CHIPOTLE STEAK:

4	New York strip steaks, 1 inch thick
⅓	cup lime tequila, *Jose Cuervo*®
¼	cup canola oil
1	packet (1.12-ounce) chipotle marinade mix, *Durkee*®
2	teaspoons Montreal steak seasoning, *McCormick*® *Grill Mates*®
¼	cup chopped fresh chives
2	tablespoons chopped chipotle in adobo, *Embasa*®

FOR TEQUILA SAUCE:

½	stick (¼ cup) butter, melted
1½	teaspoons crushed garlic, *Christopher Ranch*®
2	tablespoons steak sauce, *A.1.*®
1	tablespoon lime juice, *ReaLime*®
3	tablespoons lime tequila, *Jose Cuervo*®
1	teaspoon chopped chipotle in adobo, *Embasa*®

1. For Chipotle Steaks, place steaks in a large zip-top plastic bag. Add tequila, oil, chipotle marinade mix, steak seasoning, chives, and chipotle in adobo. Squeeze out air and seal. Gently massage bag to combine ingredients. Marinate in the refrigerator for 6 to 8 hours.

2. Set up grill for direct cooking over high heat (see page 17). Remove steaks from the refrigerator 30 minutes before cooking. Oil grate when ready to start cooking.

3. Remove steaks from marinade, shaking off excess; discard marinade. Place on preheated grate at an angle. Grill for 2 minutes. Turn steaks one-quarter turn to create cross-grill marks. Cook 3 minutes more. Turn steaks over and cook an additional 5 to 6 minutes.

4. For Tequila Sauce, in a medium saucepan, combine all sauce ingredients. Cook over medium-low heat until heated through; stir thoroughly. Serve Tequila Sauce over Chipotle Steak with extra sauce on the side for dipping.

Pizza Burgers

Prep 15 minutes **Grill** 8 minutes **Makes** 4 servings

1½	**pounds ground beef**
⅓	**cup diced pepperoni,** *Hormel®*
¼	**cup pizza sauce plus extra for topping,** *Ragu®*
¼	**cup canned mushroom stems and pieces, chopped,** *Green Giant®*
2	**teaspoons Italian seasoning,** *McCormick®*
4	**sandwich-size English muffins, toasted,** *Thomas®*
	Sliced tomatoes
4	**slices mozzarella cheese,** *Sargento®*
	Fresh basil leaves (optional)

1. In a large bowl, combine ground beef, pepperoni, the ¼ cup pizza sauce, the mushrooms, and Italian seasoning. Mix thoroughly. Form into 4 patties slightly larger than English muffins.

2. Set up grill for direct cooking over high heat (see page 17). Oil grate when ready to start cooking. Place patties on hot, oiled grill. Cook for 4 to 5 minutes per side for medium (160 degrees F).

3. Serve hot on English muffins with tomatoes and additional pizza sauce; add cheese slices. Top with fresh basil leaves (optional).

Taco Meat Loaf

Prep 20 minutes **Grill** 45 minutes **Stand** 10 minutes **Makes** 4 servings

1½	**pounds ground beef**
½	**cup bread crumbs,** *Progresso®*
½	**cup Mexican cheese crumbles,** *Kraft®*
½	**cup bottled chunky salsa,** *Ortega®*
1	**egg**
2	**tablespoons chopped fresh cilantro**
1	**teaspoon crushed garlic,** *Gourmet Garden®*
1	**packet (1.25-ounce) reduced taco seasoning mix,** *McCormick®*
2	**slices thick-cut bacon,** *Oscar Mayer®*

1. Prepare grill for indirect cooking over medium-high heat (no direct heat source under meat loaf; see page 17).

2. In a large bowl, combine ground beef, bread crumbs, cheese crumbles, ¼ cup of the salsa, the egg, cilantro, garlic, and taco seasoning. Poke several holes in bottom of an 8×4×2½-inch foil loaf pan. Shape meat mixture to fit loaf pan; place in pan. Spread the remaining ¼ cup salsa over meat loaf; top with bacon.

3. Place on grill over drip pan; cover grill. Cook for 45 minutes to 1 hour or until internal temperature reaches 160 degrees F. Transfer meat loaf to cutting board and let stand for 10 minutes. Remove from loaf pan and slice. Serve warm.

Pineapple Teriyaki Burgers

Prep 10 minutes   **Grill** 8 minutes   **Makes** 4 servings

This laid-back Hawaiian burger brings a taste of the tropics to your backyard. Lean ground beef is given a dunk in a ginger teriyaki marinade, topped with pineapple rings, and grilled to sear in the flavor. Serve on a toasted bun to treat island fever year 'round.

1½	pounds lean ground beef
1	can (8-ounce) pineapple rings, drained (reserve juice), *Dole*®
2	tablespoons ginger teriyaki marinade mix, *McCormick*® *Grill Mates*®
1	packet (1.1-ounce) beefy onion soup mix, *Lipton*®
	Salt and ground black pepper
4	whole grain hamburger buns, toasted
	Lettuce
	Grilled or raw onion slices
	Condiments (such as Thousand Island dressing)

1. Set up grill for direct cooking over high heat (see page 17). Oil grate when ready to start cooking.

2. In a large bowl, combine ground beef, ¼ cup of the reserved pineapple juice, teriyaki marinade mix, and onion soup mix. Mix thoroughly. Form into 4 patties slightly larger than buns. Gently press pineapple rings into tops of burgers (burgers may have to be reshaped back to size). Season burgers with salt and pepper.

3. Place burgers, pineapple sides down, on hot, oiled grill. Cook 4 to 5 minutes per side for medium (160 degrees F).

4. Serve hot on toasted buns with lettuce, grilled onion slices, and desired condiments.

Stuffed Chili Cheeseburgers

Prep 20 minutes   **Grill** 8 minutes   **Makes** 8 servings

The star of any All-American burger lineup has to be the chili cheeseburger. This favorite teams lean ground beef with a booster of chili seasoning to score big with burger fans. The sweet spot is the center, filled with Colby-Jack cracker snacks that melt into a tangy burst of cheese over the heat.

2	pounds extra-lean ground beef
3	tablespoons chili seasoning mix, *McCormick®*
3	tablespoons water
16	Colby-Jack cracker snacks, *Sargento®*
8	hamburger buns, toasted
	Lettuce, tomato slices, and onion slices
	Condiments (such as ketchup and mustard)

1. In a large bowl, combine ground beef, chili seasoning, and water. Mix thoroughly. Divide beef mixture evenly into 8 pieces. Form each piece around 2 pieces of cheese snacks. Form patties slightly larger than buns. (Be sure no cheese is showing.)

2. Set up grill for direct cooking over high heat (see page 17). Oil grate when ready to start cooking.

3. Place burgers on hot, oiled grill and cook for 4 to 5 minutes per side for medium (160 degrees F). Serve on toasted buns with lettuce, tomato, onion, and desired condiments.

Baby Back Ribs with Old No. 7 BBQ Sauce

Prep 15 minutes   **Grill** 2 hours   **Makes** 4 servings

3	racks pork baby back ribs
⅓	cup All-Purpose Pork Rub (below)
2	teaspoons dry mustard, *Coleman's*®

FOR OLD NO. 7 BBQ SAUCE:

1	bottle chili sauce, *Heinz*®
⅓	cup packed brown sugar, *C&H*®
⅓	cup whiskey, *Jack Daniel's*®
¼	cup molasses, *Grandma's*®
2	tablespoons Worcestershire sauce, *Lea & Perrins*®
2	teaspoons Montreal steak seasoning, *McCormick*® *Grill Mates*®
2	tablespoons soy sauce, *Kikkoman*®
¼	teaspoon liquid smoke, *Wright's*®

1. Soak 2 cups hickory wood chips in water for at least 1 hour. Set up grill for indirect cooking over medium heat (no heat source under ribs; see page 17). Remove thin membrane from the back of ribs; set ribs aside. In a small bowl, combine All-Purpose Pork Rub and dry mustard. Sprinkle over ribs and pat in.

2. Drain wood chips. Add some of the soaked wood chips to the smoke box if using gas grill or place chips on hot coals if using charcoal. Place ribs on rib rack on hot grill over drip pan (or place ribs, bone sides down, directly on hot grill over drip pan). Cover grill. Cook for 2 to 2½ hours. Rotate ribs around rack every 30 minutes. If using charcoal, add 10 briquettes and a handful of soaked wood chips to each pile of coals every hour. If using a gas grill, add a handful of soaked wood chips to the smoke box every hour.

3. For Old No. 7 BBQ Sauce, in a medium saucepan, combine chili sauce, brown sugar, whiskey, molasses, Worcestershire sauce, steak seasoning, soy sauce, and liquid smoke. Bring to a boil; reduce heat. Simmer for 10 minutes. Remove from heat; set aside.

4. About 20 minutes before ribs are done, remove ribs from rib rack and place, meat sides down, on grill. Generously brush with Old No. 7 BBQ Sauce; stack ribs over the drip pan. Cover and cook for 10 minutes. Turn ribs; brush with additional sauce and restack. Cook 10 minutes more or until tender. Serve hot with Old No. 7 BBQ Sauce on the side.

ALL-PURPOSE PORK RUB: In a small bowl, combine 2 packets (0.7 ounces each) Italian salad dressing mix, ¼ cup paprika, ¼ cup chili powder, 2 tablespoons packed brown sugar, and 2 tablespoons salt-free lemon pepper. Store leftovers for up to 3 months.

Grilled Jerk Pork

Prep 5 minutes **Marinate** 4 hours **Stand** 30 minutes + 5 minutes
Grill 20 minutes **Makes** 6 servings

1½	pounds pork tenderloin
1	bottle (12-ounce) fat-free mango salad dressing, *Consorzio*®
½	cup mango-flavored rum, *Malibu*®
2	tablespoons salt-free Jamaican jerk seasoning, *Spice Hunter*®
2	teaspoons crushed garlic, *Christopher Ranch*®

1. Trim any fat or silver skin from pork. Place pork in a large zip-top plastic bag. Add salad dressing, rum, jerk seasoning, and garlic. Squeeze out air and seal. Gently massage bag to combine ingredients. Marinate in the refrigerator for 4 to 6 hours.

2. Set up grill for direct cooking over high heat (see page 17). Remove pork from the refrigerator 30 minutes before cooking. Oil grate when ready to start cooking.

3. Remove pork from zip-top bag; discard marinade. Place pork on hot, oiled grill. Cook for 20 to 28 minutes or until internal temperature reaches 160 degrees F, turning to cook all sides evenly. Remove from grill; let stand for 5 minutes before slicing.

Caribbean Pork

Prep 20 minutes **Marinate** 1 hour **Grill** 4 minutes
Stand 20 minutes **Makes** 4 servings

1½	pounds pork tenderloin, trimmed
1	cup pineapple juice, *Dole*®
⅓	cup dark rum, *Myers's*®
2	tablespoons Caribbean jerk seasoning, *McCormick*®
½	cup mayonnaise, *Hellmann's*® or *Best Foods*®
1	teaspoon lemon juice, *Minute Maid*®
½	teaspoon Caribbean jerk seasoning, *McCormick*®
4	sweet Hawaiian dinner rolls, sliced, *Oroweat*®

1. Cut pork into 1-inch-thick slices; pound each to a ¼-inch thickness. Place pork in a large zip-top plastic bag. Add pineapple juice, rum, and the 2 tablespoons jerk seasoning to bag. Squeeze out air and seal. Marinate in the refrigerator for 1 hour. Combine mayonnaise, lemon juice, and the ½ teaspoon jerk seasoning. Cover; chill. Set up grill for direct cooking over medium heat (see page 17). Oil grate when ready to start cooking. Let pork stand at room temperature for 20 minutes. Remove pork from marinade; discard marinade. Place pork on hot, oiled grill. Cook for 2 to 3 minutes per side or until cooked through. Serve hot on rolls with mayonnaise mixture.

Thai Pork Satay

Prep 20 minutes **Marinate** 2 hours **Grill** 4 minutes
Makes 4 servings

1¼	pounds thick-cut boneless pork loin chops, trimmed
1	bottle (11.5-ounce) Thai peanut sauce, *House of Tsang*®
2	scallions (green onions), finely chopped
2	tablespoons finely chopped fresh cilantro
2	tablespoons chile-garlic sauce, *Lee Kum Kee*®
1	tablespoon lime juice, *ReaLime*®
2	teaspoons sesame seeds
1	teaspoon salt-free Thai seasoning, *Spice Hunter*®
	Finely chopped green onion (optional)

1. Slice pork into ¼-inch-thick strips. Place in a large zip-top plastic bag. In a bowl, combine peanut sauce, scallions, cilantro, the chile-garlic sauce, lime juice, sesame seeds, and Thai seasoning. Pour ⅓ cup of the peanut sauce mixture in bag. Squeeze out air and seal. Gently massage bag to combine ingredients. Marinate in refrigerator for 2 hours to overnight. Cover and chill remaining peanut sauce mixture. Soak 6-inch wooden skewers in water for at least 1 hour.

2. Set up grill for direct cooking over medium-high heat (see page 17). Oil grate when ready to start cooking. Remove pork from marinade; discard marinade. Drain skewers. Thread pork onto skewers. Place skewers on hot, oiled grill. Cook for 2 to 4 minutes per side or until cooked through; remove from grill. Sprinkle with additional finely chopped green onion (optional). Serve hot with reserved peanut sauce mixture.

Hula Hula Pork Kabobs

Prep 20 minutes **Marinate** 2 hours **Grill** 16 minutes **Makes** 4 servings

Here's a fun way to have a luau-style meal without roasting a pig. Grilling pineapple caramelizes the sugar on the surface to bring out its juicy flavor.

1¼	pounds pork tenderloin, trimmed
¼	cup sesame-ginger marinade, *Lawry's*®
¼	cup chili sauce, *Heinz*®
¼	cup soy sauce, *Kikkoman*®
¼	cup dry sherry, *Christian Brothers*®
½	cup fresh pineapple wedges, cut into 1-inch cubes, *Ready Pac*®
1	green bell pepper, cut into 1-inch cubes

1. Cut pork into 1-inch cubes. Place pork cubes in a large zip-top plastic bag. In a bowl, combine sesame-ginger marinade, chili sauce, soy sauce, and sherry. Reserve ½ cup of the sesame-ginger mixture for basting; pour remaining into bag with pork. Squeeze out air and seal. Gently massage bag to combine ingredients. Marinate in the refrigerator for 2 hours to overnight.

2. Soak 10-inch wooden skewers in water for at least 1 hour. Set up grill for direct cooking over medium-high heat (see page 17). Oil grate when ready to start cooking. Remove pork from marinade; discard marinade in bag. Thread pork, pineapple, and pepper onto skewers. Place skewers on hot, oiled grill. Cook for 4 to 6 minutes per side (16 to 24 minutes total) or until pork is cooked through, basting with reserved marinade for the first 10 minutes of cooking time. Discard remaining marinade. Serve hot.

Sausage and Bacon Kabobs

Prep 15 minutes   **Grill** 16 minutes   **Makes** 4 servings

Shish kabobs are good-time food, deliciously up-tempo whether you're entertaining guests or the family. Generous chunks of chicken and apple sausages are sandwiched between wedges of hickory-smoked bacon and onion and pepper pieces, all basted with BBQ sauce. It's an all-in-one way to get dinner on a stick!

4	chicken and apple sausages, *Aidells*®
6	slices center-cut bacon, cut into 1-inch pieces, *Oscar Mayer*®
½	red onion, cut into 1-inch pieces
1	green bell pepper, cut into 1-inch pieces
1	cup Sandra's Signature Barbecue Sauce (below) (plus some for dipping, optional)

1. Set up grill for direct cooking over medium heat (see page 17). Oil grate when ready to start cooking.

2. Cut each sausage crosswise into 5 pieces. Thread an end piece of sausage onto skewer followed by a piece of bacon, onion, bell pepper, and another piece of bacon. Repeat using center sausage pieces and finishing with end piece (center sausage pieces will be "sandwiched" between bacon). Repeat with remaining skewers and ingredients.

3. Place skewers on hot, oiled grill and cook 16 to 20 minutes, about 4 to 5 minutes per side. Brush with Sandra's Signature Barbecue Sauce with each turn.

4. Serve kabobs with additional Sandra's Signature Barbecue Sauce on the side (optional).

SANDRA'S SIGNATURE BARBECUE SAUCE: In a saucepan, combine 1 bottle (12-ounce) chili sauce, ¼ cup cider vinegar, ⅓ cup molasses, 2 tablespoons Sandra's Sassy All-Purpose Rub (below), 2 tablespoons ground black pepper, and ¼ teaspoon hickory liquid smoke. Simmer over medium heat for 10 minutes. Remove from heat; cool. Store, covered, in refrigerator for up to 1 week.

SANDRA'S SASSY ALL-PURPOSE RUB: In a small bowl, combine 2 packets (1.25 ounces each) original chili seasoning; 3 tablespoons granulated garlic; 1 tablespoon kosher salt; 1 tablespoon salt-free, all-purpose seasoning; and 2 tablespoons sugar. Store in an airtight container in cool, dry place.

Wisconsin Beef and Cheddar Sausages

Prep 15 minutes **Cook** 20 minutes **Grill** 16 minutes **Makes** 4 servings

½	stick (¼ cup) butter
2	red onions, thinly sliced
1	yellow onion, thinly sliced
1	bottle (12-ounce) beer
8	beef and cheddar sausages, *Hillshire Farm*®
4	sourdough sandwich rolls, toasted
	Stone-ground mustard

1. Set up grill for direct cooking over high heat (see page 17). Oil grate when ready to start cooking.

2. Place cast-iron skillet on grill and add butter. When butter has melted, add onions. Cook about 10 minutes or until onions are softened. Add beer. Cover and cook an additional 10 minutes. Remove cover from skillet and let onion mixture simmer.

3. If using a gas grill, turn heat down to medium (if using charcoal, it will probably be about medium at this point).

4. Place sausages on hot, oiled grill and cook 16 to 20 minutes, about 4 to 5 minutes per side. Remove from grill.

5. To serve, place two hot sausages on each toasted roll. Smother sausages with onions and top with mustard.

Sonora Dogs

Prep 15 minutes **Grill** 16 minutes **Makes** 4 servings

4	hearty beef franks, *Ball Park*®
4	slices bacon, *Oscar Mayer*®
½	of an onion, thickly sliced
4	sourdough rolls, split horizontally and toasted, *Francisco*®
½	cup refried beans, heated, *Rosarita*®
½	cup bottled chunky salsa, *Ortega*®
½	cup sour cream, *Knudsen*®
½	cup prepared guacamole, *Calavo*®

1. Set up grill for direct cooking over medium heat (see page 17). Oil grate when ready to start cooking. Wrap each frank in a slice of bacon, securing the ends with wooden toothpicks.

2. Place bacon-wrapped franks and onion slices on hot, oiled grill. Cook for 16 to 20 minutes or until bacon is crispy, turning often. Turn onion slices each time you turn the franks. Remove from grill; remove toothpicks from franks. Place hot franks and onion on toasted rolls. Top with beans, salsa, sour cream, and guacamole.

Reuben Dogs

Prep 15 minutes **Grill** 12 minutes **Makes** 4 servings

4	all-beef big franks, *Hebrew National*®
4	teaspoons spicy brown mustard, *Gulden's*®
12	slices deli pastrami, *Hillshire Farm*®
4	sourdough French rolls, halved horizontally and toasted, *Francisco*®
4	slices Swiss cheese, cut in half diagonally
1	cup prepared sauerkraut, *Boar's Head*®
	Thousand Island salad dressing, *Wish-Bone*®

1. Set up grill for direct cooking over medium heat (see page 17). Oil grate when ready to start cooking. Spread each frank with 1 teaspoon mustard, coating all sides. Wrap three slices of the pastrami around each frank.

2. Grill pastrami-wrapped franks on hot, oiled grill. Cook for 12 to 16 minutes or until heated through, turning frequently. Serve franks hot on toasted French rolls with sliced cheese and sauerkraut. Top with Thousand Island salad dressing.

Grilled Pineapple Chicken

Prep 10 minutes   **Marinate** 1 hour   **Grill** 8 minutes   **Makes** 6 servings

6	boneless, skinless chicken breast halves
½	cup crushed pineapple, *Dole*®
¼	cup Champagne vinaigrette, *Girard's*®
¾	cup canola oil
½	cup pineapple juice, *Dole*®
¼	cup pineapple tequila, *Jose Cuervo*®
¼	cup finely chopped fresh mint
	Fresh mint sprigs (optional)
	Pineapple slices, *Dole*® (optional)

1. Place chicken in a large zip-top plastic bag. Add crushed pineapple, Champagne vinaigrette, oil, pineapple juice, tequila, and chopped mint to the bag. Squeeze out and seal. Gently massage bag to combine ingredients. Marinate in the refrigerator for 1 to 4 hours.

2. Set up grill for direct cooking over medium-high heat (see page 17). Oil grate when ready to start cooking. Remove pork from zip-top bag; discard marinade. Place chicken on hot, oiled grill and cook for 4 to 6 minutes per side or until internal temperature reaches 160 degrees F.

3. Remove from grill and place on serving platter. Garnish with mint sprigs (optional) and pineapple slices (optional).

Margarita Chicken

Prep 10 minutes **Marinate** 1 hour **Stand** 30 minutes
Grill 36 minutes **Makes** 4 servings

4	bone-in chicken breast halves
1	can (10-ounce) frozen margarita mix, thawed, *Bacardi*®
⅔	cup tequila
½	cup chopped fresh cilantro
2	tablespoons chicken seasoning, *McCormick*® *Grill Mates*®

1. Place chicken in a large zip-top plastic bag. Add margarita mix, tequila, cilantro, and chicken seasoning. Squeeze out air and seal. Gently massage bag to combine ingredients. Marinate in the refrigerator for 1 to 2 hours.

2. Set up grill for direct cooking over medium heat (see page 17). Oil grate when ready to start cooking. Remove chicken from refrigerator; let stand at room temperature 30 minutes. Remove chicken from marinade; discard marinade. Place chicken on hot, oiled grill; cook 18 to 22 minutes per side or until chicken is no longer pink and juices run clear (170 degrees F). Serve hot.

Provence-Style Chicken

Prep 15 minutes **Marinate** 1 hour **Stand** 30 minutes
Grill 10 minutes **Makes** 4 servings

4	boneless, skinless chicken breast halves
½	cup light olive oil, *Bertolli*®
2	tablespoons herbes de Provence, *Spice Island*®
2	tablespoons lemonade concentrate, *Minute Maid*®
1	tablespoon citrus herb seasoning, *Spice Island*®
1	tablespoon Champagne vinegar, *O Olive Oil*®

1. Place chicken between sheets of waxed paper; pound to ½ inch thickness. Place chicken in a large zip-top plastic bag. Add remaining ingredients. Squeeze out air and seal. Gently massage bag to combine ingredients. Marinate in refrigerator 1 to 2 hours. Set up grill for direct grilling over medium heat (see page 17). Oil grate when ready to start cooking. Let chicken stand at room temperature about 30 minutes. Remove chicken from marinade; discard. Place chicken on hot, oiled grill and cook 5 to 6 minutes per side or until chicken is no longer pink and juices run clear (170 degrees F). Serve hot.

Island Chicken

Prep 10 minutes **Grill** 12 minutes **Makes** 4 servings

4	6-ounce boneless, skinless chicken breast halves
2	teaspoons extra virgin olive oil, *Bertolli®*
2½	teaspoons salt-free Jamaican jerk seasoning, *Spice Hunter®*
	Salt (optional)
1	can (20-ounce) pineapple slices (juice pack) *Dole®*
1	tablespoon packed brown sugar, *C&H®*
	Hot cooked brown rice (optional)

1. Set up grill for direct cooking over medium-high heat (see page 17). Oil grate when ready to start cooking.

2. Brush both sides of chicken pieces with olive oil and sprinkle with 1½ teaspoons of the jerk seasoning. Sprinkle with salt (optional); set aside.

3. Drain pineapple slices, reserving juice. Sprinkle both sides of pineapple slices with ¾ teaspoon of the jerk seasoning; set aside.

4. For sauce, in small saucepan, combine reserved pineapple juice, the remaining ¼ teaspoon jerk seasoning, and brown sugar. Bring to a boil over high heat; cook about 5 minutes or until mixture is reduced by half. Set aside.

5. Place chicken on hot, oiled grill. Cook for 6 to 8 minutes per side or until no longer pink (165 degrees F). Remove to a platter and cover with aluminum foil to keep warm.

6. Place pineapple slices on grill and cook for 1 to 2 minutes per side or until grill marks appear and pineapple is heated through.

7. Serve chicken with pineapple slices and sauce. Serve with hot cooked rice (optional).

Tangerine Glazed Game Hens

Prep 20 minutes **Grill** 1 hour **Stand** 10 minutes **Makes** 4 servings

3	Cornish game hens, *Tyson*®
	Salt and ground black pepper
1½	cups tangerine juice, *Odwalla*®
2	tablespoons honey, *SueBee*®
⅓	cup dry white wine
2	tablespoons ginger teriyaki marinade mix, *McCormick*® *Grill Mates*®

1. Soak about 1 cup hickory wood chips in water for at least 1 hour. Set up grill for indirect cooking over medium heat (no heat source under birds; see page 17).

2. Cut hens in half with kitchen shears, removing backbones. Rinse with cold water and pat dry. Season both sides of halves with salt and pepper.

3. Drain wood chips; add wood chips to the smoke box if using gas grill or place chips on hot coals if using charcoal. Place hen halves, bone sides down, on grill over drip pan. Cover grill and cook 1 hour to 1 hour 15 minutes or until thigh temperature registers 180 degrees F.

4. While hens are cooking, prepare glaze. In a small saucepan, cook tangerine juice over medium-high heat until reduced by half. Once juice is reduced, stir in honey, wine, and teriyaki mix. Bring to a boil and remove from heat.

5. About 20 minutes before hens are done, brush liberally with glaze every 10 minutes.

6. Remove from grill. Let stand for 10 minutes before serving, brush with glaze once more. Serve hot.

Grilled Snapper with Mango Salsa

Prep 15 minutes   **Grill** 8 minutes   **Marinate** 30 minutes
Makes 4 servings

4	**6-ounce snapper fillets**
1	**can (11.5-ounce) mango nectar, *Kern's*®**
½	**cup bottled chunky salsa, *Pace*®**
¼	**cup finely chopped fresh cilantro**
1	**fresh jalapeño chile pepper, sliced**
2	**whole peeled garlic cloves, crushed, *Global Farms*®**
½	**teaspoon salt**

FOR MANGO-AVOCADO SALSA:

1½	**cups frozen mango chunks, finely diced, *Dole*®**
1	**avocado, peeled, pitted, and diced**
1	**cup bottled chunky salsa, *Pace*®**
¼	**cup chopped fresh cilantro**
1	**tablespoon lime juice, *ReaLime*®**
	Salt and ground black pepper

1. Place snapper fillets in a large zip-top plastic bag. Add mango nectar, the ½ cup salsa, ¼ cup cilantro, the chile pepper, garlic, and the ½ teaspoon salt. Squeeze out air and seal. Gently massage bag to combine ingredients. Marinate in the refrigerator for 30 minutes to 2 hours.

2. For Mango-Avocado Salsa, in a medium bowl, combine mango, avocado, the 1 cup salsa, ¼ cup cilantro, and the lime juice. Season to taste with salt and black pepper. Cover; chill until ready to use.

3. Set up grill for direct cooking over medium heat (see page 17). Oil grate when ready to start cooking. Remove fish from marinade; discard marinade. Place fish on hot, oiled grill. Cook for 4 to 5 minutes per side or until fish flakes easily when tested with a fork. Serve fish hot with Mango-Avocado Salsa.

Napa Valley Wine Planked Salmon

Prep 10 minutes   **Marinate** 30 minutes   **Grill** 8 minutes   **Makes** 4 servings

1	**1¼-pound salmon fillet**
1	**cup Champagne vinaigrette, *Girard's*®**
2	**tablespoons Dijon mustard, *Grey Poupon*®**
	Salt and ground black pepper
⅓	**cup finely chopped fresh herbs (such as parsley, oregano, basil, and/or marjoram)**

1. Place salmon in a large zip-top plastic bag. Add Champagne vinaigrette and mustard. Squeeze out air and seal. Gently massage bag to combine ingredients. Marinate in refrigerator for 30 minutes.

2. Set up grill for direct cooking over medium-high heat (see page 17). Remove salmon from marinade; discard marinade. Place on wine-soaked plank. Season salmon with salt and pepper; cover generously with herbs.

3. Place planked salmon on grill. Cover grill; cook for 8 to 12 minutes or until salmon is pale pink and flakes easily when tested with a fork. Remove from grill and serve hot.

Grilled Trout Wrap

Prep 10 minutes   **Grill** 6 minutes   **Makes** 6 servings

2	pounds fresh trout, cleaned, heads and tails removed
1	cup olive oil-and-vinegar salad dressing, *Newman's Own*®
3	tablespoons orange juice concentrate, *Minute Maid*®
1	tablespoon Mexican seasoning, *McCormick*®
1	teaspoon chili powder, *Gebhardt*®
½	cup chunky salsa, *Newman's Own*®
¼	cup sour cream
1	tablespoon lemon juice, *ReaLemon*®
	6 soft large flour tortillas, *Mission*®
2	cups spring salad mix, *Fresh Express*®
2	tomatoes, sliced
½	red onion, peeled and thinly sliced

1. Place cleaned trout in a large zip-top plastic bag. Add salad dressing, orange juice concentrate, Mexican seasoning, and chili powder. Squeeze out air and seal. Gently massage bag to combine ingredients. Marinate in the refrigerator for 1 to 2 hours.

2. In a medium bowl, stir together salsa, sour cream, and lemon juice. Cover; chill in the refrigerator until ready to use.

3. Set up grill for direct cooking over medium heat (see page 17). Carefully oil grate when ready to start cooking. Remove trout from zip-top bag and discard marinade. Place trout on hot, oiled grill, flesh sides down. Grill for 3 to 4 minutes per side. Remove from grill. Carefully pull skin from trout (bones should come up with skin).

4. Assemble wrap by cutting trout into serving-size pieces and laying on tortillas. Top with sour cream mixture, salad mix, tomatoes, and red onion. Roll up tortillas.

TIP: Although most should come out with removal of skin, warn guests to be aware of bones.

Lemon Swordfish Brochettes

Prep 20 minutes **Marinate** 1 hour **Stand** 30 minutes
Grill 12 minutes **Makes** 6 servings

In French, en brochette means "on a skewer." Instead of lemon butter, lemonade and grilled lemon wedges flavor the swordfish for a lighter, cleaner taste that oozes vitamin C.

1½	pounds fresh or frozen swordfish steaks (at least 1 inch thick)
1	bottle (8-ounce) clam juice, *Snow's*®
⅓	cup finely chopped fresh flat-leaf parsley
⅓	cup white wine vinegar
3	tablespoons frozen lemonade concentrate, thawed, *Minute Maid*®
2	teaspoons salt-free lemon-pepper seasoning, *McCormick*®
2	teaspoons crushed garlic, *Christopher Ranch*®
24	cherry tomatoes
3	organic lemons, each cut into 8 pieces

1. Thaw fish, if frozen. Soak twelve 10-inch wooden skewers in water for 30 minutes. Meanwhile, rinse fish under cold water; pat dry with paper towels. Remove skin from fish; cut fish into 1-inch cubes.

2. For marinade, in small bowl, stir together clam juice, parsley, vinegar, lemonade concentrate, lemon-pepper seasoning, and garlic; set aside.

3. Drain skewers. Alternately thread fish pieces and tomatoes on skewers, beginning and ending each skewer with a lemon piece. Place skewers in 2 large shallow baking dishes. Pour marinade over skewers, dividing equally between baking dishes. Cover and chill in the refrigerator for 1 to 2 hours, turning skewers once.

4. Set up grill for direct cooking over medium-high heat (see page 17). Remove skewers from the refrigerator 30 minutes before grilling. Oil grate when ready to start cooking.

5. Remove skewers from baking dishes; discard marinade. Place skewers on hot, oiled grill. Cook for 3 to 4 minutes per side (12 to 16 minutes total) or until fish flakes easily when tested with a fork. Do not overcook.

Grilled Snapper with Vera Cruz Salsa

Prep 10 minutes **Grill** 8 minutes **Makes** 4 servings

Red snapper comes from warm, tropical climates, where spicy foods are the norm. So do as the natives do and season it with strong flavors. An unfussy rub of Mexican seasonings and tequila lime salsa is all you need to bring out the fish's naturally nutty flavor.

FOR GRILLED SNAPPER:

1½	**pounds snapper fillets**
2	**tablespoons Mexican seasoning, *McCormick*®**
	Salt and ground black pepper

FOR VERA CRUZ SALSA:

1	**cup tequila lime salsa, *Newman's Own*®**
½	**cup sliced Spanish olives, drained, *Star*®**
1	**tablespoon capers, drained, *Star*®**
¼	**teaspoon crushed garlic, *Christopher Ranch*®**

1. Set up grill for direct cooking over medium heat (see page 17). Oil grate when ready to start cooking.

2. For Grilled Snapper, rinse fillets with cold water and pat dry. Season with Mexican seasoning, salt, and pepper. Set aside while preparing salsa.

3. For Vera Cruz Salsa, in a medium bowl, combine salsa, Spanish olives, capers, and garlic; set aside.

4. Place fillets, flesh sides down, on hot, oiled grill. Cook for 4 to 5 minutes per side or until fish flakes easily when tested with a fork. Remove from grill. Top with salsa. Serve hot.

Slow Cooker Made Simple

These days, people use the slow cooker for just about anything—or everything. This chapter is filled with versatile recipes that cover all the courses, serving up soup, meat, and vegetables in one do-it-all dish. It's hard to have it all. But cook an entire meal in one pot, and it suddenly seems easy.

The Recipes

Cheddar-Beer Chicken

Prep 5 minutes **Cook** 3½ to 4½ hours (Low) **Makes** 4 servings

1	large onion, peeled and diced large
1	package (16-ounce) diced red potatoes, *Reser's*®
1	cup frozen diced green pepper, *Pictsweet*®
4	boneless, skinless chicken breast halves
1½	teaspoons garlic salt, *McCormick*®
1½	teaspoons ground black pepper
1	can (10-ounce) condensed cheddar cheese soup
¾	cup *Bass Ale*®
¾	cup bacon crumbles, *Hormel*®
	Fresh chives, finely chopped, for garnish

1. In a 5-quart slow cooker, combine onion, potatoes, and green peppers. Season both sides of chicken breasts with garlic salt and pepper. Place in slow cooker on top of vegetables.

2. In a small bowl, stir together cheddar soup, Bass Ale, and bacon crumbles. Pour over chicken. Cover and cook on low heat setting for 3½ to 4½ hours.

Chicken Paprika

Prep 8 minutes **Cook** 3½ to 4½ hours (Low) **Makes** 6 servings

1	large onion, peeled and quartered
1	package (8-ounce) sliced fresh mushrooms
2	pounds boneless, skinless chicken thighs
	Salt and ground black pepper
1⅓	tablespoons Hungarian paprika, divided
1	can (10¾-ounce) condensed cream of mushroom with roasted garlic soup, *Campbell's*®
½	cup sour cream

1. In a 5-quart slow cooker, combine onion and mushrooms.

2. Season chicken thighs with salt, pepper, and one teaspoon paprika. Place in slow cooker on top of the vegetables.

3. In a small bowl, stir together cream of mushroom soup and remaining one tablespoon of paprika. Pour over chicken.

4. Cover and cook on low heat setting for 3½ to 4½ hours.

5. Remove chicken from slow cooker and keep warm. Strain and defat cooking liquid. Stir sour cream into liquid and serve hot over chicken.

Italian Chicken

Prep 10 minutes   **Cook** 5 to 7 hours (Low)   **Makes** 6 servings

2	pounds boneless, skinless chicken breast halves
1	can (28-ounce) whole peeled tomatoes, drained, *Progresso*®
2	packages (8 ounces each) frozen artichoke hearts, thawed, *C&W*®
1	can (15-ounce) pinto beans, rinsed and drained, *Bush's*®
1	package (8-ounce) presliced fresh mushrooms
1	box (1.4-ounce) vegetable soup mix, *Knorr*®
1	can (10.75-ounce) condensed cream of chicken soup, *Campbell's*®
⅓	cup Italian salad dressing, *Newman's Own*®
	Hot cooked pasta (optional)
	Chopped fresh parsley (optional)

1. Trim fat from chicken; set chicken aside.

2. In a 5-quart slow cooker, combine tomatoes, artichoke hearts, beans, mushrooms, and vegetable soup mix. Add chicken.

3. In a small bowl, combine soup and salad dressing. Pour over chicken. Cover and cook on low heat setting for 5 to 7 hours.

4. Shred or cut chicken breast halves into bite-size pieces (optional). Serve chicken and vegetables over cooked pasta (optional). Sprinkle with parsley (optional).

Chicken with Red Onion Salsa

Prep 5 minutes   **Cook** 4 to 6 hours (Low)   **Makes** 4 servings

4   chicken breast halves
2   tablespoons Mexican seasoning, *McCormick*®
2   cans (10 ounces each) Mexican diced tomatoes, *Ro-Tel*®
1   can (6-ounce) tomato paste, *Contadina*®
2   medium red onions, peeled and finely diced

1. Season both sides of chicken breasts with Mexican seasoning and set aside. In a medium bowl, stir together diced tomatoes, tomato paste, and onions.

2. Pour half of salsa mixture in the bottom of a 5-quart slow cooker. Add chicken and top with remaining salsa mixture. Cover and cook on low heat setting for 4 to 6 hours.

Tomato-Garlic Chicken

Prep 10 minutes   **Cook** 3½ to 4½ hours (Low)   **Makes** 4 servings

2   zucchinis, sliced into ¼-inch-thick rounds
1   cup frozen chopped onions, *Ore-Ida*®
1   can (28-ounce) whole peeled tomatoes, coarsely broken into pieces, *Muir Glen*®
10 whole peeled garlic cloves, *Christopher Ranch*®
4   boneless skinless chicken breasts, rinsed and patted dry
    Salt and ground black pepper
1   packet (1.6-ounce) garlic herb sauce mix, *Knorr*®
1   can (6-ounce) tomato paste, *Contadina*®
½   cup olive tapenade, *Cantare*®
½   cup low sodium chicken broth, *Swanson*®

1. In a 5-quart slow cooker, combine zucchinis, onions, tomatoes, and garlic. Season chicken breasts with salt and pepper. Place in slow cooker on top of vegetables.

2. In a small bowl, stir together garlic herb sauce mix, tomato paste, tapenade, and chicken broth. Pour over chicken. Cover and cook on low heat setting for 3½ to 4½ hours.

Borracho Chicken

Prep 5 minutes   **Cook** 3 to 4 hours (Low)   **Makes** 4 servings

2	cans (16 ounces each) pinto beans, undrained, *Bush's®*
4	boneless, skinless chicken breasts
	Salt and ground black pepper
2	cans (10 ounces each) Mexican diced tomatoes, *Ro-Tel®*
¼	cup gold tequila, *Jose Cuervo®*
1	tablespoon salt-free fajita seasoning, *The Spice Hunter®*

1. Place pinto beans in the bottom of a 5-quart slow cooker.

2. Season chicken breasts with salt and pepper. Place in slow cooker on top of pinto beans.

3. In a medium bowl, stir together diced tomatoes, tequila, and fajita seasoning. Pour over chicken.

4. Cover and cook on low heat setting for 3 to 4 hours.

Chicken with Bacon and Mushrooms

Prep 15 minutes   **Cook** 3 to 5 hours (Low)   **Makes** 6 servings

2	pounds boneless, skinless chicken breast halves, cut into 1-inch pieces
1	package (8-ounce) presliced fresh mushrooms
1½	cups frozen loose-pack petite pearl onions, *C&W*®
1	can (10.75-ounce) condensed cream of mushroom soup with roasted garlic, *Campbell's*®
¾	cup Chardonnay or other white wine
8	slices precooked bacon, cut into ½-inch pieces, *Hormel*®
1	tablespoon fines herbes, *Spice Islands*®
2	teaspoons bottled crushed garlic, *Christopher Ranch*®
	Hot mashed potatoes (optional)

1. In a 4- to 5-quart slow cooker, stir together chicken, mushrooms, onions, soup, wine, bacon, fines herbes, and garlic until thoroughly combined.

2. Cover and cook on low heat setting for 3 to 5 hours. Serve with mashed potatoes (optional).

Chicken with White Wine Sauce

Makes 6 servings   **Prep** 15 minutes   **Cook** 3 to 4 hours (High) or 8 hours (Low)

This flavorful dish couldn't be simpler—or more elegant—at home on family night as it is when company comes. The secret is a subtle wine sauce that makes the chicken moist and juicy. The alcohol in the wine evaporates during cooking, leaving only the fabulous flavor that everyone fancies.

24	pearl onions, peeled
8	ounces fresh mushrooms, sliced
4	strips thick-sliced bacon
4	pounds meaty chicken pieces
	Salt and ground black pepper
1	can (10¾-ounce) cream of chicken soup, *Campbell's®*
1	cup dry white wine, *Vendage®*
2	teaspoons Italian seasoning, *McCormick®*
2	teaspoons bottled minced garlic, *McCormick®*

1. In a 4- to 5-quart slow cooker, combine pearl onions and sliced mushrooms.

2. In a large skillet, fry bacon over medium heat until crispy. Remove bacon; reserve for garnish. Discard all but 2 tablespoons of the bacon fat.

3. Season cut-up chicken with salt and pepper. Cook chicken pieces in reserved bacon fat over medium-high heat. Place browned chicken into slow cooker.

4. In a medium bowl, stir together cream of chicken soup, white wine, Italian seasoning, and garlic. Pour over chicken. Cover and cook on high heat setting for 3 to 4 hours or low heat setting for 8 hours.

5. If desired, remove skin from chicken before serving. Ladle chicken with white wine sauce and garnish with crumbled bacon.

Chicken with Mushrooms

Prep 10 minutes **Cook** 3 to 4 hours (High) or 7 to 8 hours (Low)
Makes 6 servings

2	tablespoons extra virgin olive oil, *Bertolli*®
4	pounds chicken breasts and thighs
2	cans (10.75 ounces each) condensed golden mushroom soup, *Campbell's*®
2	teaspoons Italian seasoning, *McCormick*®
1	packet (1.5-ounce) four-cheese sauce mix, *Knorr*®
10	ounces fresh mushrooms, sliced
8	ounces frozen artichoke hearts
1	cup frozen chopped onions
1	medium red bell pepper, finely chopped

1. In a large skillet, heat oil over medium-high heat. Season chicken with *salt* and *ground black pepper*. Working in batches, brown chicken on both sides. Transfer to plate; set aside. In a medium bowl, combine soup, Italian seasoning, and cheese sauce mix; set aside. In a 4- or 5-quart slow cooker, combine mushrooms, artichoke hearts, onions, and bell pepper. Add browned chicken and any accumulated juices. Pour soup mixture over chicken. Cover and cook on high heat setting for 3 to 4 hours or low heat setting for 7 to 8 hours.

Beer BBQ Chicken

Prep 10 minutes **Cook** 3 to 4 hours (High) or 7 to 8 hours (Low)
Makes 8 servings

1	teaspoon canola oil, *Wesson*®
4	pounds chicken breasts and thighs
	Salt and ground black pepper
2	medium onions, cut into wedges
1	cup dark beer or ale
1½	cups barbecue sauce

1. In a large skillet, heat oil over medium-high heat. Season chicken with salt and pepper. Working in batches, brown chicken on both sides. Place browned chicken in a 4- to 5-quart slow cooker. Add onions to slow cooker.

2. In a bowl, combine dark beer and barbecue sauce. Pour mixture over chicken and onions in slow cooker.

3. Cover and cook on high heat setting for 3 to 4 hours or low heat setting for 7 to 8 hours.

Turkey Meatballs

Makes 6 servings **Prep** 15 minutes
Cook 3 to 4 hours (High) or 8 to 9 hours (Low)

1½	pounds ground turkey
1¼	cups Italian bread crumbs, *Progresso*®
¼	cup minced onion
1	teaspoon bottled minced garlic, *McCormick*®
¼	cup chopped fresh parsley
1	egg, lightly beaten
	Salt and ground black pepper
1	jar (26-ounce) marinara sauce, *Prego*®
2	cans (14.5 ounces each) diced tomatoes with basil, garlic, and oregano, *Hunt's*®
2	teaspoons dried basil, *McCormick*®

1. In a medium bowl, combine ground turkey, bread crumbs, onion, garlic, parsley, egg, salt and pepper. With your hands, blend ingredients together and form approximately thirty 1-inch meatballs.

2. Clean the medium bowl and stir together marinara sauce, tomatoes, and dried basil. Pour half of sauce mixture into a 4- to 5-quart slow cooker. Add meatballs and top with remaining sauce. Cover and cook on high heat setting for 3 to 4 hours or low heat setting for 8 to 9 hours.

Easiest-Ever Paella

Prep 15 minutes **Cook** 2 hours plus 20 minutes (High)
Makes 6 servings

8	ounces boneless, skinless chicken breast halves, cut into 1-inch pieces
8	ounces fully cooked andouille sausage, cut into 1-inch pieces, *Aidell's*®
2	cans (14 ounces each) reduced-sodium chicken broth, *Swanson*®
1	can (14.5-ounce) no-salt-added diced tomatoes
2	packages (5.6 ounces each) Spanish rice mix
1	cup frozen loose-pack petite peas, *C&W*®
½	cup frozen chopped onion, *Ore-Ida*®
1	cup frozen cooked shrimp, thawed

1. In a 4-quart slow cooker, stir together chicken, sausage, chicken broth, undrained tomatoes, Spanish rice mix, peas, and onion until thoroughly combined. Cover and cook on high heat setting for 2 hours. Stir in shrimp. Cover; cook for 20 to 30 minutes or until shrimp is heated through.

Meatball Lasagna

Prep 15 minutes **Cook** 3 to 4 hours (Low) Makes 8 servings

2	pounds frozen fully cooked meatballs, thawed, *Armanino*®
1	large egg
1	container (15-ounce) ricotta cheese, *Precious*®
1	tablespoon dried Italian seasoning, *McCormick*®
	Olive oil cooking spray, *Pam*®
2	jars (26 ounces each) roasted garlic pasta sauce, *Classico*®
1	box (9-ounce) no-boil lasagna sheets, *Barilla*®
1	pound thinly sliced provolone cheese

1. Slice meatballs in half; set aside. In a medium bowl, beat egg with a fork. Stir in ricotta cheese and Italian seasoning until combined; set aside.

2. Coat a 5-quart slow cooker with cooking spray. Add ½ cup of the pasta sauce to slow cooker. Add a layer of lasagna noodles, breaking them to fit. Layer with one-third of the meatballs, one-third of the ricotta cheese mixture, and one-third of the provolone cheese. Add 1½ cups of the pasta sauce. Repeat layers twice more. End with noodles and remaining pasta sauce. Cover and cook on low heat setting for 3 to 4 hours.

Beefy Mac

Prep 20 minutes **Cook** 2 to 4 hours (Low) **Makes** 6 servings

12	ounces dried elbow macaroni, *Barilla*®
1½	pounds lean ground beef
1	packet (1.5-ounce) beef stew seasoning mix, *Lawry's*®
2	cups shredded four-cheese blend, *Kraft*®
1	can (10.75-ounce) condensed cheddar cheese soup, *Campbell's*®
1	cup frozen chopped onion, *Ore-Ida*®
½	cup reduced-sodium beef broth, *Swanson*®
	Chopped fresh tomato (optional)
	Chopped fresh parsley (optional)

1. In a pot of salted, boiling water, cook macaroni for 5 to 6 minutes or until almost al dente. Drain and transfer to a 5-quart slow cooker.

2. In a large skillet, cook and stir ground beef and beef stew seasoning mix until beef is browned, breaking up clumps. Drain off fat. Stir beef, cheese, soup, onion, and beef broth into pasta in slow cooker. Cover and cook on low heat setting for 2 to 4 hours. Serve with chopped tomato (optional) and parsley (optional).

Beef Roast with Madeira Sauce

Prep 10 minutes   **Cook** 8 hours (Low)   **Makes** 6 servings

2	tablespoons extra virgin olive oil, *Bertolli*®
1	3-pound beef rump roast
	Salt and ground black pepper
1½	cups roasted garlic and herb tomato sauce, *Prego*®
¾	cup Madeira wine
1	teaspoon bottled minced garlic, *McCormick*®
1½	cups frozen pearl onions
1	cup frozen sliced carrots

1. In a large skillet, heat oil over medium-high heat. Season roast with salt and pepper. Brown roast on all sides in skillet. Transfer to plate and set aside.

2. In a medium bowl, combine tomato sauce, Madeira, and garlic. Set aside.

3. In a 3½- to 4-quart slow cooker, combine onions and carrots. Add roast and any accumulated juices. Pour sauce mixture over roast. Cover and cook on low heat setting for 8 hours.

Hunter's Steak

Prep 15 minutes   **Cook** 8 to 10 hours (Low)   **Makes** 6 servings

2½   pounds beef round steak
1   can (28-ounce) whole peeled tomatoes, *Progresso®*
1   package (8-ounce) presliced fresh mushrooms
1   cup frozen loose-pack sliced carrots, *C&W®*
2   ribs celery, sliced
1½   cups reduced-sodium beef broth, *Swanson®*
1   cup condensed cream of mushroom soup,
       Campbell's®
1   packet (1.5-ounce) beef stew seasoning mix,
       McCormick®
     Hot cooked egg noodles (optional)

1. Cut steak into 6 serving-size portions; set aside. In a 5-quart slow cooker, combine undrained tomatoes, mushrooms, carrots, and celery. Place steak on top of vegetables.

2. In a medium bowl, whisk together beef broth, soup, and beef stew seasoning mix. Pour over steak. Cover and cook on low heat setting for 8 to 10 hours. Serve with cooked egg noodles (optional).

Steak and Potatoes with Blue Cheese

Prep 10 minutes   **Cook** 8 hours (Low)   **Makes** 6 servings

2   pounds russet potatoes
½   cup frozen chopped onion, *Ore-Ida®*
1   container (4-ounce) crumbled blue cheese, *Treasure Cave®*
¾   cup cooked and crumbled bacon, *Hormel®*
1   teaspoon crushed garlic, *Christopher Ranch®*
2   cans (10 ounces each) white sauce, divided, *Aunt Penny's®*
2   pounds bottom round steak
     Salt and ground black pepper
2   tablespoons beef stew seasoning, *Lawry's®*

1. Peel and slice potatoes ¼-inch thick. Soak in cold water until ready to use. In a large bowl, combine chopped onion, blue cheese, bacon, and garlic. In a 5-quart slow cooker, layer potatoes and blue cheese mixture. Pour one can of white sauce over mixture. Cut round steak into six portions and season with salt and pepper. Place in slow cooker on top of potatoes and cheese. In a medium bowl, stir together one can of white sauce and the beef stew seasoning. Pour over steaks. Cover and cook on low heat setting for 8 hours.

Creamy Steak á la Vodka

Prep 15 minutes **Cook** 10 to 12 hours (Low) Makes 6 servings

2½	pounds beef round steak
1	package (8-ounce) presliced fresh mushrooms
1	medium onion, chopped
1	can (10.75-ounce) condensed cream of mushroom soup with roasted garlic, *Campbell's*®
1	cup tomato-based pasta sauce, *Prego*®
¼	cup vodka
¼	cup reduced-sodium beef broth, *Swanson*®
2	teaspoons dried Italian seasoning, *McCormick*®

1. Cut steak into 6 serving-size portions; set aside.

2. In a 4-quart slow cooker, combine the mushrooms and onion. Add steak.

3. For sauce, in a medium bowl, combine soup, pasta sauce, vodka, beef broth, and Italian seasoning; pour over steak.

4. Cover and cook on low heat setting for 10 to 12 hours. Serve steak with sauce.

Beef Pot Roast

Prep 10 minutes **Cook** 3 to 4 hours (High) or 8 to 9 hours (Low)
Makes 8 servings

1	bag (12-ounce) frozen onions
1	bag (8-ounce) frozen carrot slices
1	4-pound beef chuck roast
	Salt and ground black pepper
2	tablespoons vegetable oil, *Wesson®*
1	can (10.75-ounce) condensed cream of celery soup, *Campbell's®*
1	packet (1-ounce) onion soup mix, *Lipton®*
1	cup reduced-sodium beef broth, *Swanson®*
¼	cup steak sauce, *A1 Steak Sauce®*

1. In a 4- to 5-quart slow cooker, combine frozen onions and carrots.

2. Season roast with salt and pepper. In a large skillet heat oil over medium-high heat. Cook roast in hot oil over medium-high heat until brown on all sides. Place in slow cooker on top of onions and carrots.

3. In a medium bowl, stir together cream of celery soup, onion soup mix, beef broth, and steak sauce. Pour over top of roast.

4. Cover and cook on high heat setting for 3 to 4 hours or low heat setting for 8 to 9 hours.

Pot Roast Smothered with Onions

Prep 8 minutes   **Cook** 8 to 10 hours (Low)   **Makes** 6 servings

1	pound whole baby red skin potatoes, rinsed
1	3-pound beef chuck roast
2	teaspoons Montreal Steak seasoning, *McCormick Grill Mates®*
1	box (1.9-ounce) pre-cooked bacon, *Eckrich Ready Crisp®*
1	can (10-ounce) condensed cream of mushroom soup, *Campbell's®*
1	packet (1.5-ounce) meatloaf seasoning, *McCormick®*
1	package (8-ounce) presliced fresh mushrooms
1	large onion, peeled and sliced

1. Place potatoes in the bottom of a 5- or 6-quart slow cooker.

2. Season both sides of the roast with steak seasoning. Place in cooker on top of potatoes. Lay bacon slices over roast.

3. In a medium bowl, stir together soup and meatloaf seasoning. Pour over roast and bacon. Top with sliced mushrooms and onion. Cover and cook on low heat setting for 8 to 10 hours.

Sausage with Caramelized Onions

Prep 10 minutes **Cook** 4 to 6 hours (Low) plus 2 hours (High)
Makes 6 servings

3	large sweet onions, cut into ½-inch slices
½	stick (¼ cup) butter, cut into chunks
1½	pounds sweet Italian sausage links
¼	cup balsamic vinaigrette salad dressing, *Newman's Own*®
2	cans (14.5 ounces each) Italian stewed tomatoes, drained, *S&W*®
	Hot dog buns

1. Place onions in a 4-quart slow cooker. Dot with butter. Cover and cook on low heat setting for 4 to 6 hours.

2. Turn slow cooker to high heat setting. Add sausage and salad dressing. Pour tomatoes on top. Cover and cook for 2 hours.

3. Serve sausage and onions in hot dog buns.

Pork Chops in Tarragon Sauce

Prep 8 minutes   **Cook** 4 to 5 hours (Low)   **Makes:** 4 servings

1	bag (14-ounce) frozen pearl onions, *C&W*®
4	boneless, thick-cut pork loin chops
	Salt and ground black pepper
3	teaspoons dried tarragon, divided
1	can (10.5-ounce) white sauce, *Aunt Penny's*®
½	cup white wine, Chardonnay

1. Place pearl onions in the bottom of a 5-quart slow cooker. Season pork chops with salt, pepper, and 1 teaspoon dried tarragon. Place pork chops in slow cooker on top of pearl onions.

2. In a bowl, stir together white sauce, white wine, and remaining 2 teaspoons dried tarragon. Pour over chops. Cover and cook on low heat setting for 4 to 5 hours.

Pork Roast with Sherry Cream Sauce

Prep 10 minutes   **Cook** 3 to 4 hours (High) or 8 to 9 hours (Low)   **Stand** 5 to 10 minutes   **Makes** 8 servings

Pork roast is classic family food, an old favorite that stirs good memories with every bite. This version has a French twist: a simmered-in sauce of creamy sherry seasoned with fragrant herbes de Provence. Give it continental flair with a très chic garnish of peppers and squash and a delicate white wine to counterbalance the herbs.

1	large onion, sliced
8	ounces fresh mushrooms, sliced
2	tablespoons extra virgin olive oil, *Bertolli*®
1	3½-pound pork shoulder roast, rinsed and patted dry Salt and ground black pepper
2	cans (10.75 ounces each) condensed cream of mushroom soup, *Campbell's*®
1	cup sherry wine
2	teaspoons herbes de Provence, *McCormick® Gourmet Collection*®
1	teaspoon bottled minced garlic, *McCormick*®

1. In a 3½- to 4-quart slow cooker, combine the onion and mushrooms.

2. In a large skillet, heat oil over medium-high heat. Season the roast with salt and pepper. Cook roast on all sides. Transfer to slow cooker.

3. In a medium bowl, combine soup, sherry, herbes de Provence, and garlic. Pour soup mixture over roast.

4. Cover and cook on high heat setting for 3 to 4 hours or low heat setting for 8 to 9 hours or until internal temperature of roast is 160 degrees F. Remove roast from slow cooker. Let stand for 5 to 10 minutes.

NOTE: Herbes de Provence is a blend of dry herbs most commonly used in Southern France. It usually contains basil, fennel seeds, lavender, marjoram, rosemary, sage, summer savory, and thyme.

Chinese BBQ Pork

Prep 5 minutes **Cook** 8 to 10 hours (Low) **Makes** 6 servings

2	cups frozen chopped onions, *Ore-Ida*®
1	3-pound boneless pork shoulder roast
1	teaspoon salt
1	teaspoon ground black pepper
1	cup hoisin sauce, *Lee Kum Kee*®
¼	cup chili sauce, *Heinz*®
2	tablespoons honey, *SueBee*®
1	teaspoon Chinese 5-spice powder, *McCormick*® *Gourmet*
1	tablespoon minced ginger, *Christopher Ranch*®
2	teaspoons crushed garlic, *Christopher Ranch*®

1. Place onions in a 5-quart slow cooker.

2. Season pork shoulder with salt and pepper. Place pork in slow cooker, fat side up, on top of onions. In a small bowl, stir together the remaining ingredients and pour over pork shoulder.

3. Cover and cook on low heat setting for 8 to 10 hours. Strain cooking liquid; skim fat from the surface. Serve as sauce on the side.

TIP: Serve pork with bowls of steamed white rice.

Dr. Pepper® Pork Roast

Prep 10 minutes **Cook** 3 to 4 hours (High) or 8 to 9 hours (Low) **Stand** 10 minutes **Makes** 8 servings

2	medium onions, sliced
2	tablespoons canola oil, *Wesson*®
1	4-pound pork loin roast
	Salt and ground black pepper
5	whole cloves, *McCormick*®
2	sticks cinnamon, *McCormick*®
1	whole bay leaf, *McCormick*®
1	can (12-ounce) *Dr. Pepper*®
1½	cups dried apricot halves, *Sunsweet*®
1½	cups dried plums (pitted prunes), *Sunsweet*®

1. In a 3½- to 4-quart slow cooker, place onions. In a large skillet, heat oil over medium-high heat. Season pork roast with salt and pepper. Cook roast in hot oil over medium-high heat until brown on all sides. Place browned roast in cooker on top of onions.

2. Add cloves, cinnamon sticks, and bay leaf to cooker. Pour Dr. Pepper® over roast and top roast with dried fruit. Cover and cook on high heat setting for 3 to 4 hours or low heat setting for 8 to 9 hours or until internal temperature of roast is 160 degrees F.

3. Remove roast from cooker. Let stand for 10 minutes. Use a slotted spoon to remove onion, fruit, and spices from cooker; discard spices. Skim fat from sauce in cooker. Slice roast and serve topped with onions, fruit, and sauce.

Southern Pulled Pork

Prep 10 minutes   **Cook** 4 hours (High) or 7 to 8 hours (Low)   **Makes** 8 servings

I created this down-home dish for an outdoor barbeque. Slow cooking blends sloppy joe mix, chili sauce, and beef broth into a simmered-in sauce that's uniquely tangy—leaving the meat so tender, it falls apart.

2	tablespoons vegetable oil, *Wesson*®
1	3½-pound pork shoulder roast
	Garlic salt
	Salt-free lemon-pepper seasoning, *McCormick*®
1	bottle (12-ounce) chili sauce, *Del Monte*®
3	packets (1.31 ounces each) sloppy joe mix, *McCormick*®
½	cup reduced-sodium beef broth, *Swanson*®
	Hamburger buns

1. In a large skillet, heat oil over medium-high heat. Season pork roast with garlic salt and lemon-pepper seasoning. Cook pork in hot oil over medium-high heat until brown on all sides. Place in a 4- to 5-quart slow cooker. In a small bowl, combine chili sauce, sloppy joe mix, and broth. Pour over roast. Cover and cook on high heat setting for 4 hours or low heat setting for 7 to 8 hours. To serve, shred pork and place on hamburger buns.

Russian Pork Stew

Prep 5 minutes   **Cook** 4 to 6 hours (High)   **Makes** 8 servings

3	pounds boneless pork shoulder, trimmed and cut into bite-size pieces
	Salt and ground black pepper
1	bag (16-ounce) frozen sliced carrots, *Pictsweet*®
1	bag (14-ounce) frozen pearl onions, *C&W*®
1	cup dried apricots, *Sun-Maid*®
1	cup dried plums (pitted prunes), *Sunsweet*®
4	cups reduced-sodium chicken broth, *Swanson*®
2	packets (1 ounce each) peppercorn sauce mix, *Knorr*®
1	can (6-ounce) tomato paste, *Contadina*®

1. Season pork pieces with salt and pepper. Place in a 5-quart slow cooker. Add carrots, onions, apricots, and prunes. Stir to combine.

2. In a medium bowl, stir together chicken broth, peppercorn sauce mix, and tomato paste. Pour into slow cooker and stir thoroughly.

3. Cover and cook on high heat setting for 4 to 6 hours. Season with additional salt and pepper. Serve hot.

Hot Honeyed Spareribs

Prep 15 minutes **Cook** 3 to 4 hours (High) or 8 hours (Low)
Makes 12 appetizer portions

	Nonstick vegetable cooking spray, *Pam®*
4	pounds baby back ribs, cut into individual rib portions
	Garlic salt
	Ground black pepper
½	cup honey, *SueBee®*
¼	cup reduced-sodium soy sauce, *Kikkoman®*
¼	cup chili garlic sauce, *Sun Luck®*
1	cup Catalina dressing
1	teaspoon ground ginger, *McCormick®*

1. Preheat broiler. Line bottom portion of broiler pan with alumiumn foil for easy cleanup. Spray top portion of broiler pan lightly with nonstick cooking spray.

2. Season cut ribs with garlic salt and pepper; place on broiler pan. Broil for 5 minutes. Turn and broil for an additional 5 minutes. Place browned ribs in a 4- to 5-quart slow cooker.

3. In a medium bowl, stir together honey, soy sauce, chili garlic sauce, Catalina dressing, and ginger. Pour sauce mixture over ribs. Move ribs around to make sure they are all coated. Cover and cook on high heat setting for 3 to 4 hours or low heat setting for 8 hours.

4. With tongs, remove ribs from slow cooker. Skim fat from sauce. Serve ribs with sauce on the side.

Brunswick Stew

Prep 15 minutes   **Cook** 6 to 8 hours (Low)   **Makes** 6 servings

1	3- to 4-pound whole roasted chicken*
1	can (15-ounce) cream-style corn, *Green Giant®*
1	can (14.5-ounce) diced tomatoes, *Hunt's®*
1	jar (14-ounce) marinara sauce, *Prego®*
1	can (14-ounce) reduced-sodium chicken broth, *Swanson®*
1½	cups frozen loose-pack baby lima beans or sliced okra, *Birds Eye®*
8	ounces smoked ham, diced, *Hormel®*
1	cup frozen chopped onion, *Ore-Ida®*
½	teaspoon liquid smoke, *Wright's®*

1. Remove skin and bones from chicken; discard skin and bones. Chop cooked chicken.

2. In a 4- to 5-quart slow cooker, stir together chicken, corn, undrained tomatoes, marinara sauce, chicken broth, lima beans or okra, ham, onion, and liquid smoke until thoroughly combined.

3. Cover and cook on low heat setting for 6 to 8 hours.

*NOTE: Pick up a whole roasted chicken at your supermarket's deli counter.

Mediterranean Vegetable Stew

Prep 10 minutes   **Cook** 4 hours (High) or 8 hours (Low)   **Makes** 8 servings

1	bag (8-ounce) Mediterranean-style frozen vegetable mix
2	zucchini, diced
1	red onion, diced
1	teaspoon bottled minced garlic, *McCormick®*
1	can (15.5-ounce) garbanzo beans, drained, *S&W®*
1	can (14.5-ounce) diced tomatoes with basil, garlic, and oregano, *Hunt's®*
1¾	cups organic vegetable broth, *Swanson®*
1	can (10¾-ounce) condensed tomato soup, *Campbell's®*
1	packet (0.5-ounce) pesto mix, *Knorr®*
	Salt and ground black pepper
	Fresh flat-leaf parsley (optional)
	Crusty bread

1. In a 4- to 5-quart slow cooker, combine frozen vegetables, zucchini, red onion, garlic, garbanzo beans, tomatoes, broth, tomato soup, and pesto mix. Cover and cook on high heat setting for 4 hours or low heat setting for 8 hours. Season to taste with salt and pepper.

2. Ladle stew into soups bowls and garnish with flat-leaf parsley (optional). Serve with crusty bread.

BBQ Chili

Prep 15 minutes Cook 6 to 8 hours (Low) Makes 6 servings

1   pound lean ground beef
1   pound beef stew meat, cut into bite-size pieces
2   cans (14.5 ounces each) kidney beans, rinsed and drained, *Bush's®*
1   bottle (18-ounce) mesquite-flavor barbecue sauce, *Bull's-Eye®*
1   can (14.5-ounce) diced tomatoes, *Hunt's®*
1   cup frozen chopped onion, *Ore-Ida®*
1   cup frozen chopped bell pepper, *Pictsweet®*
1   can (4-ounce) chopped mild green chile peppers, *La Victoria®*
1   packet (1.25-ounce) hot chili seasoning mix, *McCormick®*
    Chopped onions (optional)
    Shredded pepper Jack cheese (optional)

1. In a large skillet, cook and stir ground beef over high heat until browned, breaking up clumps. Drain off fat.

2. In a 5-quart slow cooker, combine browned beef, beef stew meat, kidney beans, barbecue sauce, undrained tomatoes, frozen chopped onion, bell pepper, green chile peppers, and chili seasoning. Cover and cook on low heat setting for 6 to 8 hours.

3. Ladle into bowls; serve with chopped onions (optional) and shredded cheese (optional).

Five-Bean Chili

Prep 15 minutes Cook 4 hours (High) or 7 to 8 hours (Low) Makes 8 servings

1½ pounds lean ground beef
2   cups chopped onion
1   can (15-ounce) light red kidney beans
1   can (15-ounce) dark red kidney beans
1   can (15-ounce) cannellini beans
1   can (15-ounce) butter beans, drained
1   can (15-ounce) pinto beans, drained
2   cans (14.5 ounces each) diced tomatoes with chiles, *Hunt's®*
2   packets (1.25 ounces each) chili seasoning mix, *McCormick®*
½   cup tomato sauce, *Hunt's®*
    Salt and ground black pepper
    Chili toppings, such as sliced green onion, shredded cheddar cheese, and/or sour cream (optional)

1. In a large skillet, brown ground beef with the onions over medium-high heat. Drain fat and add meat to a 4- to 5-quart slow cooker.

2. Add light and dark kidney beans, cannellini beans, butter beans, pinto beans, tomatoes, chili seasoning mix, and tomato sauce to slow cooker and stir together. Cover and cook on high heat setting for 4 hours or low heat setting for 7 to 8 hours. Season to taste with salt and pepper.

3. Ladle into bowls; serve with chili toppings (optional).

Hearty Beef and Root Vegetable Stew

Prep 10 minutes   **Cook** 4 to 6 hours (High)   **Makes** 6 servings

2	pounds beef stew meat, cut into bite-size pieces
	Salt and ground black pepper
2	parsnips, peeled and diced
1	leek, white part only, cut in half lengthwise, cleaned well, and sliced crosswise
2	celery ribs, diced
1½	cups frozen sliced carrots, *Birds Eye*®
2	cups diced potatoes, *Reser's*®
1	can (28-ounce) whole peeled tomatoes, each cut in half, juice reserved, *Muir Glen*®
½	tablespoon crushed garlic, *Christopher Ranch*®
1	can (14-ounce) reduced-sodium beef broth, *Swanson*®
1	packet (1.5-ounce) meatloaf seasoning, *McCormick*®

1. Season stew meat with salt and pepper. In a 5-quart slow cooker, combine the stew meat, parsnips, leeks, celery, carrots, potatoes, and tomatoes.

2. In a small bowl, whisk together juice from tomatoes, garlic, beef broth, and meatloaf seasoning. Pour liquid into slow cooker and stir thoroughly.

3. Cover and cook on high heat setting for 4 to 6 hours. Season to taste with additional salt and pepper. Serve hot.

California Black Bean Chili

Prep 10 minutes   **Cook** 4 to 6 hours (High)   **Makes** 6 servings

1¼	pounds ground turkey
	Salt and ground black pepper
2	cans (15 ounces each) black beans, drained, *S&W*®
1	can (7-ounce) diced green chiles, *Ortega*®
1	can (14-ounce) diced fire-roasted tomatoes, *Muir Glen*®
1	can (8-ounce) tomato sauce, *Hunt's*®
3	cups diced zucchini
1	cup frozen chopped onions, *Ore-Ida*®
1	packet (1.5-ounce) chili seasoning mix, *McCormick*®
1	tablespoon chili power, *Gebhardt's*®
1	teaspoon crushed garlic, *Christopher Ranch*®
	Diced avocado or guacamole (optional)

1. In a large skillet, brown ground turkey, stirring frequently; drain. Season with salt and pepper. Transfer to a 4-quart slow cooker.

2. Add remaining ingredients, except avocado, to slow cooker. Stir thoroughly.

3. Cover and cook on high heat setting for 4 to 6 hours. Serve hot. Garnish with avocado (optional).

Creamy Chicken Noodle Soup

Prep 10 minutes **Cook** 3 to 4 hours (High) or 8 to 9 hours (Low)
Makes 8 servings

1	store-bought roasted chicken
1	cup diced onion
1	cup diced celery
1	cup diced carrots
4	cans (14 ounces each) reduced-sodium chicken broth, *Swanson*®
2	cans (10¾ ounces each) condensed cream of mushroom soup with roasted garlic, *Campbell's*®
2	teaspoons fines herbes*
	Salt and ground black pepper
2	cups egg noodles, cooked, *American Beauty*®

1. Remove skin and bones from roasted chicken. Shred cooked chicken. In a 3½- to 4-quart slow cooker, place chicken, onion, celery, and carrots. Stir in broth, soup, and fines herbes. Season to taste with salt and pepper.

2. Cover and cook on high heat setting for 3 to 4 hours or low heat setting for 8 to 9 hours.

3. When soup is done, stir in cooked egg noodles and heat through. Season to taste with additional salt and pepper. Serve hot.

*NOTE: Fines herbes are a classic blend of herbs that usually consists of chervil, chives, parsley, and tarragon. You'll find it in the spice section of the grocery store.

Mexican Meatball Rice Soup

Prep 5 minutes   **Cook** 3 to 4 hours (High) or 8 to 9 hours (Low)
Makes 8 servings

1	can (7-ounce) diced green chiles, *Ortega*®
2	cans (14.5 ounces each) diced tomatoes, *Hunt's*®
2	cans (14 ounces each) reduced-sodium beef broth, *Swanson*®
2	cans (14 ounces each) reduced-sodium chicken broth, *Swanson*®
16	ounces frozen meatballs
1	medium white onion, chopped
½	cup chopped fresh cilantro
½	cup converted rice, *Uncle Ben's*®
2	teaspoons dried oregano, *McCormick*®
	Salt and ground black pepper

1. In a 4- to 5-quart slow cooker, combine all ingredients. Cover and cook on high heat setting for 3 to 4 hours or low heat setting for 8 to 9 hours.

TIP: Serve with chopped cilantro, lime wedges, and chopped onions.

All-American Favorites

By whatever name you call it—retro food, diner food, feel-good food—true American food is a culinary hug, the tried-and-true favorites that make everybody feel loved. In a stressful world, it's comforting to revisit a time when Mom's chili or Grandma's fried chicken created a feeling of warmth and safety.

This chapter offers a soul-soothing stroll down memory lane by way of the kitchen. Each dish is a time-tested throwback with a Zen spin—mouthwatering cheeseburgers made tiny but fun, pulled pork sandwiches with a spark of chipotle, and pizza twisted into a fun-to-eat braid. The point of serving American food is for flavor and fun, so make it creative. Gather your friends and eat in the kitchen, on the deck, or in front of TV trays in the den.

The Recipes

Bunny Hotcakes with Apple Butter Cream

Prep 20 minutes   **Cook** 10 minutes   **Makes** 4 servings

A few creative additions turn plain pancakes into a cute-as-a-bunny breakfast. Use one pancake for the face and a second to cut out ears and a bow tie. The icing on the cake—apple butter cream, garnished with licorice whiskers and chocolate chip eyes and nose. All kids say is "yum" and "yeah"!

2	cups just-add-water pancake mix, *Aunt Jemima Complete*®
1½	cups apple juice
1¼	teaspoons ground cinnamon, *McCormick*®
1	container (8-ounce) whipped cream cheese, *Philadelphia*®
⅔	cup apple butter
	Whipped cream cheese (optional)
	Nonstick cooking spray, *Pam*®
	Black licorice (optional)
	Large chocolate morsels, *Hershey's*® (optional)

1. In a medium bowl, whisk together pancake mix, apple juice, and cinnamon. Set aside.

2. In a small bowl, combine the 8 ounces whipped cream cheese and apple butter until smooth. Place additional whipped cream cheese (optional) in a zip-top plastic bag. Snip a small corner from plastic bag. Set aside.

3. Lightly spray a large skillet with nonstick cooking spray and heat over medium heat. Scoop pancake batter with ⅓ cup measure and add to skillet. Cook until pancakes start to bubble. Turn pancake; cook an additional 1 to 2 minutes or until golden brown. Remove to a cooling rack.

4. To make bunny, place 1 pancake in the center of the plate. On a cutting board, cut ears and bow tie from another pancake. Arrange to make bunny. Repeat with remaining pancakes.

5. To reheat pancakes, microwave on high heat setting (100 percent power) for 30 seconds to 1 minute. Remove from microwave. Spread pancakes with the apple butter mixture. Use the cream cheese in the plastic bag to pipe eyes, mouth, and a bow on the bunny. Decorate with licorice for whiskers and chocolate morsels for eyes and nose (optional).

Cheeseburger Bites

Prep 20 minutes **Bake** 16 minutes **Makes** 16 burgers

1¼	pounds extra-lean ground beef
¼	cup ketchup, *Heinz®*
2	tablespoons meat loaf seasoning, *McCormick®*
1	package (7-ounce) sunburst-shape cheese snacks, *Sargento®*
8	hamburger buns, presplit
	Iceberg lettuce leaves
6	tablespoons Thousand Island dressing
16	cherry tomatoes
16	pickle chips

1. Preheat oven to 375 degrees F. Line baking sheet with aluminum foil. Set aside.

2. In a large bowl, combine ground beef, ketchup, and meat loaf seasoning. Mix thoroughly. Form into 16 patties slightly larger than 2 inches wide. Place patties on the prepared baking sheet.

3. Bake for 14 to 16 minutes. Top each patty with a cheese snack. Return to oven. Bake about 2 minutes more or until burgers are done (160 degrees F) and cheese is melted.

4. While the burgers cook, arrange halves of hamburger buns on a cutting board, cut sides up. Using a 2-inch round cookie cutter, cut mini buns from the large hamburger buns. Chop lettuce leaves into pieces about 2 inches wide.

5. To assemble cheeseburgers, top the bottoms of mini buns with lettuce, a patty, and about 1 teaspoon Thousand Island dressing. Add the bun tops. Skewer 1 cherry tomato and 1 pickle chip on each of 16 long cocktail toothpicks; push through the centers of assembled burgers.

Fruity French Toast

Prep 15 minutes **Chill** 1 hour **Bake** 1 hour **Stand** 10 minutes **Makes** 12 servings

	Butter-flavor cooking spray, *Mazola® Pure*
1	package (20-ounce) frozen French toast sticks, *Krusteaz®*
1	package (8-ounce) cream cheese, *Philadelphia®*
⅓	cup strawberry preserves, *Smucker's®*
3	cups milk
4	large eggs
1	cup pure maple syrup, *Maple Grove Farms®*
1	teaspoon ground cinnamon, *McCormick®*

1. Spray a 9×13-inch baking dish with cooking spray. Cut French toast sticks into 1-inch pieces. Arrange evenly in a baking dish.

2. Cut cream cheese into ½-inch cubes; sprinkle over French toast sticks. Using a spoon, drop small amounts of strawberry preserves over French toast and cream cheese.

3. In a medium bowl, whisk together milk, eggs, maple syrup, and cinnamon. Pour over French toast. Loosely cover baking dish with plastic wrap. Chill for 1 hour, occasionally pushing French toast down into mixture.

4. Preheat oven to 350 degrees F. Remove plastic wrap from baking dish. Bake for 1 hour or until golden brown.

5. Place on a wire rack; cool for 10 to 15 minutes. Serve warm.

Mini Melts

Start to Finish 25 minutes **Makes** 4 sandwiches

2	cans (6 ounces each) water-pack chunk white tuna, *StarKist®*
3	tablespoons mayonnaise, *Hellmann's®* or *Best Foods®*
½	teaspoon salt-free lemon-pepper seasoning, *McCormick®*
8	slices white sandwich bread, *Sara Lee®*
4	slices cheddar cheese, *Kraft®*
2	to 3 tablespoons butter, softened
	Canola oil cooking spray, *Mazola® Pure*

1. In a medium bowl, combine tuna, mayonnaise, and lemon pepper; set aside.

2. Place 4 bread slices on a cutting board. Put 1 cheese slice on each bread slice. Place ¼ cup tuna mixture in center of cheese. Place a second bread slice on each sandwich and gently press together.

3. Using 3-inch cookie cutters, cut sandwiches into fun shapes, such as stars and moons. Spread both sides of sandwiches with softened butter, using about 1 teaspoon butter per side.

4. Spray a large skillet with cooking spray; heat over medium-high heat. Add 2 sandwiches; cook for 3 to 4 minutes per side or until bread is brown and cheese is melted. Repeat with remaining sandwiches. Serve warm.

Ball Park Dogs

Prep 20 minutes **Grill** 12 minutes **Makes** 4 servings

4	hot dog buns, *Ball Park*®
1	egg, beaten
1	tablespoon poppy seeds
¼	cup sweet pickle relish, *Vlasic*®
2	drops green food coloring, *McCormick*®
4	all-beef franks, *Ball Park*®
	Yellow mustard, *French's*®
⅓	cup frozen chopped onions, thawed, *Ore-Ida*®
1	tomato, cut into 8 wedges
4	pickle spears, *Vlasic*®

1. Preheat oven to 350 degrees F. Very lightly brush bun tops with egg and sprinkle with poppy seeds. Bake for 10 minutes. Remove from oven; set aside. Meanwhile, combine relish and food coloring; set aside. Set up grill for direct cooking over medium heat (see page 17). Oil grate when ready to start cooking. Place franks on hot, oiled grill. Cook for 12 to 15 minutes or until heated through, turning occasionally. Place franks in buns; top with mustard. Top each frank with some of the relish mixture and onions. Arrange two tomato wedges between each frank and top of bun. Place a pickle spear between each frank and bottom of bun.

Varsity Dogs

Prep 15 minutes **Grill** 12 minutes **Makes** 4 servings

FOR SOUTHERN SLAW:

3	tablespoons cider vinegar, *Heinz*®
2	teaspoons ranch salad dressing mix, *Hidden Valley*®
2	teaspoons sugar
2	cups tricolor coleslaw mix, *Fresh Express*®

FOR VARSITY DOGS:

4	all-beef franks, *Ball Park*®
4	hot dogs buns, *Ball Park*®
4	slices American cheese, *Borden*®
1	cup chili without beans, heated, *Hormel*®

1. For Southern Slaw, in a medium bowl, stir together vinegar, salad dressing mix, and sugar. Add coleslaw mix and toss. Cover; chill until ready to use.

2. For Varsity Dogs, set up grill for direct cooking over medium heat (see page 17). Oil grate when ready to start cooking. Grill franks on hot, oiled grill for 12 to 15 minutes or until heated through, turning occasionally. Remove and set aside. Toast buns on grill until golden brown. Remove and add cheese slices to hot buns. Spoon Southern Slaw in buns; place franks on slaw and top with warm chili.

Sloppy Sandwiches

Prep 30 minutes   **Bake** 13 minutes   **Makes** 8 sandwiches

8	ounces ground beef
1	packet (1.31-ounce) sloppy joe seasoning mix, *McCormick*
1	can (6-ounce) tomato paste, *Hunt's*®
1	large egg
1	tablespoon water
	All-purpose flour
1	can (16.3-ounce) refrigerated biscuits, *Pillsbury*®
½	cup shredded mozzarella cheese, *Kraft*®

1. Preheat oven to 350 degrees F. Line a baking sheet with aluminum foil; set aside.

2. In a medium saucepan, combine ground beef and sloppy joes seasoning mix. Cook and stir over medium-high heat about 10 minutes or until meat is browned. Drain off fat. Stir in tomato paste; set aside.

3. In a small bowl, beat together egg and water; set aside.

4. On a lightly floured surface, roll out each biscuit to a 4-inch circle, turning biscuit with each roll so it doesn't stick. (If dough starts to stick, use more flour.)

5. For sandwiches, spoon 2 tablespoons meat mixture and 1 tablespoon cheese on one side of each biscuit circle. Using a pastry brush, brush a thin layer of the egg mixture around the edge of each dough circle. Fold dough over meat mixture to form a half-circle. Pinch edges together to seal.* Place on prepared baking sheet. Lightly brush the top of each sandwich with more of the egg mixture.

6. Bake for 13 to 15 minutes. Transfer sandwiches to a wire rack. Cool slightly; serve warm.

*TIP: To make pleats in the crust like in the photo, use clean kitchen shears or scissors to cut small slits around the edges of the unbaked crust after sealing.

Cinnamon Buns

Prep 30 minutes **Rise** 1 hour **Bake** 15 minutes **Makes** 16 rolls

A Food Network website favorite. When it comes to naughty food, Cinnabons® take the cake. My recipe is a ringer for the original, from the sugar-cinnamon dough to the deliciously drippy cream cheese icing. Make baby ones for a quick mini munchie or jumbo ones to share shamelessly, but be sure to get the center—it's the best part!

FOR DOUGH AND FILLING:
1	loaf frozen white bread dough, thawed*, *Bridgford*®
	All-purpose flour, for dusting surface
1	cup packed golden brown sugar, *C&H*®
1	tablespoon ground cinnamon, *McCormick*®
⅔	stick butter, softened

FOR ICING:
1	stick (½ cup) unsalted butter, softened
1	cup powdered sugar, *C&H*®
⅓	cup cream cheese, *Philadelphia*®
1	teaspoon vanilla extract, *McCormick*®

DOUGH AND FILLING PREPARATION

1. On a lightly floured surface, roll out dough to a 15×7-inch rectangle. In a small bowl, combine brown sugar and cinnamon; set aside. Spread ⅔ stick softened butter over dough. Sprinkle evenly with cinnamon-sugar mixture. Starting at the long edge, roll up dough as for a jelly roll. Pinch seam to seal.

2. Cut rolled dough into 16 slices and divide slices between 2 lightly buttered 8-inch round baking pans. Set aside in a warm place and allow dough to rise until doubled in size, about 1 hour.

3. Preheat oven to 400 degrees F. Bake for 15 minutes or until golden on top. Promptly invert baking pan over a wire rack, and lift pan from buns. Scoop filling that has remained in the pan over buns. Allow buns to cool slightly, about 10 minutes.

ICING PREPARATION

4. Meanwhile, in a medium bowl, beat the icing ingredients with an electric mixer until fluffy. Spread or pipe (with a pastry bag) icing over rolls. Serve warm.

***NOTE: Thaw frozen bread dough overnight in the refrigerator.**

Soft Pretzels

Prep 20 minutes   **Cook** 30 minutes   **Makes** 14 pretzels

Every time I go to the mall, I reward myself with one of these tasty little treats. Pretzels are the perfect "mood food," seasoned sweet, savory, or spicy to suit your mood. To make them pillowy soft, boil them in water first, then bake.

1	loaf frozen white bread dough, thawed*, *Bridgford®*
	All-purpose flour, for dusting surface, *Pillsbury®*
1	egg, lightly beaten
½	cup coarse salt (optional)

1. Line a sheet pan with waxed paper. Divide dough into 14 pieces. On a lightly floured surface, roll each piece of dough into a 16-inch rope and form into a pretzel shape. Transfer dough to prepared sheet pan; cover and chill in the refrigerator until ready to boil.

2. Preheat oven to 400 degrees F. Lightly butter a sheet pan. In a large pot, bring 4 quarts of water to a boil. Add pretzels, 3 at a time, and cook about 2 minutes or until pretzels rise to the surface. Remove and drain on paper towels.

3. Arrange pretzels 3 inches apart on prepared sheet pan. Brush with beaten egg. Sprinkle with coarse salt or with choice of toppings. Bake for 15 to 20 minutes or until brown. Transfer to a wire rack.

*NOTE: Thaw frozen bread dough overnight in the refrigerator.

Garlic Cheese Pretzels

½	cup finely grated Parmesan cheese, *Kraft®*
1	teaspoon garlic powder, *McCormick®*

1. After pretzels are boiled and just before baking, brush pretzels with beaten egg (as directed above). Sprinkle with Parmesan cheese and garlic powder. Bake for 15 to 20 minutes or until brown. Transfer to a wire rack.

Cinnamon Pretzels

½	cup powdered sugar, *C&H®*
1	tablespoon ground cinnamon, *McCormick®*
1	tablespoon water
¼	cup honey, *SueBee®*

1. In a small bowl, combine powdered sugar and cinnamon. Stir in water, adding more if needed to make a thin glaze; set aside. After pretzels are boiled and just before baking (as directed above), brush pretzels with honey instead of beaten egg. Bake for 15 to 20 minutes or until brown. Transfer to a wire rack. While still warm, brush pretzels with cinnamon-sugar glaze.

Pizza Braids

Prep 20 minutes **Bake** 12 minutes **Cool** 10 minutes **Makes** 4 braids

1	large egg
1	tablespoon milk
¾	cup diced pepperoni, *Hormel*®
¼	cup grated Parmesan cheese, *DiGiorno*®
1	can (11-ounce) refrigerated breadsticks, *Pillsbury*®
1	teaspoon dried Italian seasoning, *McCormick*®
	Pizza sauce, *Enrico's*®

1. Preheat oven to 375 degrees F. Line a baking sheet with aluminum foil. In a small bowl, beat together egg and milk with a fork; set aside. Spread pepperoni on 1 plate; spread Parmesan cheese onto another plate. Set both aside.

2. Separate breadstick dough into 12 individual pieces. Place on a cutting board. Using a pastry brush, brush a thin coating of egg mixture over dough pieces.

3. Place 1 breadstick into pepperoni on the plate, pressing so pepperoni sticks to dough. Repeat with 3 breadsticks for a total of 4 pepperoni-covered breadstick pieces. Press 4 more bread sticks into cheese, pressing so cheese sticks to dough. Sprinkle the remaining 4 breadsticks with Italian seasoning.

4. To make braids, place 1 breadstick with pepperoni, 1 breadstick with cheese, and 1 breadstick with Italian seasoning ¼ inch apart on a flat surface. Starting at the top, intertwine the 3 breadsticks to form a braid. Place braids 1 inch apart on prepared baking sheet.

5. Bake for 12 to 14 minutes. Transfer to a wire rack; cool for 10 minutes.

6. Meanwhile, place pizza sauce in a microwave-safe bowl. Cover loosely with plastic wrap. Microwave on high heat setting (100 percent power) for 1 to 1½ minutes or until heated through. Serve braids with pizza sauce for dipping.

Chili Spaghetti

Prep 10 minutes **Bake** 30 minutes **Makes** 8 servings

	Canola oil cooking spray, *Pam*®
1	pound dried spaghetti, *Barilla*®
2	cans (15 ounces each) turkey chili with no beans, *Hormel*®
1	can (14.5-ounce) diced tomatoes, *Hunt's*®
1	package (8-ounce) precrumbled cheddar and Colby cheese, *Kraft*®
¼	cup plain bread crumbs, *Progresso*®
¼	cup grated Parmesan cheese, *DiGiorno*®
1	tablespoon extra virgin olive oil, *Bertolli*®

1. Preheat oven to 375 degrees F. Lightly spray a 3-quart casserole with cooking spray. In a large pot, bring 4 to 6 quarts *water* to a boil over high heat. Add spaghetti. Return to boil; cook about 9 minutes or until spaghetti is tender, stirring occasionally. Drain spaghetti and return to pot. Stir in chili, undrained tomatoes, and cheese. Transfer to prepared casserole; set aside.

2. In a small bowl, stir together bread crumbs, Parmesan cheese, and oil until well mixed. Sprinkle over spaghetti mixture. Bake for 30 to 35 minutes or until golden brown and heated through. Using a large spoon, divide among bowls.

Billiard Room Pizza Wheel

Prep 10 minutes   **Bake** 35 minutes   **Makes** 8 to 10 servings

1	package (16-ounce) fresh sage sausage, *Jimmy Dean*®
1	can (15.5-ounce) black beans, rinsed and drained, *Goya*®
8	ounces roasted garlic tomato sauce, *Hunt's*®
2	tablespoons Mexican rice seasoning, *Lawry's*®
½	cup diced green bell pepper
½	cup diced red bell pepper
	All-purpose flour, for dusting
1	can (13.8-ounce) refrigerated pizza dough, *Pillsbury*®
1	cup shredded cheddar/Jack cheese blend, *Sargento*®
1	can (2.25-ounce) sliced ripe olives, drained, *Early California*®

1. Preheat oven to 375 degrees F.

2. In a large skillet, brown sausage over medium heat, breaking meat apart with a spoon. Drain sausage and discard fat. Add beans, tomato sauce, and Mexican rice seasoning. Cook over medium heat for 5 minutes, stirring occasionally. Add peppers; simmer for 8 minutes more. Set aside.

3. On a lightly floured surface, roll dough to fit a 15-inch round pizza pan. Place dough in pan. Spoon sausage filling around edge of dough. Top with cheese and olives. Using a pie cutter, begin from the center of the dough making 8 cuts; each will end at the start of the filling. This will create 8 triangles. Gently lift each triangle over the filling and tuck the tip under the edge of the dough.

4. Bake for 20 to 25 minutes or until crust is golden brown.

Cornmeal Catfish Fingers

Prep 15 minutes **Cook** 5 minutes **Makes** 4 servings

FOR CATFISH FINGERS:
- 1½   pounds catfish fillets, rinsed and patted dry
- 1   box (8.5-ounce) corn muffin mix, *Jiffy®*
- 2   tablespoons Cajun seasoning, *McCormick®*
- 1   egg
- 1   tablespoon water
- ½   cup flour
-   Canola oil

FOR SASSY TARTAR:
- 1   bottle (10-ounce) tartar sauce, *Best Foods®*
- 2   teaspoons Cajun seasoning, *McCormick®*
- 1   scallion, finely chopped
- 6   dashes hot sauce, *Tabasco®*

1. To prepare catfish fingers, cut catfish into ½-inch strips. In a medium bowl, combine corn muffin mix and Cajun seasoning; set aside. Lightly beat egg with water to make egg wash. Dredge catfish fingers in flour; dip into egg wash, coat with corn muffin mixture, and shake off excess.

2. In a large skillet, heat ¼ inch oil over medium to medium-high heat until temperature reaches 375 degrees F.* In small batches, fry catfish fingers about 2 to 3 minutes per side or until golden brown. Transfer to a plate; keep warm. Repeat with remaining catfish fingers (if necessary, add more oil and reheat.)

3. To make tartar, in a small bowl, stir together tartar sauce, Cajun seasoning, scallion, and hot sauce. Serve fried catfish fingers hot with tartar sauce on the side.

TIP: If you don't have a candy thermometer to measure oil temperature before frying, drop a tiny piece of bread into the hot oil. If it begins to fry and immediately take on color, the oil is ready for the fish to be added.

Smoky and Spicy Baked Beans

Prep 15 minutes   **Grill** 30 minutes   **Makes** 8 servings

1	slice bacon, chopped, *Oscar Mayer®*
1	medium red onion, diced
2	cans (28 ounces each) baked beans, *Bush's®*
1	bottle (12-ounce) root beer, *A&W®*
¼	cup Worcestershire sauce, *Lea & Perrins®*
¼	cup ketchup, *Heinz®*
¼	cup yellow mustard, *French's®*
3	tablespoons molasses, *Grandma's®*
3	tablespoons chile-garlic sauce, *Lee Kum Kee®*

1. Set up grill for direct cooking over medium heat (see page 17). Set an 8-inch cast-iron skillet on grill to preheat. Add bacon and cook long enough to render fat. Remove bacon with a slotted spoon and place in a small bowl; set aside. Cook onion in bacon grease until soft. Return bacon to skillet. Stir in baked beans, root beer, Worcestershire sauce, ketchup, mustard, molasses, and chile-garlic sauce.

2. Cover grill. Cook about 30 minutes or until beans are thickened and bubbling. Serve hot.

Grandma Dicie's Spicy Fried Chicken

Prep 15 minutes **Chill** 4 hours **Cook** 20 minutes

My Grandma Dicie had so many talents. She spent her days running her Santa Monica dress shop—hand-making dresses for Hollywood stars and socialites. At the end of the day, she'd fry up batches of chicken. My grandma would be the first to tell you her dresses and fried chicken were the best around, and they were. I can remember standing in her kitchen, breathing in the tang of buttermilk batter while the breeze carried in the sweet scent of tangerines from the tree outside. She was raised in Louisiana, so she made it Southern and spicy!

1	quart buttermilk
2	packets (1.75 ounces each) hot wing seasoning mix, *French's®*
¼	cup hot sauce, *Tabasco®*
1	3½ pound frying chicken, rinsed, patted dry, and cut into serving pieces
1	box (10-ounce) seasoned coating mix, *Dixie Fry®*
2	teaspoons cayenne pepper, *McCormick®*
2	teaspoons poultry seasoning, *McCormick®*
1	teaspoon ground black pepper
	Peanut oil

1. In a large bowl, stir together buttermilk, hot wing seasoning mix, and hot sauce. Add chicken, making sure it is completely submerged. Cover with plastic wrap and chill in the refrigerator for at least 4 hours, preferably overnight.

2. In a 13×9-inch baking pan, combine coating mix and spices. Mix together thoroughly. Remove chicken from buttermilk and coat with spice coating mixture. Let chicken stand to dry in coating mixture until ready to fry.

3. In a large, straight-sided skillet, heat ½ inch oil to 375 degrees F. Add chicken to oil, skin sides down. (Do not overcrowd pan; if necessary, fry chicken in batches with additional oil.) Fry for 20 minutes, turning frequently. Drain fried chicken on paper towels or on wire cooling racks over paper towels.

TIP: If you don't have a candy thermometer to measure oil temperature before frying, drop a tiny piece of bread into the hot oil. If it begins to fry and immediately take on color, the oil is ready for the chicken.

Barbecued Ribs

Prep 5 minutes   **Cook** 2½ hours   **Makes** 6 servings

2	racks pork baby back ribs
2	teaspoons Montreal steak seasoning, *McCormick® Grill Mates®*
1	can (14-ounce) tomato sauce with Italian herbs, *Contadina®*
1	packet (1.31-ounce) sloppy joe seasoning, *McCormick®*
3	tablespoons light brown sugar
2	tablespoons mesquite steak sauce, *A.1.®*
½	teaspoon crushed garlic, *Christopher Ranch®*

1. Preheat oven to 325 degrees F. Season ribs with steak seasoning and place in shallow roasting pan. In a medium bowl, stir together remaining ingredients. Pour barbecue sauce over ribs. Cover with aluminum foil and roast for 2½ to 3½ hours.

2. Remove ribs from oven and let stand 10 minutes. Skim fat from barbecue sauce and keep warm. Cut ribs into serving portions and serve with sauce on the side.

Green Parsley Slaw

Start to Finish 5 minutes   **Makes** 6 servings

1	bag (10-ounce) finely shredded cabbage, *Fresh Express®*
1	cup finely chopped flat-leaf parsley
½	cup finely chopped scallions (green onions)
½	cup mayonnaise, *Best Foods®*
2	tablespoons sour cream, *Knudsen®*
2	teaspoons granulated sugar
1	teaspoon white vinegar, *Heinz®*
¼	teaspoon salt

1. In a large bowl, toss together shredded cabbage, parsley, and scallions. In a medium bowl, combine remaining ingredients. Pour over cabbage mixture and toss to combine. Serve immediately.

TIP: The slaw can be chilled in the refrigerator for up to one day before serving.

Slow-Simmered Chipotle Rib Sandwiches

Prep 20 minutes   **Cook** 10 to 12 hours (Low)   **Makes** 6 servings

1	onion, sliced
3½	pounds beef short ribs
1	envelope (1.1-ounce) beef onion soup mix, *Lipton*®
1	jar (16-ounce) chipotle salsa, *Pace*®
½	cup ale-style beer
	Kaiser rolls, split and toasted (optional)

1. Place onion in a 4- to 5-quart slow cooker. Add ribs to slow cooker, meaty sides up. Sprinkle with onion soup mix. Add salsa and beer.

2. Cover and cook on low heat setting for 10 to 12 hours. Transfer ribs from slow cooker to a cutting board. Tent with aluminum foil until cool enough to handle. Using tongs, transfer onions from cooking juices to a serving bowl. Remove meat from bones (it should fall off); shred. Serve on kaiser rolls (optional). Serve with onions and cooking juices.

Chili-Rubbed BBQ Pork Chops

Start to Finish 20 minutes   **Makes** 4 servings

4	pork loin chops, ¾ to 1 inch thick
	Garlic salt, *Lawry's*®
	Ground black pepper
2	tablespoons chili seasoning, *McCormick*®
½	cup or more bottled barbecue sauce, *KC Masterpiece*®

1. Preheat broiler. Line a baking sheet or broiler pan with aluminum foil. Place chops on baking sheet. Season with garlic salt and pepper. Rub with chili seasoning.

2. Broil chops 6 inches from heat for 4 minutes per side. Brush chops with barbecue sauce; broil for 1 minute. Turn chops and brush with additional barbecue sauce. Broil for 1 minute more or until cooked through (160 degrees F). Serve hot.

Onion Blooms

Prep 15 minutes   **Cook** 10 to 12 minutes   **Makes** 4 blooms

They're called many things—onion loaves, awesome blossoms, Texas tumbleweeds—and I crave them all the time. They're gorgeous, dramatic, positively perfect, but not at all difficult to make. The trick is to add club soda to the batter. It makes the crust light, fluffy, and crunchy.

	Vegetable oil, *Wesson*®
3	cups all-purpose flour, *Pillsbury*®
2	packets (1 ounce each) dry ranch salad dressing mix, *Hidden Valley*®
4	large Vidalia onions
2	boxes tempura (8 ounces each) batter mix, *McCormick*® *Golden Dipt*®
2	cups club soda, chilled, *Schweppes*®

1. Fill fryer with vegetable oil to its maximum level. Preheat oil to 375 degrees F. For seasoned flour, in a shallow bowl, combine flour and ranch dressing mix; set aside.

2. Cut about ½ inch off the onion tops and peel them. Cut 12 vertical slices to just above the bottom of onion. Do not cut all the way through the onion. Remove center of each onion and save for other recipes.

3. In a large bowl, combine the tempura batter and chilled club soda. Batter should be slightly lumpy. Cover 1 onion in seasoned flour, shaking to remove excess flour. Dip the onion into tempura batter, spreading "petals" to coat onion evenly with batter.

4. Carefully place 1 onion into fryer. Fry about 2 to 3 minutes or until golden. Remove and drain well on paper towels. Repeat with the remaining 3 onions. Serve hot.

Brilliant Bacon Burger

Prep 15 minutes   **Grill** 9 minutes   **Makes** 4 servings

1½	pounds ground beef
½	cup bottled chunky salsa, drained, *Pace*®
2	tablespoons finely chopped fresh cilantro
2	tablespoons real bacon crumbles, *Hormel*®
1	tablespoon canned chopped jalapeño chile peppers, *Ortega*®
1	teaspoon Montreal steak seasoning, *McCormick*®
4	slices pepper Jack cheese, *Tillamook*®
4	onion buns, toasted
	Lettuce leaves, sliced tomatoes, and sliced red onion
	Precooked sliced bacon, crisped in microwave, *Oscar Mayer*®
	Purchased guacamole, *Calavo*®

1. In a large bowl, combine ground beef, salsa, cilantro, bacon crumbles, chile peppers, and steak seasoning. Mix thoroughly. Form into 4 patties slightly larger than buns. (Cover and chill if not cooking immediately.)

2. Set up grill for direct cooking over high heat (see page 17). Oil grate when ready to start cooking. Place patties on hot, oiled grill. Cook for 4 to 5 minutes per side for medium (160 degrees F). Place cheese slices on burgers. Cook for 1 to 2 minutes more or until cheese is melted. Serve hot on buns with lettuce, tomatoes, red onion, bacon, and guacamole.

Beef Burgundy

Start to Finish 20 minutes   **Makes** 6 servings

4	slices thick-sliced bacon, diced
1	package (17-ounce) beef tips in gravy, *Tyson®*
1	can (14.5-ounce) diced tomatoes with basil, garlic, and oregano, *Del Monte®*
1	package (8-ounce) presliced fresh white button mushrooms
1	cup loose-pack frozen carrot slices, *C&W®*
1	cup loose-pack frozen or bottled pearl onions
1	cup Merlot, Pinot Noir, or other red wine
2	tablespoons tomato paste, *Hunt's®*
	Fresh parsley, chopped (optional)

1. In a large skillet, brown diced bacon over medium heat. Drain and discard bacon fat. Set aside some of the bacon for garnish (optional). To the remaining bacon in skillet, add beef tips in gravy, tomatoes, mushrooms, frozen carrots and onions, Merlot, and tomato paste. Bring to a boil; reduce heat to low. Simmer for 10 minutes or until heated through.

2. Serve beef mixture over Parsleyed Egg Noodles (below). Garnish with reserved bacon and chopped parsley (optional).

Parsleyed Egg Noodles

Start to Finish 15 minutes   **Makes** 6 servings

12	ounces dried wide egg noodles, *American Beauty®*
½	stick (¼ cup) butter
3	tablespoons finely chopped fresh parsley
	Salt
	Ground black pepper

1. In a large pot of boiling salted water, cook noodles according to package directions.* Drain well; return noodles to hot pot.

2. Add butter and parsley; stir to coat noodles. Season with salt and pepper.

*NOTE: Cook noodles only until they are al dente. Do not let them get soft and mushy.

Chunky Chili

Prep 10 minutes   **Cook** 25 minutes   **Makes** 6 to 8 servings

2	tablespoons butter
1	medium sweet onion, very finely chopped
1½	pounds ground beef
2	cans (15 ounces each) red kidney beans, drained, *S&W*®
1	jar (26-ounce) marinara sauce, *Newman's Own*®
1	package (1.25-ounce) chili seasoning, *Schilling*®,
	minus 1 tablespoon reserved for Chili Rolls (see recipe below)
	Chili toppings (such as shredded cheese, sour cream, chopped chives) (optional)

1. In a large skillet, melt butter over medium heat. Add onion and cook until softened. Crumble in the beef and cook until browned. Stir in beans and marinara sauce. Stir in chili seasoning. Reduce heat and simmer for 15 minutes. Ladle into soup bowls and garnish with chili toppings (optional).

TIP: Serve with Chili Rolls (below).

Chili Rolls

Prep 5 minutes   **Bake** 15 minutes   **Makes** 12 rolls

1	stick (½ cup) butter
1	tablespoon chili seasoning, *Schilling*® (see recipe, above)
1	package (12-count) brown-and-serve rolls, *Van de Kamp's*®

1. Preheat the oven according to package directions.

2. In a medium saucepan, melt butter over medium heat. Stir in chili seasoning. Brush tops of rolls with chili butter, then place rolls on a baking sheet covered with aluminum foil. Bake about 15 minutes or until golden brown.

Desserts

Like most people, I love desserts—they're my weakness. Growing up, I would sit in the kitchen for hours and watch my grandmother bake and decorate the most fabulous cakes. Unfortunately, few of us have time for this luxurious expression of love anymore. To this day, I have not forgotten my grandmother's greatest creations—her famous dessert casseroles. None of us ever knew exactly what was in them, but our mouths watered in anticipation of every bite. Now I, too, have continued her not-so-common tradition. Even my grandmother would take her hat off to the wonderful desserts included here. My decadent treats are not as time-consuming as the old-fashioned delicacies, but I promise you they are just as amazing, and only you will know how truly easy they are to make.

The Recipes

Malibu®
Rum Cake

Prep 10 minutes   **Cook** 45 minutes   **Cool** 45 minutes   **Makes** 12 servings

I created this cake in college, and it was always a big hit. I wonder if having the word "rum" in its title added to its success?

FOR MALIBU® RUM CAKE:
Nonstick cooking spray, *Pam®*
1   package (18.25-ounce) classic yellow cake mix,
       Duncan Hines® Moist Deluxe®
1   cup rum, *Malibu®*
½   cup vegetable oil, *Wesson®*
1   package (3.4-ounce) vanilla instant pudding
       and pie filling mix, *Jell-O®*
4   eggs

FOR MALIBU® RUM GLAZE:
1   cup packed golden brown sugar, *C&H®*
¼   cup water
1   stick (½ cup) butter
¼   cup rum, *Malibu®*

1. Position rack in center of oven and preheat to 325 degrees F. Spray a 10-inch (12-cup) fluted tube pan with nonstick cooking spray.

2. For Malibu® Rum Cake, in a large bowl, beat cake mix, rum, oil, pudding mix, and eggs with an electric mixer for 2 minutes. Transfer batter to prepared pan. Bake in preheated oven for 45 to 50 minutes or until a toothpick inserted into center of cake comes out clean.

3. Cool cake in pan for 20 minutes. Invert cake onto platter, then carefully remove pan. Cool cake completely.

4. Meanwhile, for Malibu® Rum Glaze, in a medium heavy-bottom saucepan, cook and stir brown sugar and the water over medium-high heat until sugar dissolves. Add butter. Simmer about 5 minutes or until mixture thickens and is syrupy.

5. Remove saucepan from heat and whisk in rum. Cool glaze completely. Drizzle glaze evenly over cooled cake and serve.

Life's a Beach Cake

Start to Finish 15 minutes   **Makes** 8 servings

1	purchased (10- to 12-ounce) angel food cake
10	large marshmallows, *Kraft Jet-Puffed*®
2	containers (16 ounces each) vanilla frosting, *Betty Crocker® Rich & Creamy*
	Blue food coloring
	Jellied octopus candy and chocolate seashell candy
3	paper wooden skewer umbrellas
½	cup sweetened flaked coconut, *Baker's*®

1. Place cake, wide end down, on serving platter. Fill hole in center of cake with marshmallows.

2. Spread contents of 1½ containers of the frosting evenly over top and sides of cake to coat completely. Stir blue food coloring, 1 drop at a time, into remaining frosting until desired color is achieved. Transfer blue frosting to pastry bag fitted with star tip. Pipe blue frosting around base of cake.

3. Starting at base of cake and swirling in semicircular upward motion, drag wooden skewer through blue-colored frosting to form wave design. Arrange umbrellas on top of cake. Arrange jellied candy octopus and chocolate seashells on cake. Sprinkle coconut around base of cake.

Fruit Custard Tarts

Prep 5 minutes **Chill** 30 minutes **Bake** 15 minutes **Makes** 6 servings

1	package (1-ounce) cheesecake-flavored sugar-free and fat-free instant pudding and pie filling mix, *Jell-O*®
1	cup milk
½	teaspoon orange extract, *McCormick*®
1	package (11-ounce) piecrust mix, *Betty Crocker*®
⅓	cup cold water
½	teaspoon raspberry extract, *McCormick*®
1	bag (16-ounce) frozen peaches, thawed and drained
1	container (½ pint) fresh blackberries
	Powdered sugar, *C&H*®
¼	cup apricot preserves, *Smucker's*®

1. In a large bowl, combine pudding mix, milk, and orange extract. Whisk to a thick consistency, about 1 minute. Cover and chill in refrigerator for 30 minutes to 1 hour.

2. Preheat oven to 450 degrees F. Line baking sheet with parchment paper. In a large bowl, combine piecrust mix, cold water, and raspberry extract. Stir until dough forms. Shape into 6 small balls. Roll out dough on a lightly floured surface to make six 4-inch disks. Fill the center of each crust with 2 tablespoons pudding mix, leaving ½-inch border. Top with peaches and blackberries. Fold edges over and pinch together to form a tart shell. Dust tops with powdered sugar and arrange on prepared baking sheet. Bake in preheated oven for 15 to 18 minutes or until crust is browned.

3. In a microwave-safe bowl, microwave apricot preserves on high heat setting (100 percent power) for 2 minutes. Remove tarts from oven. Use a pastry brush to glaze the tops of each tart with melted apricot preserves.

Raspberry Chocolate Wontons

Prep 10 minutes   **Cook** 15 minutes   **Makes** 4 servings

½	bar (5-ounce) milk chocolate, *Hershey's*®
1	egg
1½	teaspoons water
12	wonton wrappers, *Dynasty*®
¼	cup red raspberry preserves, *Smucker's*®
	Vegetable oil
	Powdered sugar
	Fresh raspberries (optional)

1. Cut chocolate bar into scored rectangles, then cut each in half; set aside. In a small bowl, lightly beat egg with water to make egg wash.

2. Lay out wonton wrappers on a flat surface. Use a pastry brush to brush egg wash around the edge of a wonton wrapper. Place 1 teaspoon of the raspberry preserves in the center of the prepared wonton wrapper. Top with chocolate bar piece. Fold wonton wrapper in half to make a triangle. Press to seal. Repeat with remaining wonton wrappers, preserves, and chocolate pieces.

3. In a medium saucepan, heat 2 inches of oil to 350 degrees F. Carefully slide four wontons at a time into the hot oil and fry for 1 minute per side. Remove and drain on paper towels. Sift powdered sugar over warm wontons. Serve with fresh raspberries (optional).

TIP: If you don't have a candy thermometer to measure oil temperature before frying, drop a tiny piece of bread into the hot oil. If it begins to fry and immediately take on color, the oil is ready for the wontons.

Raspberry Trifle

Prep 10 minutes **Cook** 1 minute **Cool** 45 minutes
Makes 6 servings

3	tablespoons butter
¾	cup powdered sugar, *C&H*®
½	cup raspberry jam, *Knott's*®
3	tablespoons water
¾	teaspoon imitation rum extract, *McCormick*®
1	frozen pound cake (12-ounce), thawed and cut into quarter-size cubes, *Sara Lee*®
3	containers (4 ounces each) refrigerated prepared vanilla pudding, *Jell-O*®
	Fresh raspberries

1. In a micro-safe bowl, microwave the butter on high heat setting (100 percent power) about 30 seconds or until melted. Whisk in powdered sugar, jam, the water, and rum extract, whisking to form a smooth sauce. In 6 small bowls or wine glasses, evenly distribute pound cake cubes. Pack cubes down slightly. Drizzle jam-rum sauce evenly over each. Spoon about 3 tablespoons of the pudding evenly over each. Serve warm or chill for 45 minutes. Garnish with raspberries and serve.

Texas Cinnamon Pecan Strudel

Prep 10 minutes **Bake** 20 minutes **Makes** 10 to 12 slices

1	package (18-ounce) frozen unbaked cinnamon rolls, thawed, *Rich's*®
3	tablespoons honey, *Sue Bee*®
½	cup chopped pecans
½	cup chopped walnuts
	Honey, *Sue Bee*®
1	teaspoon ground cinnamon, *McCormick*®

1. Preheat oven to 375 degrees F. Line cookie sheet with parchment paper. Gather cinnamon rolls into one ball. Knead dough in bowl until smooth. Roll out dough on lightly floured work surface to 12×7-inch rectangle. Brush dough with the 3 tablespoons honey. Sprinkle dough with pecans and walnuts. Gently press nuts into dough. Roll up dough, starting on the short end (as for jelly roll).

2. Place dough, seam side down, on prepared cookie sheet. Bake in preheated oven about 20 minutes or until golden brown. Cut strudel crosswise into diagonal slices. Drizzle with additional honey and sprinkle with cinnamon. Serve warm.

Frozen English Toffee Cake

Prep 15 minutes **Bake** 30 minutes **Cool** 30 minutes **Assembly** 15 minutes
Freeze 3 hours **Stand** 5 minutes **Makes** 12 to 16 servings

FOR ENGLISH TOFFEE CAKE:
1   package (18.25-ounce) devil's food cake mix, *Duncan Hines®*
          Moist Deluxe®
1⅓ cups water
½   cup vegetable oil, *Wesson®*
3   eggs

FOR ICE CREAM FILLING:
½   gallon chocolate or vanilla ice cream, softened, *Dreyer's®*
1   bag (10-ounce) English toffee bits, *Skor®*

FOR FROSTING:
1   container (8-ounce) frozen whipped topping, thawed,
          Cool Whip®

1. Preheat oven to 350 degrees F. Butter and flour two 8-inch round cake pans.

2. For English Toffee Cake, in a large bowl, combine cake mix, the water, oil, and eggs. Beat about 2 minutes or until well blended. Pour batter into prepared pans. Bake in preheated oven about 30 minutes or until toothpick inserted into centers of cakes comes out clean. Cool cakes in pans on wire racks for 15 minutes. Remove cakes from pans and cool cakes completely on wire racks.

3. For Ice Cream Filling, line three 8-inch round cake pans with plastic wrap, allowing 3 inches of the plastic wrap to hang over sides. Divide ice cream equally among pans. Using rubber spatula, spread ice cream over bottoms of prepared pans, forming smooth, even layers. Sprinkle ¼ cup of the toffee bits over ice cream in each pan. Freeze about 3 hours or until frozen solid.

4. Using a large serrated knife, cut each cake layer horizontally in half. Working quickly, remove ice cream from pans. Peel off plastic wrap and place 1 ice cream circle on each of 3 of the cake layers. Stack cake and ice cream layers on top of each other on serving platter. Top with remaining cake layer. Frost cake with whipped topping and sprinkle with remaining toffee bits. Freeze until ready to serve. Let ice cream cake stand at room temperature for 5 minutes before serving.

Orange-Spiced Cheesecake

Start to Finish 20 minutes   **Makes** 6 servings

1	package (30-ounce) frozen New York-style cheesecake, *Sara Lee®*
⅓	cup orange marmalade, *Smucker's®*
2	tablespoons orange-flavored liqueur, *Cointreau®*
1	tablespoon frozen orange juice concentrate, *Minute Maid®*
¼	teaspoon five-spice powder, *McCormick®*
1	orange, sliced

1. Let cheesecake stand at room temperature for at least 15 minutes.

2. In a large saucepan, combine marmalade, orange-flavored liqueur, frozen orange juice concentrate, and five-spice powder. Cook and stir over medium-high heat until orange juice concentrate is melted. Add orange slices. Simmer about 10 minutes or until thick and syrupy.

3. Arrange orange slices over top of cake. Spoon warm orange juice mixture over orange slices. To serve, cut into slices.

Cinnamon Roll Bread Pudding

Prep 10 minutes   **Bake** 1 hour   **Makes** 6 servings

	Butter-flavored cooking spray, *Pam®*
1	pound leftover or store-bought cinnamon rolls, cut into 1-inch cubes
1½	cups pitted dates, *Sun-Maid®*
¼	cup sliced almonds, *Planters®*
1	package (4.6-ounce) cook-and-serve vanilla pudding and pie filling mix, *Jell-O®*
2	cans (12 ounces each) evaporated milk, *Carnation®*
½	teaspoon almond extract, *McCormick®*
½	teaspoon pumpkin pie spice, *McCormick®*
2	tablespoons butter, cut into small pieces

1. Preheat oven to 350 degrees F. Lightly spray the inside of a 3-quart casserole with butter-flavored cooking spray. In a large bowl, place cinnamon roll cubes, dates, and almonds. Toss to combine.

2. In a medium bowl, whisk together pudding mix, evaporated milk, almond extract, and pumpkin pie spice. Pour pudding mixture over bread mixture. Stir together until well combined and bread is saturated. Transfer to prepared casserole dish and dot with butter.

3. Bake bread pudding in preheated oven for 1 hour to 1 hour 10 minutes or until knife inserted into center comes out clean. Remove from oven. Serve warm in martini glasses.

Glazed Doughnut Crisps

Prep 25 minutes **Freeze** 10 minutes **Bake** 12 minutes per batch
Makes 16 cookies

1	package (18-ounce) refrigerated sugar cookie dough, room temperature, *Pillsbury®*
½	teaspoon brandy extract, *McCormick®*
½	cup all-purpose flour
	Purchased vanilla frosting, *Pillsbury®*
1	recipe Yellow Icing (right)

1. Preheat oven to 350 degrees F. Cut cookie dough into 8 pieces. In the bowl of a standing electric mixer, combine cookie dough pieces, brandy extract, and flour, adding flour in 2 parts and beating until well mixed. Divide dough into 16 pieces. Roll each piece into 6-inch rope.

2. Placing 2 inches apart on ungreased cookie sheet, shape each rope into ring-shaped doughnut, pinching ends together. Freeze for 10 minutes.

3. Bake in preheated oven about 12 minutes or until cookies are light golden brown. Cool completely on wire rack. Frost each cookie with vanilla frosting. Drizzle Yellow Icing over cookies.

YELLOW ICING: In small bowl, combine 1 cup powdered sugar and 2 tablespoons milk. Tint with 1 drop yellow food coloring. If necessary, add more powdered sugar to obtain desired consistency. Drizzle icing over cookies.

Lemon Spritz Squares

Prep 25 minutes **Freeze** 10 minutes **Bake** 10 minutes per batch
Makes 42 cookies

1	package (17.5-ounce) dry sugar cookie mix, *Betty Crocker®*
4	ounces cream cheese, softened, *Philadelphia®*
1¼	cups all-purpose flour
¾	teaspoon lemon extract, *McCormick®*
2	eggs
1	tablespoon grated lemon zest
	Powdered sugar

1. Preheat oven to 350 degrees F. In the bowl of a standing electric mixer, beat cookie mix and cream cheese until crumbly. Add flour in 3 parts, mixing well after each addition. Add lemon extract, eggs, and lemon zest; mix just until incorporated. On lightly floured surface, roll out dough to 12×14-inch rectangle. Using fluted pastry cutter or sharp knife, cut dough into 2-inch squares.

2. Place squares 1 inch apart on ungreased cookie sheet. Freeze for 10 minutes. Bake in preheated oven about 10 minutes or until bottoms are golden brown and tops are set. Cool on wire rack. Sift powdered sugar over cookies.

Cherry Lattice Pie

Prep 15 minutes **Bake** 40 minutes **Stand** 20 minutes **Makes** 8 servings

1	can (21-ounce) cherry pie filling or topping, *Comstock® More Fruit* or *Wilderness® More Fruit*
12	ounces frozen mixed berries, thawed and drained
1	tablespoon cherry brandy (Kirsch)
1	package (15-ounce) refrigerated piecrust, *Pillsbury®*
1	egg, lightly beaten
	Sugar, *C&H®*

1. Preheat oven to 375 degrees F. In a large bowl, combine cherry pie filling, mixed berries, and cherry brandy. Set aside.

2. Gently press 1 sheet of the piecrust into a flour-dusted 9-inch pie plate. Pour berry filling into unbaked crust. Using a pie plate as a guide, cut a circle for the top crust from second sheet of piecrust. Use a generously floured lattice cutter to cut a pattern from circle. Top pie with lattice top. Press along rim to seal and trim edges. Press fork into edges or crimp to make decorative edge. Brush top crust with beaten egg and sprinkle lightly with sugar.

3. Bake in preheated oven about 40 minutes or until filling bubbles. Cover pie with foil halfway through baking to prevent overbrowning. Let stand for 20 minutes before serving.

Double Strawberry Pie

Prep 20 minutes **Bake** 1 hour **Makes** 8 servings

4	cups frozen unsweetened strawberries, partially thawed in refrigerator
¾	cup sugar, *C&H®*
4	tablespoons cornstarch
1	package (11-ounce) piecrust mix, *Betty Crocker®*
⅓	cup strawberry nectar, chilled, *Kern's®*
1	egg, beaten with 1 tablespoon water
	Sugar, *C&H®*

1. Preheat oven and a baking sheet to 450 degrees F. Place strawberries in a large bowl. Sift the ¾ cup sugar and the cornstarch over the partially thawed strawberries. Stir to combine; set filling aside.

2. In a medium bowl, combine crust mix and strawberry nectar. Stir until soft dough forms. Divide into 2 pieces, form balls, and flatten into disks. On a lightly floured surface, roll 1 of the disks 1½ inches larger than an inverted 9-inch pie plate. Fold rolled dough in half, place in pie plate, and unfold. Press dough into plate but do not stretch. Trim dough ½ inch beyond edge of pie plate.

3. Roll out second disk and fold in half. Pour filling into bottom crust. Place top crust over filling; unfold. Press along rim to seal and trim edges. Press fork into edges or crimp to make decorative edge. Cut vent slits in top crust or punch center with small decorative cutter. Brush with beaten egg mixture. Sprinkle with sugar. Place pie on preheated baking sheet in oven. Bake for 10 minutes. Reduce heat to 350 degrees F; continue baking for 50 to 60 minutes or until filling is bubbly and crust is golden brown. Cool completely before cutting.

Raspberry Windmill Cookies

Prep 25 minutes   **Chill** 15 minutes   **Bake** 12 minutes
Makes 9 cookies

1	package (18-ounce) refrigerated sugar cookie dough, room temperature, *Pillsbury*®
¼	cup cream cheese, *Philadelphia*®
½	teaspoon almond extract, *McCormick*®
3	tablespoons seedless raspberry jam
9	red candied cherry halves

1. Preheat oven to 350 degrees F. Cut the cookie dough into 8 pieces. In the bowl of a standing electric mixer, combine cookie dough pieces, cream cheese, and almond extract; beat until well mixed. If the dough is too soft, place in the refrigerator for 15 minutes before using.

2. Roll dough out into 9×9-inch square. With sharp knife, cut dough into nine 3-inch squares. Move squares apart slightly so they are easier to work on.

3. Stir jam and spread about 1 teaspoon on each piece of dough. On each square, cut a slice from each corner almost to center.

4. Fold cut corner from each of 4 sides to center and press to hold it. In center of each cookie, press a candied cherry half. Place on ungreased cookie sheet. Bake in preheated oven about 12 minutes or until cookies are light golden brown. Cool on wire rack.

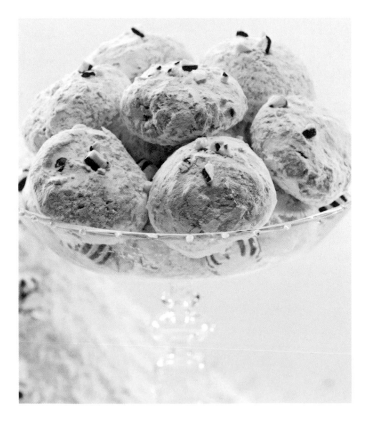

White Peppermint Snowballs

Prep 20 minutes   **Bake** 8 minutes per batch   **Makes** 36 cookies

1	package (18-ounce) refrigerated sugar cookie dough, room temperature, *Pillsbury*®
⅓	cup peppermint candies, crushed
1	cup powdered sugar
	Peppermint candies, crushed (optional)

1. Preheat oven to 350 degrees F. Cut cookie dough into 8 pieces. In the bowl of a standing electric mixer, combine dough pieces, crushed peppermint candies, and ½ cup of the powdered sugar.

2. Roll dough into 1-inch diameter balls. Place 2 inches apart on ungreased cookie sheet. Bake for 8 minutes or until set. Cool slightly on wire rack.

3. While still warm, roll cookies in the remaining ½ cup powdered sugar. Sprinkle with crushed peppermint candies (optional).

Broadway Deli Cheesecake

Prep 10 minutes   **Bake** 35 minutes   **Makes** 10 servings

FOR CRUST:

15	caramel pecan shortbread cookies, *Keebler®*
½	stick (¼ cup) butter, melted

FOR FILLING:

3	packages (8 ounces each) cream cheese, softened, *Philadelphia®*
½	cup granulated sugar
¼	cup packed brown sugar, *C&H®*
2	teaspoons ground cinnamon, *McCormick®*
1	teaspoon vanilla extract, *McCormick®*
3	eggs
1	can (21-ounce) apple pie filling, *Comstock® More Fruit* or *Wilderness® More Fruit*
	Caramel sauce, *Hershey's®*

1. Preheat oven to 350 degrees F. Wrap outside of a 9-inch springform pan with foil.

2. For crust, in a food processor, process cookies until fine crumbs form. Transfer to a medium bowl and stir in melted butter. Press mixture into bottom and halfway up sides of the prepared springform pan.

3. For filling, in a large bowl, combine cream cheese, both sugars, cinnamon, and vanilla extract; beat with an electric mixer on medium speed until creamy. Add eggs, one at a time, beating after each addition until smooth.

4. Pour filling into prepared crust and smooth top with a rubber spatula. Fan apple slices from pie filling along the outer edge and middle of the top of the cheesecake. Bake in preheated oven for 35 to 45 minutes or just until set in center. Cool on wire rack, then refrigerate for 3 hours. Slice and serve with caramel sauce on the side.

Dino Cookies

Prep 25 minutes **Chill** 15 minutes **Bake** 10 minutes per batch
Makes 28 cookies

1	package (17-ounce) sugar cookie mix, *Betty Crocker*®
¼	cup all-purpose flour
1	package (3-ounce) cream cheese, *Philadelphia*®
1	egg
1	package (12-ounce) miniature candy-coated milk chocolate pieces, *M&M's*®
	Edible rock candy (optional)
	Edible Palm Trees (optional) (below)

1. Preheat oven to 350 degrees F. In a large bowl, stir together sugar cookie mix and flour.

2. Place cream cheese in a microwave-safe bowl. Microwave on medium-high heat setting (80 percent power) for 1 minute. Add cream cheese and egg to cookie mix mixture. Stir until dough forms a ball. Divide dough in half. Lightly sprinkle a flat rolling surface and a rolling pin with flour. Using the rolling pin, roll out half of the dough on the floured surface until ¼ inch thick, turning the dough so it does not stick.

3. Dip a 3-inch dinosaur-shape cookie cutter into flour. Cut out cookies at the center of the dough and work your way toward the edge, cutting cookies as close together as possible. (Dip cookie cutter into flour as needed to prevent sticking.)

4. Place cookies on ungreased cookie sheet. Repeat with remaining dough. Decorate each cookie by pressing chocolate pieces into dough. Place cookies in the refrigerator; chill for 15 minutes.

5. Place cookie sheet in preheated oven. Bake for 10 to 12 minutes or just until browned on edges. Remove from oven. Cool on cookie sheet for 1 minute. Using the spatula, transfer cookies to wire racks; cool. Surround cookies with rock candy and Edible Palm Trees (optional).

EDIBLE PALM TREES: On a surface lightly sprinkled with sugar, roll a large green gumdrop into a flat round piece. With a small knife, cut wedges from edges to resemble palm tree leaves. Form the gumdrop over a pretzel stick. Prop the tree up with edible rock candy (optional).

Chocolate Caramel Corn Candy Cubes

Start to Finish 20 minutes   **Makes** 4 servings

These bonbons are delicious on so many levels, from their *Kit Kat*® crust to their *Cracker Jack*® center, drizzled with layer upon layer of chocolate and caramel, chilled to a crunchy candy shell. Kids can make them in the microwave…as long as they share some of them with you!

4	bars (1.5 ounces each) chocolate-covered crisp wafers, *Kit Kat*®
3	boxes (1.0 ounce each) caramel corn with peanuts, *Cracker Jack*®
15	individually wrapped caramels, unwrapped *Kraft*®
1¼	teaspoons butter
½	cup white chocolate chips, *Nestle*®
3	teaspoons shortening, divided, *Crisco*®
½	cup milk chocolate chips, *Nestle*®

1. Unwrap candy bars and place face down on waxed or parchment paper; set aside. Pour caramel corn into a medium bowl; set aside.

2. In a microwave-safe bowl, combine caramels with butter. In another microwave-safe bowl, combine white chocolate with 1½ teaspoons of the shortening. In a third microwave-safe bowl, combine chocolate chips with the remaining 1½ teaspoons shortening.

3. Microwave one bowl at a time on high heat setting (100 percent power) about 2 minutes or until contents are completely melted, stirring every 30 seconds.

4. Drizzle half of the melted caramel over candy bars. Divide and mound caramel corn on top of candy bars. Drizzle the melted white chocolate, remaining melted caramel, and melted milk chocolate over caramel corn. Place in the refrigerator; chill for 5 minutes to set.

Creamy Pudding

Start to Finish 20 minutes   **Makes** 6 servings

⅓	cup sugar
3	tablespoons cornstarch
2	cups milk
1	package (11-ounce) milk chocolate chips, *Hershey's*®
1	teaspoon vanilla extract, *McCormick*®

1. In a medium heavy-bottom saucepan, stir together the sugar and cornstarch. Gradually stir in the milk. Cook and stir over medium heat for 8 to 10 minutes or until mixture begins to boil and thicken.

2. Reduce heat to medium-low and stir in chocolate chips. Continue stirring until smooth and chocolate chips have melted. Pour into serving cups. Let stand for 5 minutes. Serve warm or chilled.

TIP: Another time, replace the milk chocolate chips with peanut butter chips, white chocolate chips, or butterscotch chips.

Lemon Pudding Brûlée with Blueberries

Start to Finish 20 minutes   **Makes** 4 servings

A luscious cross between pudding and crème brûlée, this chic dessert blends the tartness of lemon with the sweetness of blueberries. Get all the flavor and prestige of crème brûlée with the simplicity and convenience of instant pudding.

1	package (3.4-ounce) instant lemon pudding and pie filling mix, *Jell-O*®
2	cups cold milk
½	pint (1 cup) fresh blueberries
¼	cup sugar
	Fresh mint sprigs (optional)

1. Preheat broiler. Place pudding mix in a medium bowl. Add milk; whisk for 2 minutes. Place in the refrigerator for 5 minutes.

2. Count out 12 blueberries; set aside for garnish. Fold remaining berries into the pudding. Divide pudding into four 8-ounce broilerproof ramekins or soufflé dishes. Refrigerate until ready to serve.

3. Sprinkle 1 tablespoon of the sugar on top of each pudding. Place ramekins on a baking sheet. Broil 6 inches from heat for 2 to 3 minutes or until sugar has caramelized, rotating the baking sheet so the sugar caramelizes evenly.

4. Garnish with mint sprigs (optional). Serve with reserved berries.

Pears with Chantilly Cream

Start to Finish 10 minutes   **Makes** 4 servings

1   package (14-ounce) fat-free vanilla pudding cups (4 cups),
    Kraft® Handi-Snacks
1   container (8-ounce) fat-free frozen whipped topping, thawed,
    Cool Whip®
1   teaspoon almond extract, *McCormick®*
2   cans (15.25 ounces each) light pear halves, *Del Monte®*
¼   cup sliced almonds, toasted, *Planters®*

1. For chantilly cream, in a medium bowl, combine pudding, whipped topping, and almond extract.

2. To serve, arrange 3 pear halves in each of 4 serving dishes. Top each with chantilly cream and sprinkle with almonds.

Apricot Compote

Start to Finish 10 minutes   **Makes** 6 servings

1   can (15-ounce) light apricot halves, *Del Monte®*
1   cup dried apricots, cut into thin strips, *Sun-Maid®*
¼   cup golden raisins
1   tablespoon lemon juice, *ReaLemon®*
2   teaspoons finely chopped fresh mint
3   cups fat-free vanilla ice cream

1. In a medium saucepan, combine the apricot halves, the dried apricots, raisins, lemon juice, and mint. Slowly cook over medium-high heat until liquid is almost gone and dried fruit is rehydrated. Serve warm with ice cream.

Perfectly Peachy Sorbet

Prep 10 minutes **Chill** 30 minutes **Freeze** 2 hours
Makes 8 servings

¾	cup canned peach pie filling, *Comstock® More Fruit* or *Wilderness® More Fruit*
1	tablespoon sugar-free low-calorie peach-flavored gelatin dessert mix, *Jell-O®*
1	cup boiling water
1½	cups peach nectar, chilled, *Kern's®*

SPECIAL EQUIPMENT:
1-quart ice cream maker

1. Puree peach pie filling in blender until smooth. Set aside.

2. In a large bowl, stir peach-flavored gelatin into the boiling water until dissolved (about 2 minutes). When gelatin is completely dissolved, stir in chilled peach nectar and pureed pie filling until blended. Cover with plastic wrap and cool in refrigerator for 30 minutes.

3. Pour peach mixture into 1-quart ice cream maker and freeze according to manufacturer's instructions. When sorbet is frozen, transfer to airtight container and freeze for at least 2 hours. *

*NOTE: Sorbet freezes very hard—let sit at room temperature for 5 minutes before trying to scoop.

Luscious Lemon-Lime Sorbet

Prep 10 minutes **Chill** 30 minutes **Freeze** 2 hours
Makes 8 servings

1	tablespoon sugar-free low-calorie lime-flavored gelatin dessert mix, *Jell-O®*
1	cup boiling water
1	cup cold water
1	cup frozen lemonade concentrate, thawed

SPECIAL EQUIPMENT:
1-quart ice cream maker

1. In a large bowl, stir lime-flavored gelatin into boiling water until dissolved (about 2 minutes). When gelatin is completely dissolved, stir in the cold water and lemonade concentrate until blended. Cover with plastic wrap and cool in refrigerator for 30 minutes.

2. Pour lemon mixture into 1-quart ice cream maker and freeze according to manufacturer's instructions. When sorbet is frozen, transfer to airtight container and freeze for at least 2 hours (see note, above).

Really Raspberry Sorbet

Prep 15 minutes **Chill** 30 minutes **Freeze** 2 hours
Makes 8 servings

¾	cup frozen raspberries, thawed and drained
1	tablespoon sugar-free low-calorie raspberry-flavored gelatin dessert mix, *Jell-O®*
⅓	cup no-calorie sweetener, *Splenda®*
1	cup boiling water
1⅓	cups low-carb cranberry-raspberry juice, chilled

SPECIAL EQUIPMENT:
1-quart ice cream maker

1. Puree raspberries in blender until smooth. Push puree through fine mesh strainer to remove seeds. Set aside.

2. In a large bowl, stir raspberry-flavored gelatin and no-calorie sweetener into the boiling water until dissolved (about 2 minutes). When gelatin is completely dissolved, stir in chilled cranberry-raspberry juice and pureed raspberries until blended. Cover with plastic wrap and cool in refrigerator for 30 minutes.

3. Pour raspberry mixture into 1-quart ice cream maker and freeze according to manufacturer's instructions. When sorbet is frozen, transfer to airtight container and freeze for at least 2 hours (see note, above).

Holiday Parties

As much as I look forward to an intimate evening with family and friends, I'm the first to admit that a full house during the holidays is what I truly love. Two's company; three's a party. The more the merrier rings true when you plan can't-go-wrong dishes that serve up great taste with a small helping of effort.

When it comes to holiday entertaining, easy does it best. This chapter is an elegant, yet practical, resource for seasonal cooking, filled with simple favorites that are as appealing to the eye as they are to the palate. You can make some ahead to save time—for instance, Decorated Cream Cheese Sugar Cookies—while others pull together right before company arrives. When you're entertaining for special occasions and holidays, keeping it creative is the recipe for a good time for both you and your guests.

The Recipes

Screamin' Macaroni and Cheese

Prep 5 minutes **Cook** 30 minutes **Makes** 4 servings of each variation

Mexican-Style

1   package (7¼-ounce) macaroni and cheese mix, *Kraft*®
1   tablespoon Mexican seasoning, *McCormick*®
¾   cup shredded Mexican cheese blend, *Kraft*®

1. Preheat oven to 350 degrees F. Make macaroni and cheese according to package directions. Transfer to a medium baking dish or casserole dish.

2. Sprinkle Mexican seasoning over top of macaroni and cheese. Sprinkle cheese blend over top to cover. Bake for 5 minutes or until cheese is melted.

Italian-Style

1   package (7¼-ounce) macaroni and cheese mix, *Kraft*®
2   tablespoons butter
1   cup Italian-style bread crumbs, *Progresso*®

1. Preheat oven to 350 degrees F. Make macaroni and cheese according to package directions. Transfer to a medium baking dish or casserole dish.

2. In a microwave-safe bowl, microwave butter on low heat setting (25 percent power) until melted. Add bread crumbs and toss to coat with butter. Sprinkle bread crumb mixture over top of macaroni and cheese. Bake for 10 to 15 minutes or until browned on top.

American-Style

1   package (7¼-ounce) macaroni and cheese mix, *Kraft*®
1   to 1½ cups leftover broccoli florets

1. Preheat oven to 350 degrees F. Make macaroni and cheese according to package directions. Add broccoli and stir to combine. Transfer to a medium casserole dish. Bake about 10 minutes or until heated through.

Oozing Potatoes

Prep 15 minutes   Bake 18 minutes   Makes 4 servings

½   bag (22-ounce) frozen waffle fries, *Ore-Ida*®
1   can (16-ounce) refried black beans, *Rosarita*®
1   cup Mexican cheese blend, *Kraft*®
½   cup mild chunky salsa, *Pace*®
½   cup dairy sour cream, *Knudsen*®
1   can (2¼-ounce) sliced black olives, drained,
      Early California®

1. Preheat oven to 400 degrees F. Line a baking sheet with foil; set aside. Arrange waffle fries in a single layer on prepared baking sheet. Bake for 18 to 20 minutes.

2. Meanwhile, in a microwave-safe bowl, microwave black beans on high heat setting (100 percent power) for 4 to 6 minutes.

3. To assemble, evenly space waffle fries on a microwave-safe plate. Top each with 1 tablespoon beans and a sprinkle of cheese. Microwave on high heat setting (100 percent power) for 1 minute or until cheese is melted. Top each stack with 1 teaspoon salsa, 1 teaspoon sour cream, and an olive slice.

Spooky Punch

Prep 5 minutes   Makes about 2 quarts

1   can (12-ounce) frozen cranberry concentrate
3½   cups fresh orange juice, *Minute Maid*®
1   liter lemon-lime soda

1. In a pitcher, combine cranberry concentrate, orange juice, and lemon-lime soda. Serve in glasses over ice.

Scary Icee

Prep 5 minutes   Makes 6 servings

1   can (12-ounce) frozen lemonade mix concentrate
2   tablespoons packaged lemon gelatin mix, *Jell-O*®
1   tablespoon granulated sugar, *C&H*®
     Ice

1. In a blender, cover and pulse lemonade, gelatin, and sugar. Add ice to almost fill blender. Cover and continue to pulse until ice is crushed. Pour into glasses and serve.

Crunchy Doughnut Eyeballs

Prep 30 minutes **Chill** 10 minutes **Makes** 20 treats

20   glazed doughnut holes, *Entenmann's*®
1   cup premier white morsels, *Nestlé*®
2   tablespoons solid vegetable shortening, *Crisco*®
20   *Life Savers Gummies*®
20   mini candy-coated milk chocolate candies, *M&M's Minis*®
2   drops red food coloring

1. Line cookie sheet with parchment paper or waxed paper. Cut ⅛-inch-thick slices from 2 opposite sides of each doughnut hole.

2. Melt white morsels and vegetable shortening in top of double boiler or in a microwave-safe bowl in microwave.

3. Working with one doughnut hole at a time, use a fork to dip into melted morsels mixture to coat. Lift coated doughnut holes from coating, shaking excess melted morsels mixture back into bowl. Place coated doughnut holes, one cut side down, on prepared cookie sheet.

4. Place jellied candies on top of doughnuts. Dab chocolate candies with some of remaining melted morsels mixture and press onto jellied candies. Chill in refrigerator for 10 minutes or until coating is set.

5. In a small bowl, combine 2 tablespoons of remaining melted morsels mixture and 2 drops of food coloring. Using toothpick, paint colored morsels mixture on doughnut eyeballs to resemble veins. Chill in the refrigerator until ready to serve.

Vampire Kiss Martini

Start to Finish 10 minutes **Makes** 1 drink

1   part raspberry liqueur, *Chambord*®
1   part vodka, *Absolut*®
1   part Champagne, *Korbel*®
     Licorice, wax teeth, candy corn, and/or blood orange slice

1. In a chilled martini glass, layer raspberry liqueur, vodka, and Champagne. Garnish with licorice, wax teeth, candy corn, and/or blood orange slice.

Prosciutto-Tied Asparagus

Start to Finish 20 minutes **Makes** 18 bundles

1 package (3-ounce) prosciutto, *Columbus®*
1 pound thin asparagus, ends trimmed
2 tablespoons extra virgin olive oil
1 teaspoon lemon juice, *ReaLemon®*
Salt and ground black pepper

1. Preheat oven to 400 degrees F. Line a baking sheet with aluminum foil. Cut prosciutto slices lengthwise into two thin strips. Gather two to three asparagus spears and carefully tie prosciutto into a knot around asparagus bundle. Continue until all ingredients are used and place asparagus bundles on prepared baking sheet.

2. In a small bowl, whisk together the olive oil and lemon juice. Drizzle over asparagus. Season to taste with salt and pepper. Roast for 8 to 10 minutes.

Hot Apple Toddies

Prep 5 minutes **Cook** 45 minutes **Makes** 4 drinks

3 cups apple cider, *Martinelli's®*
½ cup spiced rum, *Captain Morgan®*
½ cup cinnamon schnapps, *Goldschlager®*
4 cinnamon sticks, *McCormick®*
Cinnamon sticks, *McCormick®*

1. In a medium saucepan, combine apple cider, rum, schnapps, and the 4 cinnamon sticks. Bring to a simmer over medium heat. Simmer for 45 to 60 minutes. (Or, use a 4-quart slow cooker.)

2. Serve warm in footed glasses. Garnish each with cinnamon stick swizzles.

NOTE: If using bittersweet to garnish the cinnamon stick swizzles, make sure it is faux.

Turkey with Cornbread Stuffing

Prep 45 minutes **Bake** 4 hours **Stand** 15 minutes
Makes 8 to 10 servings

1	12-pound frozen turkey, thawed
1	box (8.5-ounce) cornbread mix, *Jiffy*®
1	cup chopped celery
½	cup chopped green onions
1	can (10.5-ounce) chicken with rice soup, *Campbell's*®
2	tablespoons poultry seasoning, *McCormick*®
1	stick (½ cup) butter, softened
3	tablespoons vegetable oil
3	tablespoons all-purpose flour
	Salt and ground black pepper

1. Rinse the turkey in clean water and pat dry with paper towels. Remove the gizzards and neck. Place gizzards and neck in a saucepan and cover with water. Bring to a simmer to create broth for gravy. Simmer for 30 to 45 minutes. Remove from heat, strain, and reserve.

2. Meanwhile, prepare cornbread according to package directions. Crumble cornbread into small pieces; place on a baking sheet to air dry. In a bowl, combine prepared cornbread, celery, and green onions. Add soup and poultry seasoning. Mix well; stuff inside turkey cavities.

3. Generously cover turkey with softened butter. Tent with aluminum foil and bake according to package instructions for bird's weight. One hour before bird is done, remove foil and baste. The turkey is done when the internal temperature registers 170 degrees F deep in the thigh. The temperature of the stuffing should be 160 degrees F in the center.

4. Remove turkey from oven. Place on a serving platter; tent with foil. Let turkey stand for about 15 minutes until the temperature of the stuffing reaches 165 degrees F in the center and the temperature in the thigh rises to 180 degrees F.

5. While turkey stands, prepare gravy. In a large skillet, heat the oil over medium-low heat. Add flour; cook and stir until deep brown. Add turkey drippings and whisk until thickened. Add reserved gizzard broth and simmer. Season to taste with salt and pepper.

6. Remove stuffing from bird and place in a serving bowl. Carve turkey and arrange on a platter. Serve with stuffing and gravy.

Maple Pecan Pie

Prep 10 minutes **Bake** 50 minutes **Cool** 15 minutes **Makes** 8 servings

1¼	cups maple-flavored pancake syrup, *Log Cabin Original Syrup*®
⅓	cup packed golden brown sugar
3	eggs
1	egg yolk
2	teaspoons all-purpose flour
1½	teaspoons pure vanilla extract, *McCormick*®
2	tablespoons butter, melted
1½	cups pecan halves
1	9-inch frozen unbaked deep-dish pie shell, *Marie Callender's*®

1. Preheat oven to 350 degrees F. In a large bowl, stir together syrup, sugar, eggs, egg yolk, flour, and vanilla. Whisk in melted butter. Stir in 1 cup of pecans. Place frozen pie shell on a baking sheet. Pour maple syrup mixture into shell. Arrange remaining ½ cup of pecans on syrup mixture, pressing into syrup mixture to coat.

2. Place baking sheet in center of oven. Bake pie for 50 minutes or until edges are golden and filling is just set in center. Cool pie on cooling rack for 15 minutes. Cut pie into wedges and serve warm.

Tiered Cheeseballs

Prep 10 minutes   **Chill** 4 hours   **Makes** 6 cheeseballs

  2   packages (8 ounces each) cream cheese, *Philadelphia*®
  4   ounces blue cheese
1¼   cups finely chopped dried dates, *Dole*®
       Seedless red grapes

1. In a food processor fitted with a metal blade, combine cream cheese and blue cheese. Cover and process until smooth. Transfer to an airtight container and chill in refrigerator for at least 4 hours.

2. Once chilled, form cheese mixture into 6 even balls. Roll each ball into chopped dates. Arrange cheeseballs on tiered platter. Garnish platter with red grapes.

Let It Snow Cocktail

Start to Finish 10 minutes   **Makes** 1 drink

  1   shot vodka, *Blue Ice*®
  1   shot passion fruit liqueur, *Envy*®
½   shot orange liqueur, *Cointreau*®
  1   cup ice cubes
       Honey*
       Sweetened shredded coconut

1. In a blender, combine vodka, passion fruit liqueur, orange liqueur, and ice cubes. Cover and blend until smooth.

2. Dip rim of martini glass in honey; dip in shredded coconut. Pour cocktail into martini glass.

*TIP: You can also use corn syrup to make coconut stick to glasses.

Herb Salt-Crusted Prime Rib

Prep 15 minutes   **Bake** 50 minutes   **Stand** 5 minutes   **Makes** 4 servings

1	3½-pound beef rib roast (ribs removed*)
¼	cup Worcestershire sauce, *Lea & Perrins*®
1	tablespoon salt-free seasoned pepper, *Lawry's*®
4	pounds kosher salt
1	packet (1.12-ounce) Italian herb marinade mix, *Durkee*® *Grill Creations*®
½	cup water
1	can (14-ounce) reduced-sodium beef broth, *Swanson*®
1	packet (0.9-ounce) onion soup mix, *Lipton*®

1. Preheat oven to 500 degrees F. Line a roasting pan with aluminum foil. Sprinkle roast with Worcestershire sauce and seasoned pepper.

2. In a medium bowl, combine kosher salt and herb marinade mix. Sprinkle water over salt mixture until salt is well-moistened but not wet. Spread a ½-inch layer of salt mixture in middle of roasting pan, making it slightly larger than the diameter of the roast. Place roast, fat side up, on top of salt layer. Insert oven-safe meat thermometer into center of roast. Carefully pat remaining salt mixture onto meat, covering roast completely.

3. Place roast in oven and reduce temperature to 425 degrees F. Roast, uncovered, for 14 to 16 minutes per pound or until thermometer reads 5 degrees less than desired temperature. (Final temperature will be 130 degrees F for rare, 135 degrees F for medium-rare, or 140 degrees F for medium.) Remove roast from oven and let stand for 5 minutes.

4. For jus, in a small saucepan, bring broth to boil over medium heat. Reduce heat, stir in soup mix; simmer for 5 minutes more. Remove from heat.

5. To serve, remove salt crust from roast by breaking and peeling. Slice roast and transfer slices to a platter. Ladle a small amount of jus over meat and serve remaining jus on the side.

*TIP: Have the supermarket butcher remove ribs from the beef roast.

Sour Cream Mashed Potatoes

Prep 10 minutes   **Cook** 10 minutes   **Makes** 6 servings

2	pounds white potatoes, peeled and quartered
4	ounces sour cream
½	stick (¼ cup) butter
¾	to 1 cup buttermilk
	Salt and ground white pepper

1. Place potatoes in a large pot and cover with cold water. Bring to boil. Reduce heat and simmer for 10 to 15 minutes or until fork tender. Transfer potatoes to a large bowl.

2. With an electric mixer on low speed, break up the potatoes. Add sour cream, butter, and ½ cup buttermilk. Whip potatoes on medium speed until smooth. Add buttermilk to reach desired consistency. Season to taste with salt and pepper.

Angel Wreath Cake

Start to Finish 15 minutes   **Makes** 8 servings

1	purchased (10- to 12-ounce) angel food cake
	Green food coloring
1	container (16-ounce) vanilla frosting, *Betty Crocker® Rich & Creamy*
2	cups sweetened flaked coconut, *Baker's®*
3	purchased sugar leaf decorations, *Dec-A-Cake®*, or green decorating gel, *Cake Mate®*
3	hard cinnamon-flavored candies, *Red Hots®*, or red decorating gel, *Cake Mate®*

1. Place cake, wide end down, on serving platter. In a large bowl, stir food coloring, 1 drop at a time, into frosting until desired color is achieved. Spread frosting evenly over top and sides of cake to coat completely.

2. Press coconut into frosting to resemble snow. Arrange sugar leaves on top of cake or pipe green gel on top of cake to resemble holly leaves. Arrange cinnamon-flavored candies on top of cake or pipe red gel on top of cake to resemble holly berries.

Easter

Bacon-Wrapped Artichoke Hearts

Start to Finish 20 minutes **Makes** 4 servings

1	jar (12-ounce) marinated artichoke heart quarters, *Luna Rosa*®
9	slices bacon, cut in half, *Oscar Mayer*®

1. Preheat oven to 425 degrees F. Line a baking sheet with aluminum foil. Drain artichoke heart quarters, reserving liquid.

2. Wrap each artichoke heart quarter with a half-slice bacon. Secure with a toothpick.

3. Place on baking sheet. Drizzle with reserved liquid from artichokes. Roast for 12 to 15 minutes or until bacon is lightly browned and cooked through.

Lemon Cream Martini

Start to Finish 10 minutes **Makes** 1 drink

	Ice cubes
2	shots vanilla vodka, *Stoli*®
½	shot lemon liqueur, *Limoncello*®
	Lemon-flavor glass rimmer, *Stirrings*®
	Splash lemon-lime soda, *Sprite*®
	Fresh blueberries (optional)

1. Fill a martini shaker with ice cubes. Add vodka and lemon liqueur. Wet rim of a chilled martini glass and coat with lemon-flavor rimmer. Shake vodka mixture vigorously. Strain into prepared martini glass. Add lemon-lime soda. Garnish with blueberries (optional).

Bourbon Honey-Glazed Ham

Prep 15 minutes   **Cook** 1 hour   **Stand** 20 minutes   **Makes** 10 to 12 servings

1	cup honey,* *SueBee®*
⅔	cup bourbon or other whiskey
½	cup orange marmalade (100% fruit), *Smuckers®*
⅓	cup molasses*
1	5-pound whole bone-in smoked ham, fully cooked
⅛	cup whole cloves, *McCormick®*

1. Preheat oven to 350 degrees F.

2. For glaze, in a medium saucepan, heat honey, bourbon, marmalade, and molasses over low heat for 15 minutes or until reduced by half, stirring occasionally. Set aside.

3. With a sharp knife, cut a diamond pattern into the fatty part of the ham. Stud whole cloves in each diamond at points where lines cross. Spread half of the bourbon glaze over the ham.

4. Roast, uncovered, for 30 minutes. Baste with glaze. Roast for 15 minutes more, basting occasionally with remaining glaze. Remove from oven. Let stand for 20 minutes before slicing.

*TIP: When measuring honey and molasses, spray measuring cup with nonstick cooking spray to easily remove them from cup.

Goat Cheese Polenta

Prep 10 minutes   **Cook** 15 minutes   **Makes** 4 servings

2	tablespoons butter
1	package (24-ounce) precooked polenta, *San Gennaro*®
1	cup half-and-half or light cream
4	ounces goat cheese
1	tablespoon finely chopped fresh tarragon
	Salt and ground black pepper

1. In a saucepan, melt butter over medium heat. Break polenta into small pieces and add to pan. Whisk in half-and-half and continue stirring until smooth and heated through.

2. Add goat cheese and tarragon to polenta. Whisk until goat cheese is melted. Season to taste with salt and pepper.

Cream Cheese Sugar Cutouts

Prep 30 minutes **Bake** 10 minutes per batch   **Makes** about 24 cookies

1	package (18-ounce) refrigerated sugar cookie dough, room temperature, Pillsbury®
3	ounces cream cheese, softened, Philadelphia®
¾	cup cake flour
1	teaspoon vanilla extract, McCormick®
	Flour, for dusting work surface
	Colored sugars, frosting, and candies

1. Preheat oven to 350 degrees F. Cut cookie dough into 8 pieces. In the bowl of a standing electric mixer, thoroughly combine dough pieces, cream cheese, cake flour, and vanilla. If dough is too soft, add additional flour as needed. Place the dough in the refrigerator for 15 minutes.

2. On a lightly floured surface, roll dough out to ¼-inch thickness. Using your favorite cookie cutters, cut out cookies. Place on greased cookie sheets. Sprinkle with colored sugars. Bake for 10 minutes or until edges are light golden brown. Cool completely on a wire rack. Decorate as desired with colored sugars, frosting, and candies.

Index

Index

Index

Free
Lifestyle web magazine subscription

Just visit
www.semihomemade.com
today to subscribe!

Sign yourself and your friends and family up to the semi-homemaker's club today!

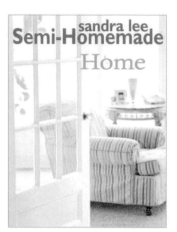

Each online issue is filled with fast, easy how-to projects, simple lifestyle solutions, and an abundance of helpful hints and terrific tips. It's the complete go-to magazine for busy people on-the-move.

tables & settings	fashion & beauty	ideas	home & garden	fabulous florals
super suppers	perfect parties	great gatherings		decadent desserts
gifts & giving	details	wines & music	fun favors	semi-homemaker's club

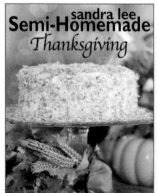

semihomemade.com
making life easier, better, and more enjoyable

Semihomemade.com has hundreds of ways to simplify your life—the easy Semi-Homemade way! You'll find fast ways to de-clutter, try your hand at clever crafts, create terrific tablescapes or decorate indoors and out to make your home and garden superb with style.

We're especially proud of our Semi-Homemakers club: a part of semihomemade.com which hosts other semihomemakers just like you. The club community shares ideas to make life easier, better, and more manageable with smart tips and hints allowing you time to do what you want! Sign-up and join today—it's free—and sign up your friends and family, too! It's easy the Semi-Homemade way! Visit the site today and start enjoying your busy life!

Sign yourself and your friends and family up to the semi-homemaker's club today!

tablescapes   home   garden   organizing   crafts

everyday & special days   cooking   entertaining   cocktail time

Halloween   Thanksgiving   Christmas   Valentine's   Easter   New Year's

Collect all of Sandra's books
Save Money ◆ Create More Time ◆ Make Life Easier

Also from Sandra Lee: *Made From Scratch, A Memoir*

0608